THE GRAND DUKES

DAVID CHAVCHAVADZE

ATLANTIC INTERNATIONAL PUBLICATIONS

By

David Chavchavadze

ATLANTIC INTERNATIONAL PUBLICATIONS

ISBN 0-938311-11-5
Library of Congress # 89-085203

Editor/Research: G. Nicholas Tantzos

For Information:

Atlantic International Publications
701 Seventh Avenue, Suite 9W
New York, New York 10036
Tel. (212) 757-6300

Published in the United States of America

ACKNOWLEDGMENT

I am most grateful to the following friends and relations who have provided information, research, and encouragement to me in the preparation of this book:

Prince Teymouraz Bagration, Dr. Nina Bouroff, Miss Marlene Eilers, Captain Tihon Kulikovsky, Prince Alexis Obolensky, Prince Paul Romanovsky-Ilyinsky, Mr. G. Nicholas Tantzos, Mr. Vladimir Tolstoy, and Princess Vera of Russia.

My thanks also go posthumously to my parents for the Imperial Russian lore they imparted to me and to my late aunt, Princess Xenia of Russia, who left me her library of rare, pre-revolutionary Russian books.

Finally, I offer sincere gratitude to the Royal Danish Library in Copenhagen and its director, Mr. Henri Dupont, for their efficient and prompt procurement of numerous grand ducal photographs.

David Chavchavadze

MOSCOW
HOUSE OF BOYAR ROMANOV

PUBLISHER and AUTHOR'S NOTES

What or who was a Grand Duke of Russia? Usually, the term is understood to mean the son or grandson of an emperor, but some historical explanation is required.

In old Muscovy, and in the previous capitals of the Ryurik Dynasty, the rulers were called 'Grand Dukes.' This is actually an early European mistranslation of the Russian *Velikiy Knyaz*, meaning Great (or Grand) Prince. Beginning with Ivan III (1440-1505) these Grand Dukes began to call themselves 'Tsar' (a derivative of Caesar), while retaining the title of Grand Duke. Ivan IV (the Terrible) (1530-1584) was the first to crown himself Tsar officially.

When the Romanovs were elected to the throne in 1613, they continued this tradition. Thus the first five Romanov rulers—Michael, Alexis, Feodor III, Ivan V, and Peter I—were both Tsars and Grand Dukes. All of their sons were called Tsarevich, meaning, simply, son of a Tsar.

In 1721 Peter I (the Great) declared his title to be "Emperor." He also abolished the automatic inheritance of the throne by primogeniture. The children or other descendents of an emperor became known as 'Grand Dukes' or 'Grand Duchesses.' There also came into being the new title of Tsesarevich. This was not just a variation on the spelling of Tsarevich, but a step up, meaning 'Son of Caesar.' This title gradually became reserved for the designated heir to the throne, who retained the title of Grand Duke as well.

The specific title of Grand Duke was regularized with the accession of Paul I to the throne in 1796. One of his first acts as Emperor was to issue a ukaze whereby succession to the throne was re-established by strict primogeniture in the male line, followed by the female only after complete failure of the male line. Grand Dukes were the descendants of an emperor through the male line, but the heir to the throne was styled "Tsesarevich," (he was also a Grand Duke.)

In 1886, Emperor Alexander III restricted the title of Grand Duke to the sons and grandsons of an emperor. Until that time, there had not been a great-grandson.

In selecting who was a 'grand duke' for the purpose of this work, we had to decide whether or not to include emperors, because they had also been grand dukes. One fact emerged: only one Emperor was born in the direct line of succession—Alexander I. None of the others at birth were in the direct line, except for the last

Tsesarevich, Alexis, who never became emperor. For example, Alexander II, the eldest son of Nicholas I, was not in the direct line at birth in 1818. His uncle, Alexander I, was still alive and on the throne; he could have produced a son. His uncle, Tsesarevich Constantine, the recognized 'heir presumptive' was alive, and while separated from his wife, could have produced an heir. Alexander II did not become Tsesarevich or heir apparent until his father Nicholas I's accession in 1825.

For these reasons, we have decided to include, as grand dukes, the emperors commencing with Nicholas I, but to limit their coverage, as the history of their reigns are already well known.

Therefore, we commence with the accession of Paul I in 1796, the point when the term 'Grand Duke' became formalized. Emperor Paul I, and Emperor Alexander I, are, however, both extensively covered in the opening "Introduction."

For those who will accuse us of discrimination because we have excluded grand duchesses from this work, there were twenty-three Russian grand duchesses by birth who reached adulthood in the period with which we are dealing. All of them married and became members of other families, except one, Maria Mikhailovna, who remained single; and one, Grand Duchess Xenia, who married a Russian grand duke; and the four daughters of Nicholas II who were murdered by the Bolsheviks. To include them would have almost doubled the size of this work. We do mention them when they play a role in the life of a grand duke, and we also cover, sometimes at length, grand duchesses by marriage, i.e., the non-morganatic wives of grand dukes.

Having now given what the publisher and author hope will be a 'satisfactory' answer as to who were grand dukes, and how we determined this, some comment is deserved as to why this book.

There is not a single biography of any of the Russian grand dukes. There are autobiographies by two grand dukes and one grand duchess written after the revolution. Nowhere has there ever been compiled even a list of all of the grand dukes, much less a combined biography of each.

David Chavchavadze, is a Russian prince, and a Romanov through his mother, Princess Nina of Russia, daughter of Grand Duke George Mikhailovich, and a direct descendant of Catherine the Great and Nicholas I. He was, for twenty-five years, a CIA officer, assigned to Soviet operations. In addition, he is a keen student of Russian history, and has had the benefit of private family lore, Romanov correspondence and documents, as well as extensive research knowledge of his family's history. Soon, all of the direct sources for information on the Romanov Family will vanish, and future generations will be left to shuffle through official records, documents, old letters and a few autobiographies.

In early 1989 Prince Vasily Alexandrovich passed away. He was the only remaining male Romanov born before the revolution. His cousins, Princes Vera Constantinovna and Catherine Ioannovna, are now the only living Romanovs born before the Revolution. After them, the direct door to this fascinating period of history will be closed forever.

Research in dusty archives is always difficult. In the case of the Romanovs, this is more true than with any other reigning royal family. Russia, before 1914, was not always in the mainstream of Europe, and much of what went on there was recorded only in Russian records. These records, in most instances, are now lost to historians and researchers because of Bolshevik policy. With the new winds blowing in Russia today, perhaps these archives will eventually be as open to researchers as the National Archives in Washington, but—more likely, they will never be completely open.

The few autobiographies written by Romanovs deal mainly with their own immediate experience before, during, and after the Revolution. These frequently leave very large gaps concerning critical events—whether by design or accident. Books which have appeared about members of the Romanov Family are virtually without exception filled with factual errors (even one autobiography of a Romanov contained incorrect birth data of family members). A biography of the Grand Dukes of Russia is, therefore, needed for historical purposes while some access to the family and records is still available; Prince David Chavchavadze is highly qualified to produce such a work; and, the little known lives of the grand dukes themselves, more than justify this book.

Most of the grand dukes were handsome men, a few were stupid, most were, however, highly intelligent—even brilliant; some were dilettantes, others highly conscientious servants of their country. All were larger than life, living only a heart-beat away from the Imperial Throne, and of becoming *Autocrat of all the Russias*! This was not an easy life. In many ways they were not as free as ordinary citizens. They had to ask the Emperor's permission each time they left the country, or wanted to get married. They were all expected to serve their country, and all of them, with the exception of those who died too young, did so. They did so, however, with very different degrees of success and diligence, and always with plenty of time off. With the power and prestige of the Imperial Throne behind them, and very substantial incomes, what they did with their time makes their story well worth preserving.

Between 1796 and 1917, there were thirty-three of these Magnificent Grand Dukes of Russia. This is their story.

ST. PETER and PAUL FORTRESS c. 1900

INTRODUCTION

In 1613 an elected body, or *Zemskiy Sobor*, elected a new Tsar, Michael Romanov, who was only sixteen years old.

Tsar Michael I was succeeded in 1645 by his only son, Alexis. Alexis had two sons by his first marriage, and another by a second marriage. He was followed by his eldest son, Feodor III in 1676. Feodor died without an heir, and was followed to the throne jointly by his brother, Ivan V, and his half-brother, Peter, in 1682.

Ivan abdicated in 1689, and Peter became sole Tsar, and known to history as "Peter the Great."

During his reign Peter made two changes in the law which had importance until the end of the Dynasty. First, he elevated his title to Emperor; secondly, he changed the succession law so that the Emperor had the right to name his own successor without consideration of primogeniture.

On Peter's death in 1725, he allegedly named his second wife, Catherine, as his heir. Whether he did or not, she claimed the throne, and was crowned as Catherine I. She reigned briefly, until 1727, and was succeeded by Peter's grandson, Peter II.

Peter's reign was brief, lasting only three years, as he died in 1730 at the age of fourteen. The death of Peter II was the end of the direct male Romanov line.

There were now many claimants to dispute the throne. The daughter of Ivan V, Anna, Duchess of Courland, was elected. Anna ruled for ten years, and before her death named her grandnephew, Ivan as her heir. Ivan was the infant son of Anna, Princess of Brunswick, the daughter of Empress Anna's older sister, Catherine. Within a short time, Peter the Great's daughter by Catherine I, Elizabeth, seized the infant Tsar and his parents, and with the help of the Guards, was proclaimed Empress. The baby Tsar, Ivan VI, lived in captivity until 1764, when he was murdered.

Empress Elizabeth ruled until 1762, and named as her successor her nephew, the Duke of Holstein, son of her eldest sister, and thus another grandson of Peter the Great. He became Tsar as Peter III in 1762. Elizabeth also arranged for his marriage to Princess Sophie Augusta of Anhalt-Zerbst, who was to become Catherine the Great.

Peter III succeeded his aunt, Empress Elizabeth, in 1762.

Within a year, his wife, Catherine, had had him imprisoned, seized the throne herself, and then Peter was murdered. While it is not thought that Catherine ordered, or was aware of the plans, she received the blame, and this event had repercussions down through the years.

Catherine was succeeded in 1796 by her son, Paul I. While Paul was officially the son of Peter III, there is some doubt as to his paternity.

With Paul I there came many changes in the Dynasty, and all the Romanovs to the present are descended from him.

At his birth, Empress Elizabeth had immediately taken the baby under her care, removing him from his parents, and Catherine had nothing to do with his upbringing during Elizabeth's lifetime.

There was talk that Empress Elizabeth would name the little Paul as her heir, passing over the dissolute Peter; nothing came of this, but plots abounded. Catherine, like Elizabeth, believed that Peter should not be allowed to reign. Peter's mistress, and lady-in-waiting to the Empress, Elizabeth Vorontzova, and her relatives had their own plan, which Peter was not displeased with. Peter would divorce Catherine, deny the legitimacy of Paul, and marry Elizabeth. Peter's supporters acted quickly, and immediately on the death of the Empress, proclaimed Peter Emperor.

Within a year, using loyal guards, Catherine had seized Peter, forced his abdication, and proclaimed herself Empress.

Her two chief rivals disposed of, Catherine was faced with a third—her son Paul, the rightful Tsar. It was, however, out of the question to do away with him, and in her own way, Catherine loved the boy, and was always alarmed at his slightest indisposition.

She always found time to spend a few minutes with him each day, and took an interest in his games and studies. This was not easy, as Paul was a difficult, mistrustful child, and was jealous of Catherine's lover, Gregory Orlov, and told her so.

Paul also suffered tremendously from his ugliness. As a baby, he had been 'cute' with his turned up nose and blond hair. But as he grew older, his nostrils became flat and he had thick lips. He soon began to ask questions about his father, and his own position. Bérenger wrote to the Duc de Praslin, "This young Prince gives evidence of sinister and dangerous inclinations . . . A few days ago . . . he asked why they had killed his father, and why they gave the throne to his mother that rightfully belonged to him. He added that when he grew up he would get to the bottom of [it]."

The hostility between mother and son increased, and Catherine virtually gave up on involving Paul with the government. She arrange a marriage, hoping this would have a beneficial influence. Princess Wilhelmina of Hesse-Darmstadt was selected, and the marriage took place 29 September 1773.

Catherine soon had reason to be displeased with her new daughter-in-law. Natalia, as she was known in Russia, was soon plotting to overthrow Catherine and place Paul on the throne. Catherine called the two of them before her and contemptuously threw the evidence in their face. Natalia, however, was not touched. She was pregnant. On 15 April 1776, a child was stillborn, and Natalia died.

Another bride had to be found, and the funeral was barely over before Catherine had put out the word. This time she found Sophia Dorothea of Württemberg, rechristened Maria Feodorovna. Catherine wrote that Sophia had a lily-and-rose complexion, the loveliest skin in the world, tall and well built; ". . . . she is graceful; sweetness, kindness and innocence are reflected in her face."

Paul was also impressed. He wrote to Henry of Prussia, "She has the art not only of driving out all my melancholy thoughts, but she gives me back the good humor that I had completely lost."

Paul and Maria made their principal residence at Gatchina, and Paul continued to be barred from politics. He took up military matters, and soon had a small private army at Gatchina, where he outdid his father in the absurdity of his orders, the cruelty of punishment and continuous drills. Catherine was not pleased to see him sliding into military mania.

The one bright spot was that Maria was expecting. On 12 December 1777, she gave birth to a boy.

Catherine promptly took custody of the boy, removing him immediately to her own quarters, and named him Alexander. The baby brought out Catherine's latent maternal instincts, frustrated when Empress Elizabeth had virtually kidnapped Paul. She now proceeded to do the same thing. She supervised every detail of Alexander's upbringing and education. She was crazy about her grandson, referring to him at length in her widespread correspondence as Monsieur Alexandre. To hear her tell it, there had never been a child so good looking, intelligent, even tempered, and healthy. As time went on, the toddler would spend more than three hours a day with his grandmother.

Her prescription for bringing up a baby was plenty of fresh air, cold baths, with no excessive rocking of the cradle or carrying the infant around. To this end, she installed an iron cot so that it could not easily be rocked. Each time she allowed the boy to spend a few days with his parents, she suffered, claiming that they undid all her efforts.

As Alexander grew older he developed a passion for books, but also rode, fenced, chopped wood, learned crafts such as carpentry and painting, and grew a vegetable garden. When he was four, Catherine wrote a special illustrated alphabet book for him, which was published and sold 20,000 copies in Petersburg in the first three days. Later she wrote books on Russian history for him, which were also used for Alexander's brother Constantine, born eighteen months later. The two boys were inseparable companions, but Catherine's enthusiasm for Constantine was not comparable to what she felt for Alexander, which she openly admitted in her correspondence with the French philosophers Diderot and Grimm, with whom she consulted about the boys' education.

At the age of six Alexander was taken away from his English nurse, Mme. Gessler, who was married to a Russian, and put into the hands of male educators. A courtier, N. I. Saltykov, was put in charge, mostly because of his ability to get along at both courts, Catherine's and Paul's, which few people were able to do. The actual instructors were very able men. One was a very unusual Russian priest called Samborsky, whom Catherine allowed to shave his beard and go about without wearing ecclesiastical robes. It is not surprising that he never succeeded in instilling an orthodox brand of Orthodoxy in Alexander. The instructor in Russian subjects was Protasov, who had a much more objective view of Alexander than did Catherine. Fortunately, he kept a diary. While he found Alexander to be honest, fair, modest and very sympathetic to people in distress, he also thought Alexander sly, lazy, critical of people, eager to imitate their mannerisms, too interested in trifles and fashions, and with a very early fascination with pretty women. Laharpe found Alexander to be very intelligent, but mentally lethargic, unwilling to think problems through.

The most important influence on Alexander's young life, from 1784 to 1795, was the Genevan Swiss, Frédéric César Laharpe, who first had to teach Alexander French in order to communicate with him. Laharpe was a man steeped in the ideas of the Enlightenment and an avowed republican. He and his associate, Protasov, a believer in absolute monarchy, were able to instill in both Alexander and Constantine a love and loyalty toward their father! Ironically, Paul, after the French Revolution had started, could not stand Laharpe, who was, in his eyes, a murderous Jacobin. Alexander and Laharpe grew extremely close to each other, an attachment which continued for years after Laharpe left, although he had always warned Alexander that rulers could never have true friends.

Catherine very early on commenced looking for a suitable bride for Alexander. She sent Count Rumyantsev on the search, and he eventually selected the eleven year old Princess Louise of Baden. She arrived for approval in St. Petersburg in 1792. Everybody, even Paul, agreed that Louise was pretty, charming, intelligent and modest. Alexander, however, never said a word to Louise when they first met. He soon came around, however. They were engaged at the age of fifteen and fourteen, and immediately provided with a court much more elaborate than Paul had had in a similar situation. The

Alexander Palace at Tsarskoye Selo, which would one day be the home of Nicholas II and Alexandra, was commenced in 1792, and was designated for them. The marriage took place at the Winter Palace on 28 September 1793. Louise took the name of Elizabeth. The marriage was not very successful. She did not produce a child for six years, when a daughter was finally born in 1799, and another in 1806, but neither survived infancy. Alexander always treated Elizabeth with the greatest consideration in public, but became estranged from her. Later, he had many affairs, notably a long and stormy one with Marie Naryshkin, who bore him two children. But in the early years, which coincided with a very difficult period in his life, Alexander confided his inner thoughts to Elizabeth and claimed that she understood and sympathized with him.

Although there were many interruptions, Alexander's education was better than that received by any previous grand duke or tsarevich. It was further interrupted beginning in 1795 when Alexander and Constantine began to go out to Gatchina or Pavlovsk four or five times a week to visit their father, who was exclusively occupied in drilling his Prussian-uniformed private army.

In spite of the liberalism absorbed from Laharpe, Alexander appeared to enjoy taking part in Paul's petty details and drill, and savage disciplinary measures. Here, Alexander met and formed a lifetime friendship with the sinister, sadistic martinet known as the "Corporal of Gatchina," Paul's right hand man, Alexis (later Count) Arakcheyev.

In the evenings, Alexander had to listen to his parents' complaints about, and criticism of, everything that went on at Catherine's court. Torn between loyalties, it is perhaps no wonder that Alexander throughout his later life struck contemporaries as being two-faced, enigmatic, secretive, and trying to be all things to all men. He seemed to hold diametrically opposite views with equal conviction. A lot of self-deception must have been involved. How was it possible to be equally loyal to Paul and Catherine? Or to form equally sincere friendships with Arakcheyev and Laharpe?

To add to Alexander's concerns there was the question of the succession. Catherine, even before his birth, had had in mind to bypass Paul and name Alexander Emperor on her death, something she was entitled to do under Peter the Great's decree. In 1793, when Alexander was sixteen, she tried to enlist Laharpe's help in this, but, much to her surprise, the liberal Swiss refused. Not only that, but in April 1795, already put on notice by Catherine that his services were no longer needed, Laharpe managed to obtain an audience with Paul, during which he begged the Tsesarevich to trust in the loyalty of both Alexander and Constantine. Four years after his departure, Laharpe became the President of Switzerland.

In 1796, Catherine asked Grand Duchess Maria Feodorovna

to agree to her husband's being passed over for the succession. Maria refused, but did not inform Paul, apparently. Then Catherine approached Alexander himself. He seemed to agree. In a letter he thanked his grandmother profusely for the honors bestowed on him, but did not specify what these were.

At about this same time, Alexander remarked that if Paul's rights were taken away, he and Elizabeth would flee to America and disappear! He also wrote Laharpe that he hated court life and would like to retire from it all.

Catherine went ahead with her plans. An act declaring Alexander to be her successor was drawn up and ready to be signed when Catherine had a stroke in November of 1796, which deprived her of the power of speech, and she died a few hours later.

Paul was now Emperor. Alexander and Constantine greeted him in their Gatchina uniforms, and Paul's troops marched into Petersburg to be integrated into the regular Imperial Guards.

Emperor Paul set about immediately to undo whatever he could of Catherine's work, and to at last gain his revenge on her. At every step the memory of Catherine was cursed or ridiculed.

Plato Zubov, Catherine's last lover, was soon relieved of all his duties, his estates were confiscated, and he was sent into exile.

Emperor Paul, not satisfied with this, had his father's coffin removed from the burial vaults at Alexander Nevsky monastery, and had it placed next to that of Catherine in the Winter Palace, giving it full Imperial honors. Above the coffins he had placed a banner which read, "Divided in life, joined in death." He then rounded up the few survivors of that 1762 murder. Alexis Orlov was made to carry Peter III's crown on a cushion at the head of the procession. Passek and Bariatinsky, Orlov's accomplices, were pallbearers. Paul marched in the procession, his head high, confident that he had avenged his father's death.

Paul's revenge against his mother was not yet complete. He remembered her long-time lover, and had his remains removed from their burial place in the St. Catherine church in Kherson, and Potemkin's bones were scattered to the four winds.

Like everyone else, Alexander was terrified of Paul. He soon tired of the Gatchina life, now extended to the whole army and the capital. In 1797 he wrote Laharpe again, complaining that after a brilliant beginning, Paul's reign had become impossible.

Alexander began meeting with four liberal friends, Novosiltsev, Kochubey, Stroganov, and the Polish Prince Adam Czartorisky, who would become known in his reign as the "special committee," or "the committee of public safety." Paul soon became suspicious of Alexander, and reminded him of the fate of Peter's son, the Tsarevich Alexis. He talked of adopting his new favorite, his wife's nephew Prince Eugene of Württemberg, and making him heir, which would have been in contradiction to the new law of succession [Pauline Law] by primogeniture that he himself had introduced.

The Emperor had become impossible, even to his own family, by 1800, and it was clear that he had to go. Alexander was made privy to a conspiracy by Counts Panin and Pahlen to depose Paul. He agreed, but stipulated that his father must not be harmed and must even be allowed to stay in his damp, new, moat-surrounded Mikhailovsky Castle. Alexander was actually agreeing to a regency with himself as regent, similar to what was going on in England during the insanity of King George III.

The conspirators had no such illusions. Paul was choked to death in his supposedly impregnable fortress on 24 March 1801. Ironically, one of his chief murderers was Plato Zubov, Catherine's last lover.

Alexander was present in the rooms below, and the Empress Maria was in an adjoining suite. She was awoken by her maid with the news, and immediately rushed to Paul's chambers. Her entrance was blocked by the guards. Here the conspiracy almost took an unexpected twist. Maria drew herself up and ordered the guards out of her way, proclaiming that she was now Empress! Even when brought to Alexander she insisted, stating that she had been crowned with Paul, and would now claim the throne. It took several days to persuade her to relinquish her claim.

Catherine's victory over her son was now complete, he was dead, and her grandson, Alexander, came to the throne as she had long-planned.

The murder of his father was a heavy load on the conscience of Alexander, and one that he carried to his grave.

Alexander I did not share in the general rejoicing. This man, born with the talents to be a great ruler, delivered very little. He remained an enigma, a sphinx, but one capable of charming everybody—for awhile. When one looks beyond the external glory of the victory over Napoleon, one sees that his good intentions were rarely translated into action, the few that were being limited to the first years of his reign. During the last ten years Alexander I became increasingly mystical and turned the internal rule of the empire over to none other than the former "Corporal of Gatchina," Count Arakcheyev, with predictable results. When Alexander unexpectedly died on 19 November 1825 at the age of forty-eight, he left a mess behind—an unclear succession, and a conspiracy against him in the army and Guards. He knew all about the conspiracy, but could not bring himself to act, or even to keep his brother Nicholas informed. It was left to Nicholas to clean up the mess.

There is a persistent story that Alexander I did not die at all in 1825, but took advantage of being in the small Sea of Azov port of Taganrog to disappear, living on for another forty years as the mysterious hermit, Fedor Kuzmich. Supporting this story is the fact that Fedor Kuzmich had a physical resemblance to Alexander and knew a lot of things about the great world, and also the undoubted fact that Alexander I's grave at the Peter and Paul Fortress cathedral was empty in the late 19th century. Other supposed "facts" such as the presence of a British yacht at Taganrog on which Alexander departed and visits to Fedor Kuzmich by Nicholas I, have been exploded. Against this admittedly intriguing and very Russian story, is the difficulty of believing it when not a single person of those who surrounded Alexander I in Taganrog, beginning with his wife, ever came out with at least a death bed account of what happened, other than the official version. Let us also give this crowned enigma the benefit of believing that he would have left affairs in a little better state for his brother Nicholas if he really carried out his frequent dream of abdication in this clandestine way.

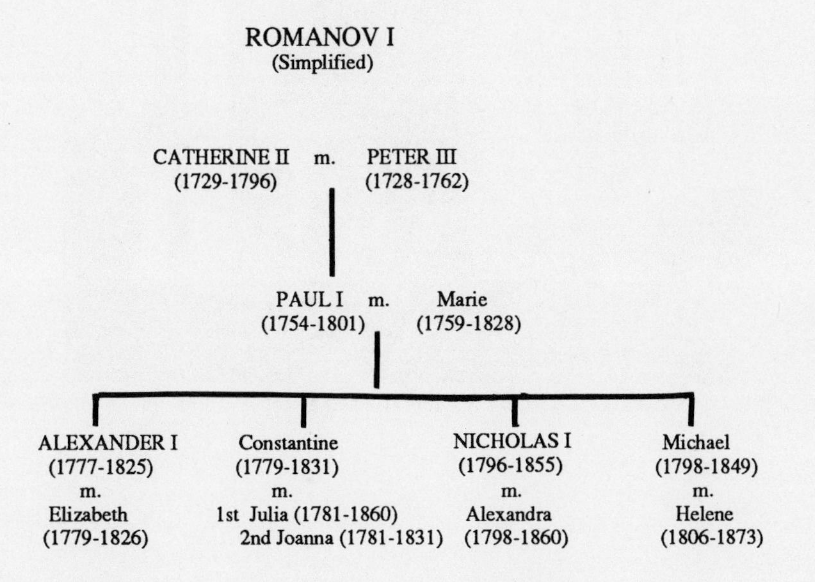
ROMANOV I
(Simplified)
CATHERINE II m. PETER III
(1729-1796) (1728-1762)
PAUL I m. Marie
(1754-1801) (1759-1828)
ALEXANDER I
(1777-1825)
m.
Elizabeth
(1779-1826)
Constantine
(1779-1831)
m.
1st Julia (1781-1860)
2nd Joanna (1781-1831)
NICHOLAS I
(1796-1855)
m.
Alexandra
(1798-1860)
Michael
(1798-1849)
m.
Helene
(1806-1873)

GRAND DUKE CONSTANTINE PAVLOVICH

CHAPTER I

GRAND DUKE CONSTANTINE PAVLOVICH (1779 - 1831)

Grand Duke Constantine Pavlovich was the second son of Grand Duke Paul Petrovich, later Emperor Paul I. Born at Tsarskoye-Selo on 8 May 1779, his mother was the strong-minded Maria Feodorovna, born a Princess of Württemberg.

Like his older brother Alexander, Constantine was taken away from his parents and brought up under the supervision of his grandmother, Empress Catherine, just as her son had been taken away by Empress Elizabeth.[1] It must be admitted, she did keep the parents well informed of the progress of Alexander and Constantine. Catherine adored Alexander and considered Constantine to be sickly and in no way comparable. Catherine wrote to Grimm, "I wouldn't give ten sous for . . . Constantine: unless I am much mistaken, it will not remain on earth." This did not stop her from having great plans for him. Someday he would sit on the throne of a new Orthodox empire based on Constantinople and would start a new, independent branch of the Romanov dynasty. Hence his name, Constantine. A Greek nurse was found, as Constantine had to be nursed on milk from Olympus.[2] Needless to say, nothing ever came of this scheme. She recounted how both accompanied her daily in her sledge, ". . . . baby Constantine on my knee while Sasha hops about on one leg like a bird." The Empress notes later ". . . . What an angel little Sasha has always been. . . ." and described Constantine as a demon with his biting, scratching, and rudeness.[3]

Grand Duke Constantine was eighteen months younger than his brother, Alexander, and they grew up very close, with a genuine affection between them. Their tutor was the Swiss, Laharpe, a man of strong republican and constitutional principles. According to the boys mother, Empress Maria, Laharpe was too severe and broke the boys' spirits, forcing them to keep records of their own shortcomings,

1. *Mother of Czars*, C. Grant
2. *Catherine the Great*, Henri Troyat
3. *A Czarina's Story*, Empress Alexandra

and afterwards insisting on their abasement. A lot of his liberalism influenced Alexander in his youth and early reign, but not much, if any, rubbed off on Constantine.

As the two young Grand Dukes grew older they were allowed to visit their parents for increasingly longer periods. This arrangement, shuttling back and forth from St. Petersburg or Tsarskoye-Selo to Gatchina, that is, between their grandmother and their father, caused complications. It was, as Schilder remarks, ". . . . like moving back and forth between Athens and Sparta for the two boys."

Their father, Paul, estranged from his mother and resentful of her, rarely went to St. Petersburg, having established himself at Gatchina, where he recruited and ran a small private army. Paul dressed his soldiers in Prussian uniforms, introduced Prussian forms of drill, and generally followed all the precepts of the out-dated army of Frederick the Great. Alexander and Constantine loved drilling the little Gatchina army, but also were aware that their father was suspicious of their loyalty to him. Grand Duke Paul had reason to be suspicious, since, at least from 1792 on, his mother was seriously considering disinheriting him and passing the succession directly to Alexander. The boys, thus, grew up with divided loyalties, but managed to maintain good relations with both camps. This difficult situation led, in Constantine's case, to extreme behavior.[4]

At Gatchina, Constantine acquired the passion of his life, the métier of military martinet, and the army was always his first love. Constantine was much like his father in character and temperament, and closer to him than was Alexander. His sister-in-law, Empress Alexandra Feodorovna, described Constantine as "an ugly charicature of Emperor Paul".

Empress Catherine arranged for Alexander's marriage when he was only sixteen to Princess Louise of Baden, who became Grand Duchess and later Empress Elizabeth Alexeyevna. Constantine, who was probably the only one of Catherine's grandchildren to stand up to her, angrily rejected her suggestions of princesses that he should marry. Nevertheless, Constantine was married at the age of seventeen, in the last year of Catherine's reign, to a pretty fifteen-year-old girl, Princess Juliane of Saxe-Coburg-Saalfeld, who became Grand Duchess Anna Feodorovna, a future aunt of Queen Victoria. They did not get along very well, and the marriage was not a success. His personal life was too irregular and licentious, and he had numerous affairs. His grandnephew, the historian Grand Duke Nicholas Mikhailovich, gives no quarter in describing him at the time of his first marriage. "Rude, impossible, totally lacking in tact," was his verdict. Constantine was never a favorite of the Russian nobles,

---

4. *Catherine the Great*, Henri Troyat

and, in fact, was detested by them.

In character, Constantine was a ruthless and rigid disciplinarian, and was subject to sudden and violent rages. He was a taciturn, morose man, and committed deeds of cruelty such as his brother, Nicholas, would never have perpetrated.

Eventually, after about five years, Grand Duchess Anna left Constantine and Russia for good. One can sympathise with her. Constantine's habit of occasionally firing a cannon in the Marble Palace, where they lived, while placing her in a large vase for safe-keeping, was hardly conducive to a good marriage! The Grand Duke is also reported to have once honored the birthday of his brother, Alexander, by having a salute cannon loaded with rats and fired, for which he received a public tongue lashing from Alexander.

Constantine did not appear unduly disturbed by the departure of his wife, and had as early as 1803 suggested that the marriage should be dissolved. At that time he wanted to marry Princess Janetta Antonovna Chetvertinskoi, the sister of Maria Antonovna Naryshkin—long the mistress of Alexander I—but his mother opposed the plan, she was violently against a divorce or a morganatic marriage.

Shortly after his wife left, Constantine commenced a long affair with a French actress, Mlle Friedrichs, by whom he had an illegitimate son, Paul Constantinovich Alexandrov, for whom he cared very deeply. Even so, he would see his wife from time to time in Europe, and in 1814 there was even talk of a reconciliation, but nothing came of it and the marriage was finally terminated by divorce in 1820.

The reign of Emperor Paul ended in 1801, with his murder. It is clear that Paul's son, Alexander, was made aware of the plot to remove his father, but it is highly improbable that he knew the conspirators intended murder. There is no indication that Constantine had any knowledge of the plot, but with his brother's accession to the throne, Constantine became the heir presumptive, and was named Tsesarevich. He retained this title for the rest of his life, using it even after his brother, Nicholas, became Emperor and had heirs of his own.

After the fall of Napoleon, the part of Poland belonging to Russia was granted a constitution by Emperor Alexander I—something that Russia herself did not have—with the Emperor as King. He appointed Constantine Viceroy.

Grand Duke Constantine arrived in Warsaw in 1814, and found a home there for the rest of his life. It was difficult to get him to leave. He lived in considerable state at the Belvedere Palace with his mistress Mlle Friedrichs.

His first job was to establish a Polish army, which by 1817 reached 35,000 men, plus a corps of Lithuanians; Constantine was very proud of this army. He also took the Polish constitution very seriously, in spite of his basic lack of sympathy for such things. It was, for the period, one of the most liberal constitutions in Europe. In 1828, when his younger brother, Nicholas I, was on the throne, Constantine refused him the use of Polish troops in the war against Turkey, saying that it was unconstitutional. Even so, the Poles had to endure his parade ground methods. On one occasion five Polish officers of the Third Regiment committed suicide, considering themselves dishonored by Constantine's having temporarily reduced two others to the ranks. A sixth officer challenged the Viceroy to a duel. What is not so widely known is that Constantine was horrified by the suicides, regarding them as the results of a misunderstanding, and agreed to shed his vice-regal and grand ducal status to give this officer the satisfaction he desired with a duel. Indeed, he insisted on it. The Polish officer withdrew his challenge, and Constantine made peace with him, insisting on the exchange of hugs and kisses, and twice apologized to the whole regiment as it stood in ranks.

Even with all of these incidents, which writers of the day used to justify characterizing him as having an odious reputation, that he was a tyrant and a maniac, and saying that he was an illiterate oaf, a boor and a bully, Constantine also had a good side.

During Paul's short reign, for example, while Constantine commanded the Horse Guards, Paul severely punished an officer of this regiment for a minor infraction in carrying out drill commands. Constantine, thinking this unfair, later went on his knees to his father, saying that he would gladly give up the decoration he had been promised for the 1799 campaign in Italy if Paul would pardon the officer. Showing a similar kind side, which he undoubtedly also had, Paul agreed not only to pardon the officer but reinstate him with a promotion.

To the charge that he was an illiterate oaf, Grand Duke Constantine spoke Polish, French, German and English in addition to Russian, and his correspondence, particularly with his sister Anna Pavlovna, Princess of Orange and later Queen of the Netherlands, shows him to be a writer of clarity and precision, capable of perception, understanding, sympathy, generosity and loyalty. His temperament did fluctuate wildly, from joking good humor—and he could be extremely witty—to sudden and fierce rages. The point is, Constantine suffered from bouts of insanity, like his father Paul, and could not always control his behavior.

Nor were his military excesses uncommon for the day. Queen Victoria's father, the Duke of Kent, was recalled from Gibraltar because of his excessively severe military discipline; the Duke of Cumberland insisted on the most rigid attention to parade ground drill; and the Duke of Wellington, who was never thought to be exacting, always believed in the lash to keep soldiers under control.

Shortly after his arrival in Poland, Grand Duke Constantine met and fell in love with Countess Joanna ("Jeannette") Grudzinska, of a distinguished Polish family, and he soon disposed of Mlle. Friedrichs. The Countess refused to become his mistress because he was still married. When his divorce came through, they were married morganatically, meaning that their issue would have no rights to the throne, and that she did not rank as a grand duchess. This was the first Romanov morganatic marriage, not counting the probable secret marriages of Empress Elizabeth to Alexis Razumovsky, and of Catherine the Great to Grigory Potemkin. There would not be another morganatic marriage until toward the end of the century. The Countess was created Princess Lovich (Lowicka).

Writing to his sister, Anna Pavlovna, on May 27, 1820, Grand Duke Constantine explained the marriage:

> "Dear Anne,
>
> . . . .Your good wishes went straight to my heart which is very grateful to you. I shall not go into the motives which made me wish to take action, but shall write here everything which has to do with the matter. Let me tell you purely and simply that I felt I should do it to bring about a permanent solution. It becomes painful to remain separated from my wife and involved in an illegal union as I grow older; a youthful folly may be excused, but at the age of reflection, and especially after the age of forty, it is no longer good. Nor do I feel called to become a monk. . . Were I to remarry with a princess of my rank, able to have children, I would be putting them all directly in front of my brother Nicholas. This is repugnant to my conscience and my scruples. . . To resolve everything and to give me some peace in a home, I felt it best to seek the hand of a private person who, according to the stipulations of the manifesto of last 20 March, would in no way hinder the established state of affairs. For all this I had the Emperor's authorisation. . . for the confirmation of the new union which I have just concluded by remarrying a lady of the court named Grudzinska, and astonishing person and kind, a lady of twenty-five or twenty-six years . . . I have sought her for almost six years, and thanks to the goodness of the Lord . . . I married her on 24 May. I am happy, content, and I have my home established the way I wish it, with a wife who is not, thank God, a Grand Duchess and does not wish to be one. . . Kiss your children for me, and ever count upon the tender and

unchanging friendship of your grateful, faithful brother and friend."

What the letter did not say was that as part of the agreement with his brother, Emperor Alexander I, Grand Duke Constantine had renounced his rights to the throne. There are several variations as to exactly when and how this was done. The account given by Constantine's mother, the Empress Maria, is probably the most accurate. According to her, at the time of his second marriage, she had finally agreed for Constantine to renounce his rights; he sent his abdication in the form of a letter, and the Emperor confirmed it, also in writing. In January 1822, in the presence of the Emperor, the two Empresses, and the Grand Duchess Maria Pavlovna, Constantine again formally renounced his rights. The agreement, however, was still kept secret; not even Nicholas, now the heir presumptive, was told.[5] Constantine did tell his brother Michael, saying that he felt the "wings of death over the Imperial Family," and that his repugnance to become Emperor was "constitutional and invincible," and that in any case he had disqualified himself from the succession by remarriage to a person of unequal rank, and who was not Orthodox. He stated that he was ready to place "my knee as mounting-block for my brother Nicholas."

Constantine continued pressing to have the decision made public, arguing that Nicholas should be officially recognized as heir, and that he wanted his own position made clear.

Alexander, always prone to balance between two opinions, and hating to take decisions, continued to delay. Two of his favorite proverbs were, "One scarcely ever repents of having waited," and "Try ten times cut once." He feared that if he let Constantine slip completely out of the succession he might be condemning himself to remain on duty until death, and by this time, Alexander seriously wanted to escape into private life.

Finally, in the summer of 1823, The State Act concerning the succession was made. The Emperor decided to consult with two great friends, Count Arakcheyev and Prince Alexander Golitsin as to the steps he should take. It was finally decided to draw up a document setting out the agreement arrived at between Alexander and Constantine. Alexander did not trust any copyist or clerk with so important a secret, so Golitsin made four copies of the rescript with his own hand. Constantine's letter of abdication, and the manifesto, were placed in a sealed cover, on which the Emperor wrote with his own hand, "*Guardez jusqu'à ma rèclamation, mais dans le cas ou je viendrais mourir ouvrez ce pacquet en séance extraordinaire avant de procéder à tout autre acte.*"[6] One copy was deposited in the

5. *Mother of Czars*, C. Grant
6. *A Czarina's Story*, Empress Alexandra

Church of the Assumption in Moscow, one with the Synod, one with the Senate and one with the Council of the Empire.

The words on the envelope—"Till I demand it," indicate that his resolution was not irrevocable, which helps explain why even with the document formally done, the deed was not made public.

Constantine continued his life as Viceroy of Poland. He swore by the loyalty of his Polish army, even though there was a conspiracy to assassinate him in 1823, which was foiled. At the same time the future "Decembrists" were in touch with elements in Poland, exhorting them to do to Constantine in Warsaw what they would do to Alexander in St. Petersburg. They promised Polish independence when they took power.

On 19 November 1825, Emperor Alexander I died at Taganrog. Now, his secrecy over the abdication of Grand Duke Constantine and the succession of Nicholas, led to an interregnum. Upon receiving the news in St. Petersburg, Grand Duke Nicholas swore allegiance to his older brother Constantine, while in Warsaw, Constantine swore allegiance to Emperor Nicholas I! Even though is wife implored him to renounce his love for her and take what was his by right of birth, Grand Duke Constantine stood by his denunciation. This historically unique Alfonse-Gaston act between the two brothers, while their youngest brother, Michael, rode posthaste back and forth between Petersburg and Warsaw, created a perfect opportunity for a revolutionary attempt in St. Petersburg by liberal and radical secret societies of army and guards officers, who became known as "Decembrists."

The revolution was put down by the firm action of the new Emperor, and Grand Duke Constantine continued on his own way in Warsaw.

The Grand Duke tended to uphold Polish interests, and spent a lot of his own, as well as crown funds, for the development of the country, which was probably better off than any part of Russia itself, and many parts of Europe as well. Many Poles, however, were not satisfied to be part of the Russian Empire, in spite of their autonomy, and yearned for total independence. It was probably naive of Constantine not to see this and not to remember that many older men in his pet Polish Army had fought fanatically for Napoleon against Russia not so many years before.

It all came to a head in 1830. This was a revolutionary year in Europe. Charles X of France was overthrown and replaced by Louis Philippe, and in the Netherlands the Belgians revolted against the Dutch king. In Poland there were rumors that Nicholas I intended using Poles to put down the Belgian revolt under the terms of the "Holy Alliance."

Neither Nicholas nor Constantine worried about Poland, not even after Constantine had to flee out of the rear of the Belvedere

Palace when it was occupied by rebellious cadets. He could have easily crushed the revolt in its early stages by using the Russian troops also under his command, but he hesitated for two months. His dispatches convinced Nicholas to do the same, while they pleaded for moderation. This gave time for Constantine's beloved Polish Army to organize itself and join the revolution. Soon the disorganized rebellion grew into a full scale war, which the Russians, after several months of severe fighting, crushed. Nicholas I eliminated the Polish constitution and the Polish army, introducing a considerable amount of russification and a degree of autonomy that was only a shadow of the former arrangement.

Constantine had withdrawn from Warsaw with the Russian troops, surprised and horrified at the scale of what had happened. Half way through the Russo-Polish war he died from cholera at Vitebsk on 27 June 1831. His wife outlived him by only several months, but before she died in November of 1831, she was cordially received by Nicholas I and his wife, and even invited to live with them.

Whatever his faults, Grand Duke Constantine was a man who, realizing his weaknesses, voluntarily and without any pressure, gave up his rights to the Russian throne and, even when circumstances made it easy for him to change his mind and take the throne, he stuck by his pledged word. For the next six years he loyally served his younger brother. This alone makes him something of a rarity among men or princes.

Grand Duke Constantine Pavlovich lies in the cathedral of the Fortress of St. Peter and Paul, even on his coffin retaining his title of Tsesarevich.

PETERHOF

GRAND DUKE NICHOLAS PAVLOVICH c. 1817
(Nicholas I)

CHAPTER II

GRAND DUKE NICHOLAS PAVLOVICH (1796-1855)

EMPEROR NICHOLAS I (1825 -1855)

Grand Duke Nicholas was born at Gatchina on 5 June 1796, the third son of Grand Duke Paul (later Emperor Paul I) and Grand Duchess Maria Feodorovna. Until he was a full grown man, there appeared no prospect of his ever coming to the throne, as both of his older brothers, Alexander and Constantine were married. In fact, Nicholas was neither raised nor trained to be Emperor.

Nicholas spent almost half of his life as "third son and Grand Duke." Much has been written about him as Emperor, but little is known of his years as Grand Duke. It is from him that all of the present House of Romanov descend.

Five months before the death of his grandmother, Catherine the Great, she described the infant as being "two feet long, with hands not much smaller than hers, and a loud, low voice. I have never seen such a knight," she wrote. "If he continues this way his brothers will look like dwarfs next to this colossus. It seems to me," she added, prophetically, "that he is destined also to rule, even though he has two older brothers."[1]

Nicholas was nineteen years younger than his eldest brother, the future Alexander I, and seventeen years younger than his second brother, Constantine. He also had five older sisters ranging in age from thirteen to one year in age. Altogether, his parents had ten children.

Unlike his two older brothers, Nicholas was not raised and educated by his grandmother, who died shortly after his birth. Madame de Lieven was initially in charge of Nicholas, handling him

1. *History of Catherine II*, V. A Bilbasov

with dignity, and Nicholas treated her like a grandmother. As he grew older, his education was entrusted to General Lamsdorff, a harsh disciplinarian. The pedagogical methods of this tutor consisted of beating his pupil's knuckles with a ruler. Nevertheless, Nicholas grew up a hard worker, handsome, neat, modest, demanding of himself and others, and developed a taste for command and a love of everything military, particularly military engineering. His style of command, unlike his brothers and father, was for maneuvers and alarms, rather than parades. He also showed talent and enthusiasm for the arts and languages, speaking Russian, French, German and English. He was grounded in the classics, as well as economics, law and political science. Early on, he indicated that he had no real interest in what he called "abstracts," which perhaps explains why in later life he complained about his education, except for the benevolent influence of an English nanny, Miss Lyon. Nicholas was fond of music, and played the flute, patronised the opera and, to a degree, was a balletomane. He had considerable artistic talent, showing an aptitude for painting and collected pictures assiduously.[2]

When Emperor Alexander made his god-like entry into Paris at the head of the Allied troops in May 1814, Nicholas rode close to him. Nicholas also accompanied the Emperor to London, and then to Vienna for the Congress called by the four great Powers—Austria, England, Prussia and Russia. At Vienna, Nicholas remained in attendance on his brother through the winter of 1814-1815, and it was not until March, when Napoleon escaped from Elba, that he returned to his regiment. The Congress calmly continued its sittings during the hundred days before the victory at Waterloo, but after this battle, at which no Russian troops were present, Nicholas found himself once again riding into Paris in the Tsar's suite.

While in Paris, Nicholas received an intimation of the surprising fate that awaited him; a mystic, Madame de Krüdener, the friend and spiritual adviser of Alexander I, told him that one day he would be Emperor. When Nicholas protested, she said, "Remember that princes are in the hands of God, who makes and unmakes kings and emperors. It is from God they hold their mandate and their power. . . ."[3]

In 1814, shortly after Napoleon's abdication, Princess Charlotte, daughter of King Frederick William III of Prussia and Queen Louise, had been called upon to entertain two of the Russian grand dukes, Nicholas and Michael as they were in Berlin enroute to join the staff of their brother, Emperor Alexander I. Although only seventeen years old, Nicholas managed to fall in love with his fair-haired, blue-eyed hostess. Fascinated by his good looks and ardour,

---

2. *Empress Alexandra*, A. Grimm
3. *A Czarina's Story*, Empress Alexandra

Charlotte hastened to exchange vows of eternal love with the handsome Grand Duke.

In October, Nicholas was granted leave to go to Charlottenburg to see his beloved. The betrothal ceremony took place in the royal chapel in Berlin with his brothers, Alexander and Michael, and his sister, Catherine, widow of Prince George of Oldenburg, present. At the banquet following the betrothal the health of the young couple was drunk. Next morning, Princess Charlotte invited the Tsar and her fiancé to accompany her to the Charlottenburg mausoleum where her mother was buried, and at the tomb she solemnly dedicated herself to Russia, and vowed to be to Nicholas what Queen Louise had been to her father.

Charlotte had not come from a home endowed with riches. She was born in troubled times, in 1798, and was baptized three days after the battle of Aboukir. For nearly two years after the dreadful events of 1807 the royal children of Prussia traveled about with their parents as fugitives rather than members of a reigning family, and their education was somewhat intermittent. At Memel the life of the Royal Family was not merely simple, it was frugal to the point of privation. Every piece of plate or article of value was converted by the King into money to help lighten the burden which Napoleon had laid on the people. The Princesses could not afford new dresses, and so great was the poverty that they could not bear strangers to see their limited household means. A diplomat who spent an evening with them at Memel said, "I would not exchange my memories of that spectacle for a thousand court festivals with gold-laced uniforms and stars. At a shabby table which was devoid of all outward show was seated a Queen, whose charm, loveliness, and dignity stood all the stronger."

At the Berlin betrothal of Nicholas and Charlotte, it was decided by their families that because of their youth, eighteen months must be allowed before the wedding. This would give the couple time to see something of the world and to educate themselves for the duties they would face as married adults.

Nicholas returned to St. Petersburg before Christmas of 1815. He assisted at the New Year's wedding of his sister Catherine to the Crown Prince of Württemberg, a marriage celebrated with great pomp at the Winter Palace. After official visits to the Odessa region in May, and the Don in August, Nicholas begged permission to travel abroad till the date of his majority and marriage. This was granted, on the condition that he not spend more than a month in Berlin, then to make a stay of at least three months in England.

Nicholas found Charlotte in good spirits and already being called "Alexandra" by her family, the name she would take as his wife. Time went swiftly for the lovers, but at the end of four weeks Nicholas, true to his promise, set off for England, paying short visits to his sisters, Marie of Saxe-Weimar, and Catherine. Travelling by way of Paris he reached Calais on 17 November and went aboard the yacht *Royal Sovereign*, sent by the Prince Regent of England [later George IV].

For three months Nicholas attended balls, routs, dinners and plays in London and race meetings in the provinces. More serious occupations also filled up part of his time. He inspected arsenals, industrial centres, coal mines, prisons and hospitals. The Duke of Wellington paid him particular attention and volunteered to be his guide during visits to Brimingham and Manchester.

The Grand Duke invited the Prince Regent and his brothers, the Dukes of York and Sussex, to join him aboard a Russian frigate that was in the Thames. The crew were put through their drills for the amusement of the guests. The Prince Regent applauded enthusiastically, and observed condescendingly that the men were really "as good as English tars." Nicholas murmured how insignificant the Russian fleet was in numbers compared to the English armada. The Prince replied jocularly, "Let us divide the empire, the empire of the seas. We will keep the ocean and leave the North Sea to you!" There was not much reply the Grand Duke could make.[4]

The more Nicholas saw of England and her statesmen, the less in sympathy he was with representative government. The debates in the House of Commons seemed silly and wasteful, confirming him in his leanings towards absolutism.

On 12 June 1817 Princess Charlotte set out for Russia, accompanied by her brother, William, her mistress of the robes, Countess Haake, her lady-in-waiting, Countess Truchsess, her gouvernante, Mademoiselle Wildermatt, her Grand Chamberlain, Baron von Schilden, her Chamberlain, Count Lottern, her secretaries Chambeau and Schiller, her doctor, Busse, and her chaplain, Father Voussovsky. With her servants, it took twelve large carriages to accommodate the entire party.

Princess Charlotte wrote of her arrival in Russia as follows:

> "My betrothed, the Grand Duke Nicholas, with sword drawn, at the head of a guard of honour, received me at the frontier turnpike with a court composed of the old Princess Wolkonsky, Countess Catherine Shouwaloff and Mlle. Barbe Ouchakoff, of Count Zachar Tehernicheff, grand echanson, of M. Albedyll, maitre de la cour, of Prince Basil Dolgorouky, chamberlain, and Mr. Sologoub, gentleman-in-waiting.
>
> "The journey was made in great heat and by

4. *A Czarina's Story*, Empress Alexandra

unimaginable roads! At Tchoudovo on the 5th June I cried a lot at the idea of having next day to make the acquaintance of the Empress Mother as they had frightened me about her. It was on the evening of the 6th June, at Krukova, that I found myself squeezed in the arms of my future mother-in-law who received me with a tenderness so caressing that she won my heart from the first moment. The Emperor Alexander and Grand Duke Michael had also come to meet me. The Emperor received me with the charm of manner and the cordial, well-chosen words that are peculiar to him.

"Next day . . . I continued my journey passing by Gatchina and skirting the gardens of Tsarskoi Selo. I was escorted by the Cossacks of the guard, which gave me childish pleasure. As we approached Pavlovsk, it made a most pleasant impression on me. . .I think that the whole Court was formed up in this little garden, but I took in nothing; I only remember that beautiful roses were in bloom, the white roses especially delighted my eyes and seemed to bid me welcome.

"I don't think they found me as pretty as they had expected, but my feet were admired and my light step, which led several people to call me *ptichka* (little bird). The ladies were presented to me by the Empress Mother . . . Mademoiselle Nelidoff [Catherine Ivanovna] taken as a specimen of these ladies of the Community at Smolny seemed to me astonishingly ugly, bad-mannered and she smelt quite horribly. . . We dined in the great mother-of-pearl saloon. I remember the Emperor pointing out to me two young women as being the prettiest and the most sought after at Court: Princess Barbe Dalgorouky and Princess Sophie Troubetzkoi[5]. . .

"My official entry into St. Petersburg took place on the 19th of June. We breakfasted at Tatarinoff, a country house near the fortifications, and there the two Empresses and the two Württemberg Princesses arranged themselves with me in a gilded landau which was open. I was placed on the left of the two Empresses so as to be on the side on which the troops were parading. It was a great pleasure to see the Guard Regiments again, especially the Semenovsky,

---

5. There are many variations in spellings of Russian names. We have tried to conform these, except where they appear in direct quotes.

the Ismailovsky and the Preobrajensky regiments, for I had got to know them at a review near Peterwaldau in Silesia during the armistice of 1813.

"We ascended the grand ceremonial staircase of the Winter Palace and proceeded to the chapel. . . Then from a balcony we watched the troops parade; the march past, I was told later, was not a great success. From this same balcony I was shown off to the people. The balcony no longer exists, it was made of wood. I made the acquaintance of several of the ladies-in-waiting: Countess Litta, white-skinned, dimpled and with the smile of a child, still appeared beautiful; old Countess Pouschkine was painted white, pink and lilac, which made her old face even uglier; Countess Lopoukhin was ignoble of presence and false of face."

While a week would pass before the wedding, the time was filled with ceremony. Lunches, dinner parties and dances, and becoming familiar with the court. The Princess described these events in detail. The details of her betrothal to Grand Duke Nicholas were recorded with obvious pleasure:

"Next day, the 25th of June, our betrothal was celebrated, and I, for the first time in my life, put on Russian costume; the dress was rose-coloured and I wore diamonds and put a little rouge on my cheeks which suited me very well. The Empress Mother's maid dressed me and her hairdresser did my hair. We exchanged rings and drove together through the city. The 25th of June was the twenty-first birthday of the Grand Duke Nicholas. This ceremony was followed by a grand dinner and a ball at which the polonaise was the only dance. Each evening I was taken driving through the streets of St. Petersburg."

Alexandra wrote that the city itself did not make a grandiose impression on her . . . "save for the view over the Neva seen from the rooms of the Czarina Elizabeth." Every day they dined on the roof garden of the Hermitage or in the adjacent galleries.

Of the wedding itself, Alexandra wrote:

"The day on which our wedding was to be solemnised, Sunday, the 1st July, was drawing near. My betrothed became more and more tender and impatient to call me wife and to live with me at the

Anitchkov Palace, which had been allotted to us as a residence. On the day before the 1st, which happened to be my birthday, I was given charming presents of pearls and diamonds; I enjoyed it all immensely as never in Berlin had I worn a single diamond, for my father had brought us up with unusual simplicity.

"They began to dress me in my own room, but half-way through my toilet and hair dressing I was moved into the chamber of the Crown diamonds, which adjoined the bedroom of the Dowager Empress. There the crown was placed on my head, and in addition there were hung on my person a very large number of huge crown jewels. Under the weight of these I felt I should die. My dress was of cloth of silver with a cramoisie train lined with ermine. To this magnificent finery I added a single real white rose which I fastened to my waist belt. I felt very happy when our hands were joined, and with the utmost confidence I placed my life in the keeping of my Nicholas and he has never betrayed that trust.

"After the ball we were invited to descend the ceremonial staircase and enter a gold coach with the Empress Mother, whose escort of Chevaliers Gardes followed us to the Anitchkov Palace . . . at the top of the stairs stood the Czar Alexander and the Czarina Elizabeth to receive us with the customary offerings of bread and salt."

Their family life was easy and pleasant. Grand Duchess Alexandra wrote, "I was forgiven my trivial sins against etiquette because of . . . the kindliness of my high spirits. Mama (Empress Maria) was much amused to see me stealing cherries, a thing which formerly she would never have forgiven her own children; she really spoilt me by her indulgence. Old Lieven said to me, "*O Sie sind das Herzblatt der Kaiserin Mutter!*"

And, "Mama found William (her brother, later Emperor William I of Germany) very agreeable socially, for he danced around and chattered as a young man should, and she went for her own sons Nicholas and Michael because at parties they retired into corners and looked bored. She thought they behaved like bears with sore heads and pulled long faces like a marabou stork. It is true that my Nicholas, as soon as he found himself in a court circle or, above all, at a ball, put on what for his twenty-one years was a very staid philosophic look. He and I were only really happy and pleased when we were alone in our rooms with me sitting on his knees while he was being loving and tender."

Almost exactly nine months after their marriage, Nicholas and his bride, now Grand Duchess Alexandra Feodorovna, had a son, the future Emperor Alexander II.

In preparation for this event, Grand Duke Nicholas and Alexandra were taken to Moscow by Maria Feodorovna, who was careful to impress on her daughter-in-law that she belonged not to herself but to Russia. The Grand Duchess wrote, "This was to raise the spirits of the inhabitants of the old capital which, in the year 1812 had been almost destroyed by fire. Before starting, we stayed at the Anitchkov Palace in which we had hardly lived at all. There we gave a masked evening party. Everybody was masked from top to toe: Mama as a witch; the Empress Elizabeth as a bat; I myself as an Indian Prince . . . On the 18th September we left St Petersburg. . ."

On the birth of the future Emperor Alexander II, his mother wrote, "In Holy Week, on the most beautiful of spring days, while the bells were still ringing in the great feast of the Resurrection, on Wednesday the 17th April, 1818, I experienced the first symptoms at one o'clock in the morning. The midwife was called and then the Empress Mother . . . at 11 o'clock I heard the first cry of my first child. Niki kissed me and burst into tears and we thanked God together."

Subsequently, Nicholas and Alexandra had three other sons and seven daughters, three of whom survived childhood. It was an extraordinarily close family group. The young couple lived in the Anichkov Palace, while Nicholas was busy organizing a military engineering school. He also commanded a brigade of Guards. On one occasion he had his children serve dinner to his engineer cadets.

They arranged their home to their own taste. Alexandra liked hothouse flowers, singing birds, and fountains, so her rooms were transformed into a fairyland of exotic blooms, Hartz canaries, and other trilling birds. She played the piano well, and Nicholas took great interest in regimental music, had a good ear, a sense of rhythm and composed operatic airs and religious chants. Nicholas also ordered a theatre to be constructed in their home, and both he and his wife sang and danced in it and enjoyed themselves greatly.[6]

As Nicholas and Alexandra's family grew, Emperor Alexander gave them the estate known as Peterhof. The Grand Duchess wrote:

> ". . . . When we started out for Peterhof Nicholas made me take the lower road after passing Strelna. When I discovered the sea, the old trees close to the shore, and all the fountains in the garden, I gave continuous little squeals of pleasure. I was really enchanted, for this place immediately impressed me far more than

---

6. *Empress Alexandra Feodorovna*, A. Grimm

Pavlovsk and Tsarskoi Selo.

"At Peterhof we occupied pretty well the whole of the wooden wing which had been recently decorated for us—the newly married couple. It was all pretty and fresh with silk hangings, but one room of our suite depressed us badly the moment we went into it. It was the bedroom, hung with dark green velvet, and it produced a lugubrious gloomy effect."

Little was done with Peterhof while Alexander I was alive, but upon becoming Emperor, Nicholas and Alexandra commenced making immense improvements, and by the end of his reign Peterhof combined the splendour of the Imperial Court with the most simple and retired domestic life.

Grand Duchess Alexandra had been charmed by the view of the sea and the gardens and fountains when she first saw it shortly after her marriage. Nicholas, however, was offended by the desolate wilderness. In the summer the wind blew clouds of dust, and the wooden houses of the gentry formed a painful contrast to the palace. Beside the most brilliant court equipages were to be seen coachmen in rags driving the different officials, and even the ministers were obliged to occupy miserable dwellings. The Russian was inured to such things, but they revolt the stranger, so Alexandra prevailed on Nicholas to introduce more harmony into the whole.

After thirty years of effort, Peterhof became the most enchanting spot in all of Russia.[7]

There were three ways to reach Peterhof from the capital—by water, by rail or by the old highway. The road was lined with fine country houses and gardens all the way from the capital, with forests of birch and pine trees. On the right, the sea appears and vanishes by turn. A guard house marked the beginning of the Emperor's property, and a road ran straight ahead for about a league, at which point it turned left on reaching a park with ancient trees through which walks had been cut. It was usually solitary and deserted, serving only as the abode of falcons, kites and crows. At some considerable distance there was a pleasant lake with islands, cottages and Swiss chalets. From the water a road led to the lower part of the town. To the left of the high road there was a second garden decorated with trees, and traversed by flowing waters on which there were islands adorned with pretty little palaces, and a succession of columns and belvideres. The most lovely flowers grew wild, reminding one of the Borromean Islands. Today, Emperor Nicholas I would feel perfectly at home on the grounds and in the

---

7. Description of Peterhof is drawn from various sources, including the autobiography of Empress Alexandra, Grimm, Beckhendorf, and others.

palaces of Peterhof, for little has changed.

In these winding paths the aristocratic world of the Court of 1835 were to be seen driving, at every hour of the day, in open *caleches.* A boat conveyed you across the water to one of the little islands, where the interior of a little palace was intended for one family only, as the largest room could not hold more than ten people; it owed its origin to the domestic inclinations of the Emperor and Empress, who, in the morning or evening, wished to enjoy each other's society exclusively for half-an-hour.

From the gardens you could cross over the brook and enter the cadet camp, a town of tents—erected for the summer, where there were the most varied collection of uniforms you could imagine. When the Emperor appeared among the Cadets, he was no longer the stern Autocrat of all the Russias, to those martial youths he was the father of a numerous family of soldiers, and those youths would spring forward to meet him with more confidence and cordiality than his own kindred at home. He took part in their exercises and sports, visited their tents, tasted the food at their table, and summoned a certain number to test their strength against his.

Next to the Cadet Camp was a stately park called the English garden, which still exists today. Its palace, avenues of trees, and grounds were designed to transport the wanderer far away from Russia into England. In summer, especially in June, the park was filled with the songs of innumerable nightingales.

Catherine the Great caused all of her crowned contemporaries to send her their portraits, and thus the picture gallery of the palace is crammed with historical treasures. There is Frederick William III as a child, with his father, and Frederick the Great, Maria Theresa and Joseph II, Caroline Matilda of Denmark, the younger brothers of Louis XVI, and even the Sultan, and the Pope.

Past the Imperial residence, up a gentle incline, to the left the old Dutch garden slopes down to the sea. It was the work of Peter the Great's own hands, and none of his successors ever ventured to make any changes. The straight avenues were marked out by himself, the oaks and elms planted by his own hands. There was a modest Dutch cottage close to a square pond. At twelve o'clock noon a bell rang, summoning the pond's inhabitants—carps—to the shore to be fed. People assembled on the opposite bank to see this spectacle. Adjoining the pond is a small house once inhabited by Peter the Great when he gave up his palace to his Court attendants. There are clumsy chairs, tables, benches and beds that Peter manufactured himself; the simple clothes he wore are preserved like sacred relics.

After crossing the canal leading down from the palace, there is another favorite resort of Peter the Great, called *Mon Plaisir*; it is a garden encompassed by strong hedges overtopped by high shady oaks and other trees, without any turf, but adorned with innumerable flower beds and several fountains.

At the back of the palace you are close by the shore of the Finland Gulf, and stone benches under spreading lime trees offer a marvelous view.

It is not true, as so often stated, that Nicholas was totally unprepared for the throne. Since the age of eighteen in 1814, he was involved by his brother in Russia's foreign relations, including European conferences. But it was not until 1822 that Alexander consulted him with any frequency. Alexander by then, of course, realized that Nicholas would become emperor, as he had only daughters, and Constantine was married morganatically, and had renounced his rights to the throne, although he kept the title Tsesarevich. Nicholas was neither informed of these events nor declared the heir.[8]

In 1825 Alexander I died unexpectedly at Taganrog, on the Black Sea, at the age of forty-eight.

When the news reached St. Petersburg on 27 November 1825, Nicholas hurried to his mother. She read the fatal news in the face of her son as he appeared during mass, and she fell to the ground senseless. While the swooning mother, accompanied by her daughter-in-law, was carried into her apartments, Nicholas announced the death of the Emperor to the palace guard, commanding them at once to take the oath of allegiance to the Emperor Constantine Pavlovich. He himself, with several generals, set the example by taking the oath and subscribing it in the Palace church, and then he went again to his mother and told her what had been done.

"What have you done, my son!" she exclaimed, "do you not know that an act of state long ago named you successor to the throne?"

According to Grimm, Nicholas was shocked, and refused to believe what his mother said.

"Neither I nor others know anything of the kind," Nicholas protested, "but everyone does know that after the Emperor Alexander, my brother Constantine is the rightful ruler of this country, and to him, therefore, I have sworn allegiance."[9]

Shortly thereafter Prince Golitsin, who, with the Empress Mother, were the only ones in on the secret in Petersburg, arrived at the palace. He severely reproached Nicholas for what he had done.

At two o'clock in the afternoon the Council of the Empire assembled, and Golitsin informed them of the existence of the document, which was opened and read. Many acknowledge Nicholas as Emperor, others maintained that he had renounced the throne by

---

8. *Mother of Czars*, C. Grant
9. *A Czarina's Story*, Empress Alexandra

taking the oath of allegiance to Constantine. Nicholas still insisted on recognizing Constantine as Emperor.

Meanwhile, in Warsaw, Grand Duke Constantine had learned of his brother's death, and he promptly swore allegiance to Nicholas, and dispatched his brother Michael to St. Petersburg to confirm his abdication. Thus occurred an incident unparalleled in history—two brothers at the same time renouncing the throne, and each devolving the crown on the other, as couriers rode back and forth between St. Petersburg and Warsaw.

An interregnum, of course, occurred, which Nicholas had to fill. When Grand Duke Michael reached Petersburg and went to the Empress Mother, she summoned Nicholas and told him, "My son, do homage to the honourable conduct of your brother Constantine; his renunciation was no mere idle words; he give up the throne to you."

"Well, mother," Nicholas replied, "I almost believe it is easier to renounce than to accept."

This situation was perfect for the revolutionary officers to strike, which they did, leading regiments of guards onto Senate Square in St. Petersburg. The enlisted men, who had no idea what was going on, were told to shout, "Constantine and Constitution," and they assumed that *Konstitutsiya* must be Constantine's wife. This was a false slogan, because if Constantine had ever become emperor, the last thing he would have granted would have been a constitution.

For hours on that short, winter day, Nicholas with loyal troops, including artillery, stood facing the regiments led by the Decembrists, loath to open his reign by shedding blood. But after General Miloradovich, a hero of the Napoleonic wars and commander of the guards had been shot down while trying to parley with them, and then another general, Nicholas ordered the artillery to fire. Three shots were enough to clear the square, except for fifty-nine killed and wounded. His generals had begged Nicholas to fire since the Decembrist-led regiments first appeared. It was a terrible way for a well-meaning ruler to start his reign.

Nicholas was horrified that treason would come from officer ranks, particularly those from the guards, many of whom he knew personally. Five hundred and seventy-nine officers were investigated, 121 were tried, of whom the court condemned thirty-one to death. Nicholas personally took part in the interrogations. He called off all but five of the death sentences. The rest were sent to Siberia, or broken to the ranks. Nicholas also gave strict orders that none of their relatives should be discriminated against.

This opening of Emperor Nicholas I's reign does much to explain the strictness of his thirty year rule.

Emperor Nicholas I died at St. Petersburg, 18 February 1855.

PETERHOF

GRAND DUKE MICHAEL PAVLOVICH

CHAPTER III

GRAND DUKE MICHAEL PAVLOVICH
(1798 - 1849)

Grand Duke Michael was the fourth son of Emperor Paul I, and the only one "born in the Purple[1]." He was born at Tsarskoye-Selo on 8 February 1779. As a child, Michael was cheery, gay and somewhat irresponsible in character, and obviously much petted by the family. He and his older brother Nicholas were favorites of their father. Emperor Paul called them, ". . . . my little lambs," and was fond of caressing them and otherwise demonstrating his affection, while their more Spartan mother never relaxed her dignity with her children.[2]

For a dynasty where there had rarely been siblings, there was a surprising closeness between the nine children of Emperor Paul. They were basically divided into two groups—the elder, consisting of Alexander, Constantine, Alexandra, Helen and Marie, and the younger, of Anna, Nicholas and Michael.

Michael and Nicholas became inseparable, just as their older brothers, Alexander and Constantine, were, and were very much alike, just as Alexander and Constantine were of a type. Oddly enough, however, in character and intellect, Michael resembled Constantine; they were very similar, and in later years the two became very close.

The early training of Michael was given over to a nurse of British nationality, a Mrs. Kennedy, whose maiden name had been Ramsbottom. Nicholas and Michael often had arguments about which of their English governesses was the better. Michael, unable to get the better of his brother in argument, according to Hodgetts, maintained that they were at least equally clever. Nicholas, conceding the point, would insist that his, Miss Lyon, was the kinder hearted—he may have been correct, for Mrs. Kennedy would lose her

---

1. "Born in the Purple," means a child whose father was Emperor at time of birth.
2. *Empress Alexandra*, A. Grimm

temper when vexed.

Both were shy, and even deficient in physical courage as boys,[3] but exhibited a love for military matters, and while they enjoyed listening to the piano played by their sister Marie, declared that they preferred drums! Michael had the livelier disposition, and a sense of humor and love of jokes which remained with him throughout his life.

Nicholas was a creator in his childhood, loving to erect toy fortifications and buildings; Michael, on the other hand, was so destructive that Nicholas dreaded his arrival on the scene, because Michael would promptly destroy whatever Nicholas had built. Although Michael would make fun of his brother's timidity, he clearly idolized Nicholas and deferred to him in most matters, and seemed never to tire of singing Nicholas' praises.

In spite of Michael's frequent teasing, Nicholas was fond of him, but treated him with some condescension, and asserted his intellectual supremacy, rarely allowing Michael to take part in serious discussions; Michael was little inclined to serious matters in any event. His education was later entrusted to General Paskevitch, whom Alexander I regarded as his best general. The General acted as his "bear-leader," and escorted Michael on his various journeys through Russia and on the Continent.

As Michael reached his teen-years, Grand Duke Constantine conceived a very strong affection for his amiable and unassuming brother. Sometimes Michael would journey to Warsaw, and at others Constantine would make a flying visit to St. Petersburg. On these occasions Constantine, smoking interminable cigars and drinking tea, would sit up all night with young Michael and tell him stories of his own past experiences, of the reign of the Empress Catherine and of Emperor Paul, of the Suvorov campaigns, and of olden times in general. Before these conversations, Michael had to take supper with his mother, which was a daily duty. At ten o'clock punctually, he presented himself to the Dowager Empress, and after his meal he was dismissed and supposed to go to bed.[4]

Michael's loyalty to his brothers, and his personal bravery is nowhere better demonstrated than in the confusing days of December 1825, when Emperor Alexander died and the succession was in doubt while brothers Constantine and Nicholas swore allegiance to each other. Had the view of some of the Council of State held—that Nicholas had abdicated himself by swearing allegiance to Constantine—and that Constantine had done the same, in addition to his actual abdication—Michael would have been Emperor. Instead of taking advantage of this situation, Michael, serving as courier between the two brothers, served both loyally.

---

3. *The Court of Russia*, E. A. Hodgetts
4. *Secret Memories of the Court of St. Petersburg*, Charles F. Masson

In 1822 Grand Duke Michael was betrothed to Princess Charlotte of Württemberg, who took the name of Helen on being converted to the Orthodox faith. Emperor Alexander met her on his return from Verona and was charmed. Writing to his sister-in-law, Grand Duchess Alexandra, wife of Grand Duke Nicholas, Alexander says, "I will content myself by simply telling you that she unites infinite calm with aplomb to a very great sweetness and affability. In short I do not think there are many of our fellow mortals who have been so well favoured as Nicholas and Michael. I consider the latter should thank God, for it is not conceivable that he could have done better for himself."

On 19 February 1824 Grand Duke Michael and Grand Duchess Helen were married in St. Petersburg. They were given the Michael Palace for a residence [now the Russian Museum], and the Grand Duchess Alexandra, writing to the Emperor at Taganrog on 7 November 1825 said, "Helen is established in her splendours, and is quite happy. Whilst admiring her handsome rooms, I would not exchange my little study for all Helen's salons."

Grand Duchess Helen was one of the few members of the Imperial Family for whom Ivan Golovine in his *Russia Under Nicholas I* has a good word. He speaks of her as a woman of superior understanding, which, he adds, "Often exposes her to a degree of jealousy on the part of the Empress, which is betrayed in frequent petty domestic quarrels." Golovine also had a word of praise for Grand Duke Michael, writing, ". . . . he has a kind disposition, but a rough exterior, and has a propensity to make puns. It is affirmed that he has been seen to weep at seeing Russian soldiers slain in Poland, while his brother Constantine rubbed his hands, saying, 'What do you think of my Poles?' It is not said whether Michael shed tears for the soldiers whom he sacrificed at Brailoff, but it is said that he would not wear the Order of St. George, conferred upon him for the deplorable siege of that place. He is, however, the greatest courtier in Russia; in public he is always seen bent double while speaking, with manifest veneration, to his brother. He is the first servant of the Tsar. I once heard him say, with regret, at a ball, 'All my colleagues have preceded me in the service.' At one time, however, there was a coolness between the two brothers, after which Michael went to Moscow or abroad, where he pretended to amuse himself excessively, and sought popularity not only among the nobles, but likewise among the officers. The Emperor reprimanded him severely for fraternising with his inferiors, to which he answered that he had not expected to be so treated by his brother and his Sovereign."

While Golovine may have been an expert on history, he was clearly no friend of the Imperial Family. There is no other record of any alleged coolness between Nicholas and Michael, nor of any over-

obsequeness towards Nicholas. Michael was always respectful, naturally, and a great fan and supporter, but equally easy and comfortable about the Emperor.

As Alexander had once had to deal with the erratic behaviour of Constantine, Nicholas had to dèal with that of Michael. While Michael always felt close to his soldiers, and helped them financially as well as professionally, he was not popular in the army. Schilder writes that when Michael was appointed Chief of the Corps of Guards Nicholas had to restrain the outbursts of passion of his brother. "The severity and meticulous pedantry of the Grand Duke were inevitably bound to give rise to discontent among his subordinates. Kind, chivalrous, noble-minded, filled with paternal solicitude for the welfare of the troops confided to his care, the Grand Duke, carried away by zeal for drill, to which he was passionately devoted, and by the excitability of his temper, occasionally indulged in excessive manifestations of displeasure." Golovine said that Michael "used even to knock the men about on the parade ground, and Nicholas I's Prussian wife thought Michael ran the Guards like a tyrant."

Beckendorff puts the matter more strongly. "For some time past complaints against the petty exactions and severity of the Grand Duke Michael had so grown in volume that they began to give cause for anxiety: Count Kotchubey, General Vassilchikov and finally I myself spoke about this to the Emperor, but without preconcerted action, thus proving that the matter was one of general comment. I was instructed to talk to the Grand Duke about it. The result has been that for the last four days His Highness is completely changed, he is polite and affable, in short just what he should always have been, whilst I have probably estranged myself from him forever."

The Grand Duke once told Count Kleinmichel, Chief of the Department of Public Works, who had caused some cadets to be flogged and drafted as private soldiers into the Caucasus, "You have cast a stain on the reign of my brother." Unfortunately, these periods of reformation did not last. Soon the Grand Duke would break out again and arouse a veritable storm of indignation. The distracted Emperor would write little notes to Benckendorff to accompany the reports and complaints against his brother, "This is painful to read," he would write, "I do not know how this nuisance is to be abated. I have argued, ordered and implored in vain. What am I to do?"

The following description of Grand Duke Michael is from Grimm's *Life of the Empress Alexandra*, translated by Lady Wallace. "Nicholas was, as we know, grave and formal; Michael, on the other hand, always in a good humour and gay, meeting the most annoying events with a witticism. He fulfilled the duties of his service with the fidelity and conscientiousness of a subject, and at his public appearances before soldiers and officers he assumed his proper dignity. This same man, whom the careless officer avoided in the street, or only formally greeted in prescribed form, cherished his regiment with the heart of a father, and in his own house, and to his friends and intimates, was all heart and feeling, cheerfulness and benevolence. He was better informed than any one in the empire of the position and the good or bad fortune of the various officers. He supported their requests to the Emperor, rewarded and punished with the same impartiality, and his generous hand, like that of the Empress, was too lavish for his means." Michael's wit was keen, but not personally offensive. Thus we get somewhat differing views of the Grand Duke.

During the Turkish and Polish campaigns he showed himself as fearless in danger as he had during the rebellion in December 1825. Like the Tsar, he was often seen in the streets of St. Petersburg wrapped in a soldier's cloak, walking slowly and observingly, greeted by everyone with the same respect as the Emperor himself.

In 1847 Grand Duke Michael thought of taking a holiday abroad for his health. "At first," he said, in a letter to his sister Anna, "I shall look quite ridiculous in my own eyes out of uniform, but after I have worn other clothes for a month I shall rather like them. When I travel I become a private individual in every respect. I should like to move about from town to town with only one friend and one servant, without seeing one single soul of my thirty relatives in Germany; above all, I should wish to be one month in Paris, which I had only a glimpse of when young. I would give a good deal to see a review in Paris as an unknown civilian."

Grand Duke Michael was a devoted family man, even with the heavy duties he imposed upon himself in the service of his brother. Even so, he was not blessed with sons; five daughters were born of the marriage, two of whom died in infancy. His eldest, Maria, died in Vienna unmarried at the age of twenty-one. The second daughter, Elizabeth, married Adolf, Duke of Nassau, who, forty-five years after her death in 1845, became the first Grand Duke of Luxembourg of the present line. The third daughter, Catherine, in 1851, married Duke George of Mecklenburg. They had a son, George, through whose morganatic marriage Grand Duke Michael has numerous descendants. A second son of Catherine, Karl Michael, was in line to become Grand Duke of Mecklenburg-Strelitz, but he chose to become a naturalized Russian subject in 1914. From 1918 to 1934, however, he assumed the courtesy title of Grand Duke of Mecklenburg-Strelitz.

On 9 September 1848, Grand Duke Michael died as a result of a fall from a horse while in Warsaw.

Grand Duchess Helen, who had always looked young and handsome, could not withstand the sorrow and became dejected.

Her seclusion did not last long, however.[5] Her house and salon had always been separate from that of her husband, and she received all kinds of society, including distinguished foreigners, travellers, artists, and *savants*.

Grand Duchess Helen continued her liberal salon through the rest of Nicholas I's reign, and through a large part of Alexander II's. Her brother-in-law, Nicholas I, called her the "scholar of the family," and refused to allow the police to file reports on her activities. During the Crimean War she played the part of a Russian Florence Nightingale by founding the first organization of nurses for the army in Russia. She also founded the St. Petersburg Conservatory of Music in 1862. The Grand Duchess was an enthusiastic supporter of Alexander II's reforms, including the liberation of the serfs in 1861.

Grand Duchess Helen died at St. Petersburg in 1873.

---

5. *The Court of Russia*, E. A. Hodgetts

EMPEROR ALEXANDER II

ROMANOV II
(Simplified)

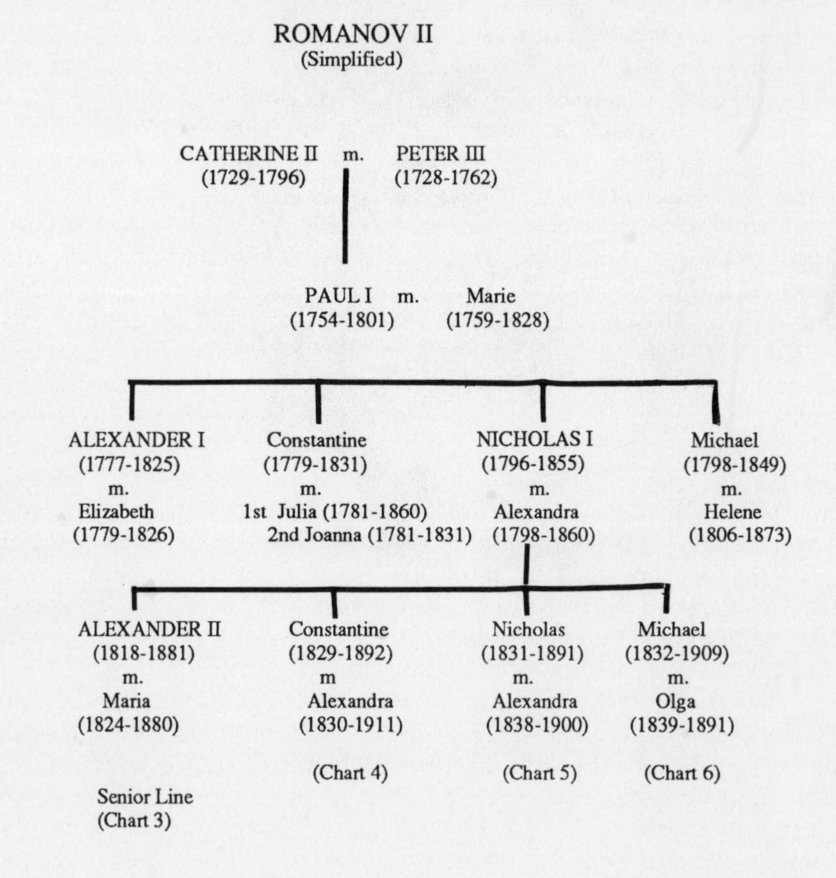

CHAPTER IV

GRAND DUKE ALEXANDER NIKOLAYEVICH (1818 - 1881)

EMPEROR ALEXANDER II (1855 - 1881)

Grand Duke Alexander Nikolayevich was born in Moscow on 29 April 1818, the first child of Grand Duke Nicholas Pavlovich and his wife, Alexandra Feodorovna. He was the first of a new generation of Romanovs. Although third in line to the throne at birth, after his uncle Constantine, and his father, his chances of one day becoming emperor were high, even though Constantine had not yet renounced his rights. In fact, the birth of Alexander was probably a factor in Constantine's later abdication.

About the birth of Alexander, his mother wrote, "White, plump, with big eyes of deep blue, and, already at the age of six weeks, smiling. The baptism took place in the church of the Tchudovsky Monastery on May 5th [1818], when our little one received the name of Alexander. It was another wonderful moment for me when I carried my new-born son in my arms to the church of the Tchudovsky Monastery and to the tomb of St. Alexis."

At his father Nicholas' accession in 1825, Alexander, at the age of seven, became Tsesarevich and official heir to the throne. Thirty years later he became Emperor Alexander II, arguably one of Russia's most outstanding rulers. Since, actually, if not officially, he was bound to inherit the throne sooner or later, and most of his upbringing was in expectation of it, he will be given undeservedly short treatment in this work devoted not to emperors but to grand dukes.

Remembering his own unsatisfactory education, Nicholas made sure that his heir received quite the opposite. His chief tutor was the outstanding Russian intellectual, poet, and liberal, Zhukovsky, at first glance a curious choice for this Tsar, generally considered so reactionary. As Alexander grew older, Nicholas eagerly confided in him and kept him close to himself in preparation for his destiny.

Alexander was almost too good to be true. Intelligent, a quick learner in all subjects, amiable, and handsome, the only criticism leveled at him during his apprenticeship to the purple was that he was prone to fall in love too easily—seemingly a prevalent characteristic of the Romanovs.

In 1841, at the age of twenty-three, he married the seventeen-year-old Princess Marie of Hesse and by Rhine, by whom he had six sons and two daughters. Marie, the only daughter to reach maturity, married Queen Victoria's second son, Alfred, Duke of Edinburgh.

After the death of his wife in 1880, Alexander II married morganatically Princess Catherine Dolgorukov, created Princess Yuryevsky. This was a long standing romance which, before the marriage, had produced a boy and two girls, the eldest born in 1872, and the youngest in 1878.

Alexander II's twenty-six year reign produced a period of great reforms in almost all aspects of Russian life, beginning with the liberation of the serfs in 1861. It also became a flourishing environment for extremely radical intellectuals, including a small but determined group of revolutionary terrorists.

Russia abounds in legend. There is one about a beautiful lady dressed all in white carrying a wreath of white roses, who is supposed to be the death messenger of the Romanovs. A story is told of how, on the morning of his assassination, Alexander II found a bunch of white roses veiled with crape on his bed, supposedly left there by the ghost.[1]

After six unsuccessful attempts on his life, the terrorists succeeded in blowing-up the Tsar-liberator with a bomb on 13 March 1881. On his desk, ready to be signed, was a manifesto introducing a limited constitution, which his successor tore up. The bomb of 13 March was thus a fateful turning point in Russian history.

---

1. *Within Royal Palaces*, Countess de Planty

GRAND DUKE CONSTANTINE NIKOLAYEVICH

CONSTANTINOVICH

(Simplified)

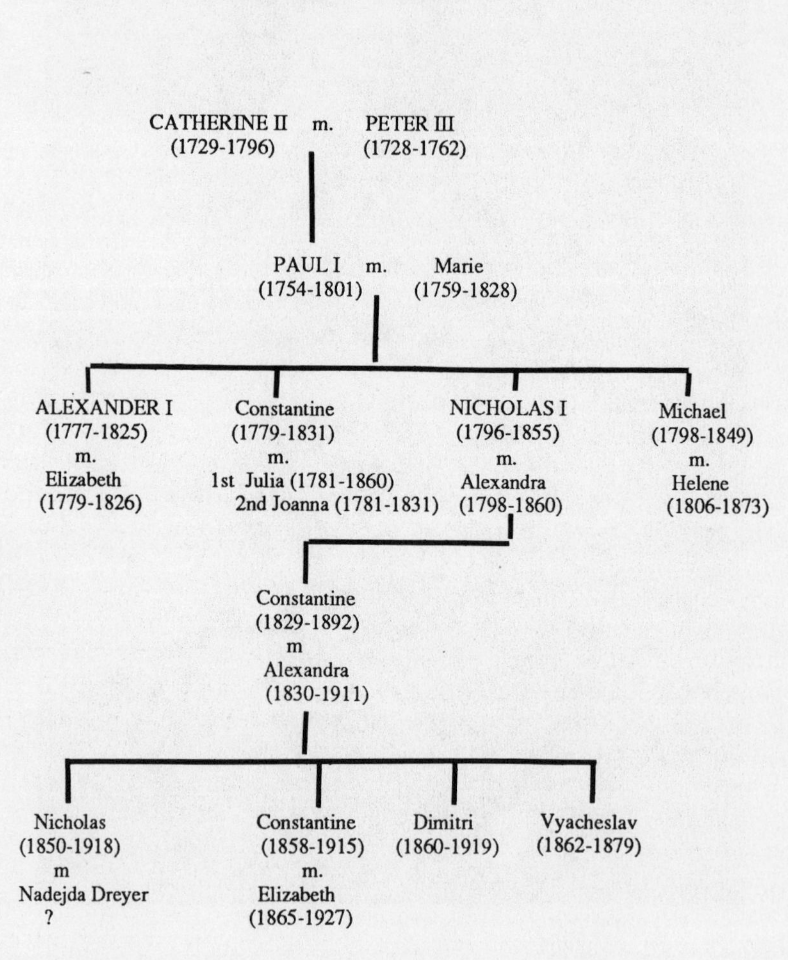

CHAPTER V

GRAND DUKE CONSTANTINE NIKOLAYEVICH (1827 - 1892)

Grand Duke Constantine was the second son of Emperor Nicholas I. He was born at St. Petersburg 21 September 1827.

Until the age of seven, all of the Imperial children were under female auspices, generally an elderly English nanny. Constantine had, however, been given a tutor when he was five because the Emperor found that he showed great spirit, and a very decided will. The Emperor had already decided that Constantine was to become Grand Admiral of the Russian navy, so the naval profession was to be specially considered in his education. For this purpose Frederick von Lutke was chosen. At that time Lutke was the youngest man to have circumnavigated the globe. The tales he told, and his lively conversation, delighted the young Grand Duke, and awoke in him a love for seafaring, even though his nature did not seem to fit him for this life.

"When the boy was seven years old, he was almost too early developed by intercourse with Lutke; he showed eager interest in the histories and discoveries of all circumnavigators," wrote Grimm, a tutor of Constantine.

"In a hall where the Imperial children practised gymnastic exercise, the Emperor would arrive. His appearance had an imposing effect on all strangers, and no one could maintain his usual state of self-possession. He was well aware of the effect his glance had . . . The tone of his voice had nothing imperious about it, and soon became confidential. After a brief conversation, saying that his son Constantine had rendered him desirous to make my acquaintance, and that he hoped for a good result from so happy a commencement, he left the room with a courteous bow."[1]

"You have succeeded in making this boy like you very much; I am glad of it for both your sakes," the Empress Alexandra stated.

1. *Empress Alexandra*, A. Grimm

"The cabinet of the Empress was splendidly furnished," Grimm reported. "I saw the Empress in a far corner of the room, she rose, and in a sweet gentle voice invited me to come nearer. Her youngest child was in her arms, and another played at her feet, and at a little distance stood two ladies-in-waiting."

During the first few years, the education of Constantine did not differ from that of others of his age; the man must be fashioned and cultivated earlier than the prince or the grand duke. All titles were dispensed with, and the only privilege accorded him was that dishes were handed to him first, at a table which was simple and nourishing. He was not permitted to use the slightest harsh word to the servants, of which people in Russia were only too lavish."

Constantine's day was strictly portioned out; while there were only three hours of actual study, a number of gymnastic exercises were required. Conversation during walks and hours of recreation, were aimed at making the Grand Duke acquainted with burgher life in all its gradations and requirements; the views imparted by the palace and its seclusion were too often mistaken ones. "It is possible to live with princes day by day for years and yet find them imbued with the most singular errors. The story of a queen once asking why poor people, during a bread famine, could not eat cakes, is too accurate, alas! Once, the Grand Duke protested that 1500 francs was too large a sum to give to an invalid officer for a journey to some baths, declaring that, 'I would only give him 1000 ducats!'" wrote Grimm.

"The privileges of childhood, if repressed, are sure to be asserted at an inappropriate time. Moreover, royal children are too often presented with the most valuable objects—pictures and other rarities, which neither suit their inclinations nor their comprehension, and, instead of awakening a taste for art, produce indifference towards it. They are accustomed to be surrounded by works of art and regard them as common household furniture, and feel neither joy nor gratitude when bestowed on them. I have observed," wrote Lutke, "that when rare and costly objects are within their reach, they eagerly seize the most ordinary toys, like Achilles grasping his weapons."[2]

Empress Alexandra arranged that another young man should be educated with Constantine, the son of her dearest companion, Baroness Krüdener. They went through life together like brothers. As a child, Constantine spoke only two languages, Russian and English, so his lessons commenced with the learning of German and French. He made equal progress in both, and in eight months was able to translate a German rendition of the Odyssey. He made equal progress in French, and lived and breathed the Homeric age, and

---

2. *Royal Destiny*, E. Tisdall

sought out in the Hermitage all the pictures that represented Homeric or other mythical objects, repeating with the greatest animation what he had learned to his playmates on Sundays, and urging them to perform scenes from the Trojan War.

In 1835 Grand Duke Constantine accompanied his parents on their visit to Germany. His great ambition was to be able to speak German with the Prussian Royal Family.

During the summers Constantine was, by design, cautiously introduced to the sea. The Emperor's favorite residence, Peterhof, was perfectly suited for this purpose.

At the back of the palace you are close by the shore of the Finland Gulf, and stone benches under spreading lime trees offers a marvelous view—to the right, the great city of Petersburg, to the left, Kronstadt, where a forest of masts rise up from the sea; across, is the shore of Finland.

It was here that Grand Duke Constantine grew up, and his training for the navy commenced. He was presented with a small English yacht, which was named after him. He sailed back and forth between Peterhof to Kronstadt, or to the shores of Finland. He received his afternoon's instructions aboard the vessel, dined, and got a slight idea of sea life. Nothing further was attempted to influence him until the following summer when a frigate was named for him, and the command of a squadron given to Admiral Lutke, who escorted Constantine on a voyage to Revel, Helsingfors and Hango Udd.

Constantine was taught to keep a diary from the age of eight, and his observations were astute. The small port, Hango-Udd, where Peter the Great gained a naval victory, had a powerful effect on his imagination.

Constantine also showed an inclination for the fine arts—music and drawing, at which he was particularly talented, but his training for the sea continued. From his tenth year on, his duties on board became more serious. He went through all the work of a naval cadet, kept watch at midnight in rain and storm.

After three years of studies, the Emperor decided that he wished to examine Constantine's progress. For this purpose he named the evenings of the next fortnight. The first evening was devoted to religion, taught by the priest Bashanov; one evening was appointed for each language; and two for a short course of natural history; two for arithmetic and geometry; another for naval science and ship building. Grand Duke Constantine, appearing before the Imperial Family and select members of the society of the city, acquitted himself with flying colors.[3]

As a young officer in 1849 Grand Duke Constantine

3. *Russian Under Nicholas I*, Ivan Golovine

participated in the campaign to put down the anti-Hapsburg uprising in Hungary, fighting in three engagements and receiving the St. George's Cross from the Russian commander, General Paskevich. It might be noted here that this expedition, so unpleasant to the Hungarians, was undertaken by Nicholas I not to acquire territory, but to return Hungary to its legitimate sovereign, under the treaty of the *Holy Alliance* (1815). Constantine wrote long letters in the field to his father, who stated that they were the best reports he received. Consequently, the following year Constantine was appointed a member of the Council of State.

This was the prelude to a brilliant career, which has not received the historical recognition it deserves. Grand Duke Constantine was a small, undistinguished man for a Romanov; he had a forked beard, and sharp, intelligent eyes. He wore glasses, hanging from a broad black silk ribbon. He had a sharp, brisk voice, and Tisdall wrote that, "he kept his brother, Alexander II, up to mark." Constantine liked to display his voice, and the sight of a new servant was more than he could resist. He usually reserved his joke for when guests were present. Suddenly, and for no apparent reason, he would fix the servant with a withering glance and scream out the victim's name till the ceiling rang. Once, a new servant fled the palace never to return; others stood frozen with terror, fainted, hurled down a tray and fled to the attic. The Grand Duke would bend over the table with hysterical laughter. Old servants looked forward to his antics, it was a kind of initiation.[4]

In 1846 Grand Duke Constantine accompanied his sister, Grand Duchess Olga to Stuttgart, then from Berlin by way of Altenburg for the express purpose of making the acquaintance of Princess Alexandra, the youngest daughter of Duke Joseph of Saxe-Altenburg. Duke Joseph's mother was the sister of Queen Louise of Prussia, and consequently, was a first cousin of Empress Alexandra.

Constantine surprised his parents when a letter arrived from him announcing that he intended to marry the Princess Alexandra, "She or no other," he said. Emperor Nicholas said to the Empress, after some consultation, "When I first knew you, I was also firmly resolved to marry you or no one, and I was then only eighteen; write to him therefore that I give my consent." He added, "It is remarkable that four different persons who have seen the Princess bestow equal praise on her, and that my opinion is the same. So let it be—only they must wait two years."[5] The Princess was at that time only sixteen, and the Grand Duke nineteen.

In spite of the illness of both his parents, Constantine set off to England at the close of his education, where he remained for several months, and won the esteem of most English statesmen. He

4. *Royal Destiny*, E. Tisdall
5. *The Court of Russia*, E. A. Hodgetts

passed through Germany on his way, and visited his betrothed in Altenburg.

Princess Alexandrina made her entry into Russia on 12 October 12 1847, and brought new life into the family circle. Although educated at a petty court, she adopted the tone of the family with such ease that it seemed as if she had been born in the Winter Palace. They were married at St. Petersburg 11 September 1848, and she took the name Alexandra Iosifovna, and was later known in the family as "Aunt Sanny."

Upon his accession in 1855, Alexander II immediately appointed Constantine to take charge of all naval affairs. In 1856 the Emperor and Constantine traveled to the Crimea, where the war against Britain, France and Turkey was still in progress, and Constantine supported the new Emperor in the necessity to admit the war was lost and to make peace.[6] This was the start of a long collaboration between the two, covering the period of Alexander II's dramatic reforms, notably the liberation of the serfs. Constantine was appointed chairman of the Committee for Peasant Affairs in 1859, where he enthuiastically supported emancipation against considerable opposition, and freed his personal serfs. He also undertook diplomatic missions to Paris to patch up relations with Napoleon III, and to the Chinese border for inspections.

True to his reformist principles, Grand Duke Constantine agitated for the Kingdom of Poland, under Russian rule, of course, to be administered by Poles, and in 1863 he was appointed Viceroy, a position his uncle, Grand Duke Constantine Pavlovich, had held. He and his wife were greeted with wild enthusiasm on their arrival. On his second day in Warsaw, however, he was wounded in the shoulder by a nationalist assassin named de Jonza. After that, Constantine and his wife were always escorted by Cossacks, who often struck out with their *nagaikas*. The only member of his entourage who protested was Khan Krym-Guirey.[7]

Nevertheless, Constantine opened universities, and encouraged exiles to return, but it was too late for conciliatory gestures, and the Poles revolted. Constantine had to declare martial law and take command of the Russian army, using severe methods of repression.

During his stay in Poland as Viceroy, Grand Duke Constantine was visited by his nephew, Grand Duke Alexander. Constantine treated Alexander, the future Emperor, as a child or nonentity, calling him *Kossolapy Sachka*, meaning "clumsy Sasha,"[7] perhaps explaining Alexander III's later dislike of his uncle.

Relieved from the post of Viceroy in August 1863, Grand Duke Constantine returned to St. Petersburg where he was received with

---

6. *Imperator Aleksandr II*, S. S. Tatismchev
7. *Memories of a Shipwrecked World*, Countess Kleinmichel

great warmth by his brother the Emperor. Thereafter, Constantine devoted most of his activities to improving the navy. He abolished corporal punishment and made many other improvements in service conditions. The navy was in terrible shape when he took it over. The Black Sea Fleet had ceased to exist by the treaty ending the Crimean War, and of the 125,000 enlisted men in the navy, only 25,000 had anything to do with sea duty. By 1879, Constantine had cut down the number of enlisted men to 27,000, all but 941 of them on sea duty. At the same time he improved the quality of the ships and personnel. Under him the fleet went from sail, to steam, and then to armor plate. His principles were to cut down dependence on foreign shipyards and all sorts of administrative overhead. In addition to his duties with the Navy, Grand Duke Constantine was appointed to the Council of State in 1865.

During his sixteen year tenure as President of the Council of State, Grand Duke Constantine, while far from an ideal chairman from the point of view of tact and diplomacy, always had his brother's ear, and effectively defended the council's view. His reformist zeal, plus a fiery temper, made him many enemies.

In spite of these extensive duties, or perhaps because of them, he had many critics. Some accused him of mismanagement of navy funds, and after his retirement, commented how surprised they were that ships could suddenly be built so cheaply.[8]

Stories of his ladies had always been a favorite topic of conversation in St. Petersburg. People soon began to discuss his friendship for a lady belonging to the highest social circles who had recently been divorced, and gossip became even busier when it transpired that the lady in question was established in a lovely villa in the Crimea close to the Grand Duke's palace, where he spent the greater part of the year. This villa was surrounded by beautiful gardens in which her pretty children, none of whom had the slightest resemblance to her divorced husband, used to play.

Like all of the grand dukes and grand duchesses, at least prior to Alexander III, Grand Duchess Alexandra lived lavishly. In *Mother Dear*, Polaykov describes one of her trips to Switzerland in 1868: "She arrived at the Hotel Monnet at Vevey, on the lake of Geneva, with one of her young sons. In her suite was the Marshal of her Court, Admiral Baron Boye; two Ladies-in-Waiting, a physician and a pianist. . . There was a masseuse, a hairdresser, a keeper of the jewels, and of the purse, two footmen, a woman of the wardrobe, four maids and a N.C.O.—a veteran of the Caucasian wars—specially attached to the young Grand Duke. The gentlemen and ladies of the suite had their own private valets and maids, about fifteen in all. In addition to a mountain of luggage, the Grand Duchess arrived with

8. *Behind the Veil of the Russian Court*, Count Paul Vasili

her grand piano because she refused to play on any other." You can imagine the difficulty and surprise which this instrument must have caused at the railway stations! All of these expenses were, of course, covered by the Imperial Court, and a miniature court was established.

Among the visitors to the villa was Don Carlos, the Spanish Pretender. He lived in an adjoining villa, surrounded by a court of Spanish Legitimists, *Les blancs d'Espagne*, they were called.

Countess Kleinmichel described Don Carlos as, ". . . very handsome, and all his person breathed romance and adventure. He used to ride a fine white horse, draped in a black cape and wearing the béret which suited his tanned skin so well."

A number of Russians had settled in the area, and were frequent visitors to the Grand Duchess. Among these were Prince André Troubetskoi and his wife, née Smirnov; Count and Countess Schouvalov; Princess Biron of Courland née Mestchersky; and Baron Gustav von Gersdorff, a chamberlain of the King of Saxony, who was in attendance on the Grand Duchess during her visit.

Prince Wilhelm of Prussia (the future William II) and his brother Henry were also staying nearby at Clarens. They came often to visit the Grand Duchess. Countess Kleinmichel describes him as being "a very lively little boy, very wide-awake, with a gift for easy repartee and jokes. He was very self-assertive and confident; Prince Henry was modest, shy and retiring."

As early as 1865, Constantine had pushed for some form of constitution, and backed his brother Alexander II when the latter was about to grant a partial constitution just before he was assassinated—a document which the new Emperor Alexander III promptly destroyed.

The Grand Admiral's actions had never been questioned until the day his nephew, Alexander III, ascended the throne in 1881. The Emperor had never liked his uncle, and he hastened to put an end to his career. The Grand Duke was told that the best thing he could do was resign, which he did. Alexander III had no use for such a "liberal" powerhouse as his uncle was.

Grand Duke Constantine spent much of the rest of his life abroad, or on his Crimean estate, making friends with the writer Turgenev, and large numbers of luminaries of the arts and sciences. Emperor Alexander III was not pleased with this arrangement, partly because he feared that Constantine would become a center for malcontents in the Crimea, or, for that matter, wherever he went; and, because of his living arrangements.

Grand Duke Constantine had a second family in the Crimea where for many years he had kept a ballerina, the divorced lady mentioned before, Anna Vasilyevna Kuznetsova, as his mistress. They had two sons, and when they died of scarlet fever, his wife,

Alexandra Iosifovna, sent him a telegram of condolence. Constantine referred to her as his "government-issue" wife up north.[9]

Constantine never stopped making suggestions for reforms. One of his ideas was that the Fortress of St. Peter and Paul, as the burial place of the Romanovs, should not also be a prison but rather a home for invalids. Nobody seems to have paid any attention to this.

In spite of his liberal views, Constantine was furious at the new law promulgated by Alexander III in 1886, limiting the title of grand duke or grand duchess to the children and grandchildren of an emperor. He considered this a slap aimed at his own grandchildren who would soon begin to appear, and would be only 'princes' and 'highnesses' instead of imperial highnesses. The timing of the law certainly was inspired by the pregnancy of his daughter-in-law, the wife of his son Constantine. Alexander III, who considered the measure one of liberal intent, was amused but not deterred. Nevertheless, he avoided holding a meeting of the whole family about this measure, to avoid a personal confrontation with his formidable uncle.[10]

In 1889, Grand Duke Constantine Nikolayevich suffered a stroke, losing the power of speech, and on 25 January 1892, the old Grand Admiral died at his palace at Pavlovsk.

His two daughters became Queens—Grand Duchess Vera, of Württemberg, and Grand Duchess Olga, of Greece. His eldest son, Grand Duke Nicholas, was banished to Tashkent after a scandal, and was probably murdered there by the Bolsheviks in 1918; Another son, Grand Duke Dimitri, was also murdered by the Bolsheviks, as were three of his grandsons; another grandson, Oleg, was killed in the early days of World War I, the only Romanov to die in the war.

There are numerous descendants of Grand Duke Constantine alive today, including King Constantine of Greece, the Prince of Wales, Infante Felipe of Spain, King Michael of Roumania and Crown Prince Alexander of Yugoslavia; and his granddaughter, Princess Vera of Russia, who resides at the Tolstoy Foundation near Nyack, New York.

---

9. *Dnevnik Gos. Sekretarya, 1883-1892*, A. A. Polovtsev
10. *Dnevnik Gos. Sekretarya*, A. A. Polovtsev

GRAND DUKE NICHOLAS NIKOLAYEVICH, SENIOR

NIKOLAYEVICH
(Simplified)

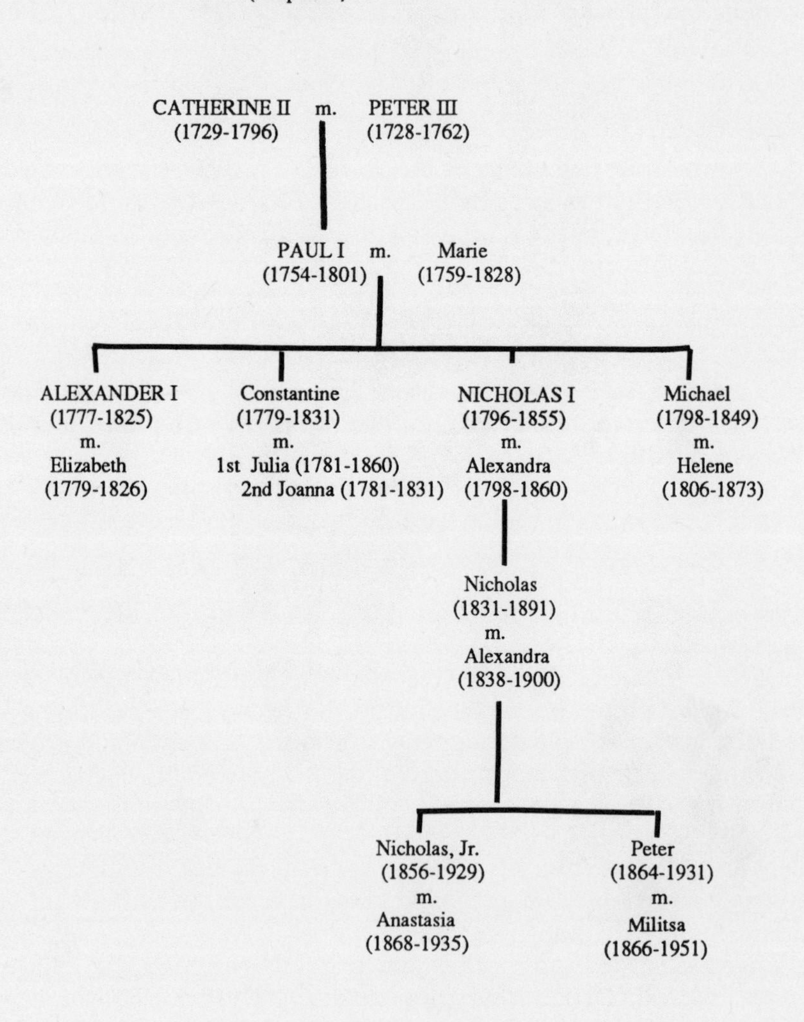

CHAPTER VI

GRAND DUKE NICHOLAS NIKOLAYEVICH, SR. (1831 - 1891)

Grand Duke Nicholas Nikolayevich, brother of Alexander II, was born at St. Petersburg on 8 August 1831. Emperor Nicholas I wrote several letters expressing his joy that his consort had been delivered of a third healthy son, to be named Nicholas. Perhaps the Emperor remembered that in his own generation the succession had not been safe until a third son, he himself, had been born to Paul I's wife.

Like all his siblings, the boy benefited from the extraordinary warmth of his immediate family and the good, if spartan, education provided to all the sons of Nicholas I. His eldest brother, Alexander, thirteen years older, was the heir to the throne and his next brother, Constantine, was devoted to naval affairs. Thus it was inevitable that young Nicholas' career would be in the army, to which he had no objection whatever, showing a special interest in military engineering. He grew up very tall, like his father and brothers, with a prominent, long thin nose.

When Nicholas was twenty-three the Crimean War with Britain, France, Turkey and Sardinia broke out, and Nicholas took part in the Battle of Inkerman. In 1855, as it became clear that Russia was losing the war, Emperor Nicholas I died. There were persistent rumors that he took his own life to make it easier for Russia to make peace. The new Emperor, Alexander II, took his brother Nicholas to the Crimea, appointed him to supervise the engineering part of the defense of Nikolayev, and later that year made him Inspector General of Engineers.

After the war was over, Nicholas married Princess Alexandra of Oldenburg in 1856. She was the daughter of Prince Peter Georgiyevich of Oldenburg, the son of Grand Duchess Catherine Pavlovna by her first marriage, and hence Alexandra was Nicholas' first cousin once removed. She was known in Russia thereafter as Grand Duchess Alexandra Petrovna. They had two sons—Nicholas, born in 1856, destined also for a very prominent military career as Commander of the Russian Armies during the early part of World War I, and Peter, born in 1864.

Alexander II believed in using his brothers to the fullest extent. In 1864 Nicholas became the commander of the Imperial Guard Cavalry. In 1873, nine years later, he accompanied his brother the Emperor to Berlin for a meeting of the three emperors—Russia, Germany and Austria, which led to the significant Three Emperors Pact of alliance. By this time he was already in command of the entire Imperial Guard, a very substantial body of troops.[1]

Nicholas struck it lucky as far as wars were concerned. Already an adult in the Crimean War, by the time the next war came along against Turkey in 1877, he was in a position for very high command. Being the Emperor's brother and the senior one in the army, of course, did not hurt. But Nicholas was popular in his own right, not the least because of his wit and humor.

This war, the last one ending in victory for Imperial Russia, was set off by atrocities committed by the Turks against their rebellious Bulgarian subjects. There was tremendous pressure for Russia to intervene by the Pan-Slavic elements of Russian society. Volunteers and funds were raised for the Slav brothers. Even so, it was some time before Alexander II agreed to active Russian intervention. When war did come, there were two theaters—the lesser Caucasian front, commanded by Alexander II's youngest brother, Michael, and the principal European theatre, commanded by Grand Duke Nicholas. In a few months total victory was had over the Turks on both fronts.

On Nicholas' European front, there were many setbacks and a very difficult crossing of the Danube. The Turkish commander, Osman Pasha, unexpectedly gathered his troops in an almost impregnable position on the heights of Plevna. Twice the Russians stormed it unsuccessfully.

At this point Nicholas showed himself to be a cautious commander. He wanted to retreat from Plevna to the north side of the Danube, considering his reserves insufficiently strong for another attempt. He was overruled, on the advice of the Minister of War, by Alexander II, who sent for the main forces of the Imperial Guard from St. Petersburg. In this case Nicholas had been wrong. A third attack on Plevna, with Nicholas himself leading troops to close the trap on the Turks in their rear, resulted in the surrender of Osman Pasha with his 2,000 officers and 44,000 men, breaking the back of Turkish resistance in Europe.

Though rarely interfering in operations, Alexander II insisted

---

1. *Imperator Aleksandr II*, S. S. Tatishchev

on being close to the front for a good part of this short war, which must have cramped the style of Nicholas and his generals. They begged him to go home because of his health, which he finally did, after decorating Nicholas with the Order of St. George, Second Class, for the Plevna victory. As commander-in-chief, Grand Duke Nicholas was well-served by a number of brilliant generals—Skobelev, Dragomirov, Gurko and Prince Bagration-Emeritinsky, to mention a few, and to whom belongs a great deal of the credit.

After Plevna, Nicholas regained confidence and led the army to Ardianople, which he reached in December 1877. The Turks sued for peace to prevent the Russians from taking their capital, Constantinople, Russia's ancient dream.

Ironically, the incredibly successful conclusion of this campaign led to the greatest problems the Grand Duke had ever faced. It involved him not only in dealing with the Turks on the truce, but into the very complicated international situation caused by the war, notably problems with Austria-Hungary, and particularly Great Britain. It did not help matters that Nicholas' telegraph links with St. Petersburg were so indirect that sometimes it took five days to exchange messages.

He had been involved in relatively minor diplomatic problems before, such as placing the Roumanian volunteers under over-all Russian command, to which Prince (later King) Charles of Roumania objected. Nicholas managed to remain on good terms with Prince Charles during these negotiations, and even took a liking to the Turkish Sultan, Abdul Hamid, in the far more complicated situation at Adrianople.

In spite of the long lines of communications, supply and disease problems of the Russian army so far from home, Grand Duke Nicholas observed the panic of the Turkish population, the sad state of the Turkish armed forces, and the most melancholy expressions on the faces of the Turkish emissaries, and felt that the war should be continued if the Turks did not accept his truce terms. The Turks stalled for time, concentrating what forces they had in front of their capital. Meanwhile, a British naval squadron was approaching with intentions that could only be guessed at.

Nicholas threatened to take Constantinople and the Gallipoli peninsula if the Turks did not immediately accept the truce. Alexander II, however, told him to give them three days before moving on their capital, but not to take Gallipoli because of promises made to Britain. The Turks signed the truce in time, granting autonomy to Bulgaria and Bosnia-Herzegovina, recognition of the independence of Roumania, Serbia and Montenegro, reparations to Russian in land and cash for war expenses, and a discussion of Russian rights in the Bosphorus and the Dardanelles.

The British fleet entered the Sea of Marmora in February of

1878, and Nicholas moved his headquarters, on his own initiative, to San Stefano, really a suburb of Constantinople, eight miles away, where he could keep a better eye on the British fleet's movements, and if necessary to mine the straits. From San Stefano he began negotiating with Sultan Abdul Hamid.[2]

What would happen if the British moved on Constantinople? Would the Turks help the Russians defend it, side with the British, or remain neutral? War with Britain was very close. A preliminary peace with Turkey was signed at San Stefano on 3 March 1878.

Meanwhile a congress of the great powers was being organized in Berlin to settle the whole complicated question. Grand Duke Nicholas wrote, prophetically, to Alexander II, "I hope Gorchakov (the foreign minister) does not give all we have won away and that Bismarck remains a loyal ally." Of course Gorchakov, as it turned out, did give a great deal away and Bismarck was anything but a loyal ally. At least war with England and Austria was avoided.

The Congress of Berlin overturned the preliminary peace signed by Abdul Hamid and Grand Duke Nicholas. Nicholas had done the best he could in a very difficult situation. Nevertheless, Alexander II gently told him he could have done more. At one point Constantinople could easily have been taken. By April 1878 typhus had broken out among the Russian troops in Turkey, and Nicholas himself fell ill. He was recalled to St. Petersburg, and replaced by the old Crimean War hero, General Todleben. Grand Duke Nicholas was promoted to the rank of field marshal, and decorated with the highest Russian military honor, the Order of St. George First Class.

This was the epitome of the Grand Duke's career. All else was anti-climatic. He became inspector general of calvary, retaining his popularity in the army. He was also the chairman of a commission to fight revolutionary "nihilism" in the army, and another commission, in 1888, to study supply problems in the event of another war.

An amusing anecdote is related about his service on the commissions. One afternoon he was presiding at one of the numerous committee meetings of which he was chairman. It was a business meeting connected with the financial affairs of the army, and the Grand Duke had made some remarks not at all to the point which at last exasperated an old general who noticed that Nicholas was working his fingers under the tablecloth in the manner of a school boy when confronted with some arithmetical problem. Unable to control his irritation, the General interrupted the Grand Duke with the brutal remark, "When a person can only count on his fingers, he would do better to hold his tongue."[3]

In 1880, the last full year of his brother Alexander II's reign, an article came out in a French magazine lauding Grand Duke

---

2. *Imperator Aleksandor II*, S. S. Tatishchev
3. *Alexander II*, S. Konovalov

Nicholas Nikolayevich for all the successes in the Turkish War, and blaming Alexander II for the failures. This made the Emperor quite annoyed, and he again brought up the matter of Nicholas' not taking Constantinople.

"But Sasha," Nicholas said, "I have telegrams from you forbidding me to take it!"

"I never could have forbidden any such thing," Alexander replied, apparently forgetting that he had indeed told Nicholas to delay his advance.

When Nicholas' nephew, Alexander III, ascended the throne in 1881, Nicholas was afraid of his nephew. For his part, Alexander III disapproved of his Uncle Nicholas' mode of life, which he felt set a bad example to society.

Grand Duke Nicholas had developed a permanent relationship with Yekaterina Gavrilovna Chislova, a ballerina, although not divorced from his wife. The Grand Duke was quite open about the affair, on one occasion cabling the Russian Consulate in Milan to rent a house for him and his mistress in San Remo. On another he requested permission from the Metropolitan of St. Petersburg to build a chapel on his mistress's property, explaining to the prelate that he needed a family life which his wife, Alexandra Petrovna, could not give him.[4]

Yekaterina did not belong to the gentry, so Nicholas arranged a change of class for her, with the new surname of Nikolayev. He and Chislova-Nikolayeva had a daughter and two sons together, all with the surname Nikolayev. The daughter, who looked very much like her grandfather, Nicholas I, eventually married a Prince Cantacuzen.[5]

Chislova-Nikolayeva nagged Nicholas to provide for their family, and he finally sold his palace in the capital to raise money. According to Princess Radziwill, Grand Duke Nicholas was a very handsome man, ". . . . but inexpressibly stupid, although he considered himself clever. He was fond of spending money, which he squandered right and left, until he became seriously financially embarrassed toward the end of his life."

Grand Duke Nicholas kept this second family at his estate in the Crimea. According to his nephew, Grand Duke Vladimir, he was waiting for his wife to die so he could marry Chislova-Nikolayeva. However, Grand Duchess Alexandra outlived him by nine years, and he outlived his mistress by one, so the marriage never took place.

After the death of Chislova-Nikolayeva, Grand Duke Nicholas remained in the Crimea, so ill that he could no longer recognize anybody. He died at Alupka in the Crimea 25 April 1891, at the age of sixty.

---

4. *Dnevnik Gos. Sekretarya, 1883-1892*, A. A. Polovtsev
5. *Behind the Veil of the Russian Court*, Count Paul Vasili

MIKHAILOVICH

(Simplified)

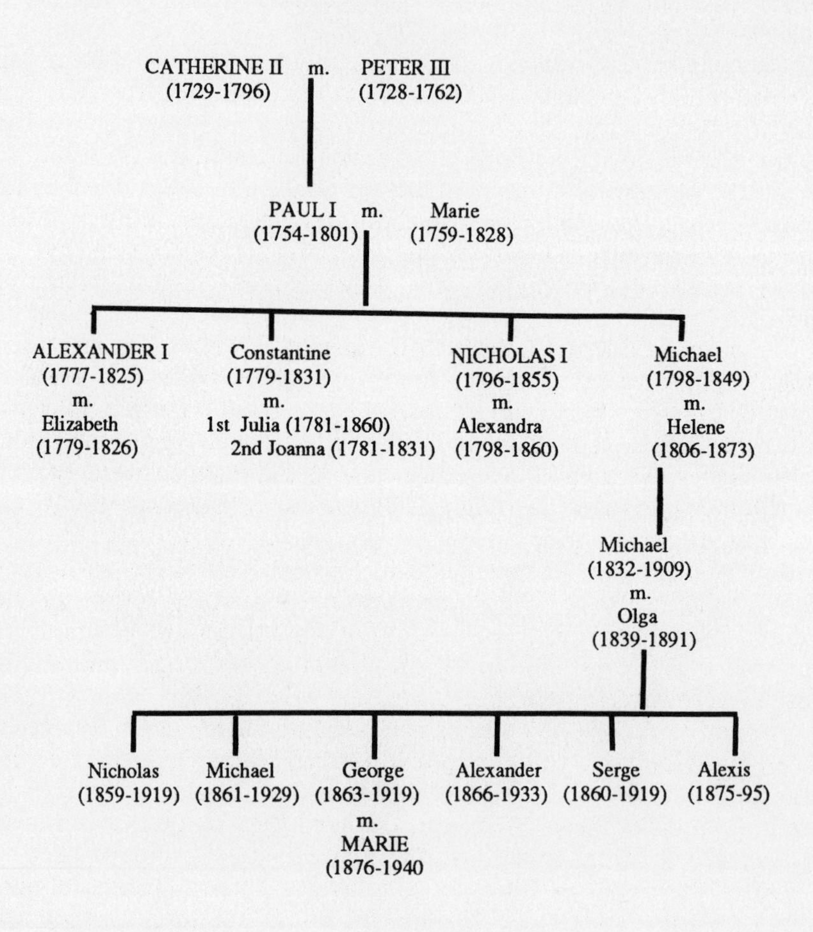

GRAND DUKE MICHAEL NIKOLAYEVICH

GRAND DUKE MICHAEL NIKOLAYEVICH

CHAPTER VII

GRAND DUKE MICHAEL NIKOLAYEVICH
(1832 - 1909)

Grand Duke Michael Nikolayevich was born at Peterhof 25 October 1832, the fourth son of Emperor Nicholas I. It is indeed rare when any man or monarch has four sons, all of them able, intelligent, and eager to serve their father and their country. Emperor Nicholas I had this good fortune. Michael was born after his father had been on the throne for seven years, and was thus "born to the purple."

His spartan military education produced a soldier with a passion for the artillery and no doubts whatever about his religion or the system he had been born into. He became not only an able soldier, but a very good administrator. Michael was tall, with piercing blue eyes and a long beard with substantial sideburns. In character, Michael was quiet, dignified and unpretentious, although he lived in grand ducal style. His St. Petersburg home, was located on the Quay with a view of the Peter and Paul fortress across the Neva. His daughter-in-law, Grand Duchess Marie, described the interior. "There was a grand marble staircase . . . there were numerous state rooms, and the furniture was rather Victorian looking and stiff. All the state rooms had beautiful parquet floors inlaid with rarest woods of different colours in lovely designs. The walls of the dining room were covered with beautiful Cordova leather."[1]

The Palace was so large that several of Grand Duke Michael's adult sons had their own apartments there. Grand Duchess Marie described how her brother-in-law, Grand Duke Serge, ". . . . who lived quite at the other end of the house, always bicycled from his rooms to ours."

In 1855 Michael was in charge of the artillery preparations for the defense of Nikolayev during the Crimean War, and in 1856 his brother, Alexander II, appointed him general in charge of ordinance for the army, and in 1862 named him Viceroy of the Caucasus.

---

1. *A Romanov Diary*, Grand Duchess George

The Caucasus was still wild, exotic, and not very tame in those days. There were scores of nationalities and languages, and great antagonism between Moslem and Christian, a situation which still exists today. The two ancient Christian countries of Georgia and Armenia looked to Russia for protection. Eastern and Central Georgia had become part of the Russian Empire sixty years before, the Western part somewhat later, one principality having been absorbed as late as 1856. Armenia was liberated from the Turks in 1828. Only in 1859 had the Moslem North Caucasians, under Imam Shamil, surrendered to the Russian general Prince Bariatinsky after a heroic thirty year resistance. There was still fighting in the northwest when Grand Duke Michael arrived to take command.

It was no easy task for the thirty-year-old Grand Duke. He had to organize this colorful and difficult area, and somehow create a degree of calm and prosperity. His predecessor as viceroy, the old and sick Prince Bariatinsky, gave him one piece of advice, "Respect local customs, Your Imperial Highness," he said. This Grand Duke Michael took to heart.

Michael had to supervise combat against the Moslems in the North Caucasus, and by the end of 1863 all of the Kuban was in Russian hands. In that year the young Grand Duke established residence in the Georgian capital of Tiflis [Tbilisi in Georgian], the administrative capital. By the following year all fighting had stopped, and Michael saw to it that serfdom was abolished as it had been in Russia in 1861. For these early successes Michael received the Order of St. George Second Class from his brother.

Grand Duke Michael was married at St. Petersburg 28 August 1857 to Cäcilie Augusta, youngest daughter of the Grand Duke of Baden; she became Grand Duchess Olga Feodorovna. Through her mother, Olga had a most interesting genealogy, bringing to this youngest branch of the Romanovs theoretical rights to the British throne, as descendants of George II; and, most interesting for Russians, the blood of Ryurik, the founder of Russia's first dynasty. Through the Kings of France she was descended from Anna Yaroslavna, daughter of Yaroslav the Wise of Kiev, who had married Henry I of France. The marriage of Michael and Olga was very close and also fruitful. Olga was intelligent, sharp-tongued, and very critical of others, and she dominated her family.

Her son, Grand Duke Alexander, tells how when his brother, Grand Duke Michael, wanted to marry morganatically, being aware of his mother's determination, went ahead with the marriage, then informed her. After reading the telegram at the train station in Kharkov, the Grand Duchess had a heart attack and died.

Grand Duke Michael remained Viceroy of the Caucasus for nineteen years, acquiring tremendous administrative experience, operating largely on his own with minimal instructions from St.

Petersburg, and succeeding probably as well as anyone could have done in making the Caucasus a viable and prosperous entity. He was greatly respected by most Caucasians, including Moslems, and there was a certain regional pride that the Russian Emperor, or "Great White Tsar," had honored them by appointing his brother as Viceroy. In 1871 the Emperor visited the Caucasus and declared himself delighted with the progress achieved under his brother's rule.

Grand Duke Michael had seven children, six sons: Nicholas (1859), Michael (1861), George (1863), Alexander (1866), Serge (1869) and Alexis (1875); and a daughter, Anastasia (1860).

All of the family loved the Caucasus and regarded it as their home, feeling cold and uncomfortable on their visits to St. Petersburg so far in the north. Together they formed a clique of grand dukes, the Mikhailovichi, inclined to be somewhat rebellious, and known in the rest of the Imperial Family as "the Caucasians."

When war broke out against Turkey in 1877, Grand Duke Michael, as Viceroy, was also in command of all Russian troops in the region, and automatically became the commander of the Caucasian front. Although the main theater of war was in the Balkans, the Caucasian front was very important, as it forced the Turks to fight on two fronts. Grand Duke Michael's operations were quite successful, and he captured considerable territory. Perhaps the most famous operation was the capture of the fortress of Kars, garrisoned by 20,000 Turks. Designed by European engineers, it was considered impregnable. The Russians took it in a night attack, losing only 500 men. Grand Duke Michael was, like his brother Nicholas, served by very able generals. He was good at making simple, soldierly speeches to the troops, explaining the purpose of the war to them, and thus instilling morale. He insisted that Turkish prisoners be treated with consideration. It was a matter of pride to him that so many Caucasians volunteered to fight in the war, although there were also instances of Moslems collaborating with the Turks. Michael was awarded the Order of St. George First Class, and a field marshal's baton for his part in the War. He was the last Russian field marshal.

During his years as Viceroy, Grand Duke Michael lived in considerable state. There were seldom less than thirty or forty guests for dinner at the Tiflis palace, and near Borjomi he had an estate roughly the size of Holland. Near St. Petersburg the Grand Duke had another summer home, Mikhailovskoe, on the Baltic. The house was in Italian style, with a lot of terraces and fountains, pergolas and balconies. The stables were huge, with room for a hundred horses and apartments for the grooms and their families

In 1881 Michael and most of his family were in St. Petersburg when his brother Alexander II's life was ended by a terrorist's bomb, and he was present at his brother's death. Ten years later, when

Michael's wife died, he was devastated, and paced the floor of his palace outside St. Petersburg, chain-smoking cigars.

Unlike his older brothers Constantine and Nicholas, Grand Duke Michael's career after the accession of his nephew, Alexander III, was not an anti-climax. Michael was the favorite uncle of Alexander III, and the only one of the three kept in important office. Partly this was due to Michael's blameless personal life, and his tact, which the others totally lacked. He became Inspector-General of Artillery, but, more important, after leaving the Caucasus in 1881, his administrative experience was put to good use by his appointment as President of the Council of State, succeeding his older brother Constantine. He served there with distinction, although one of the ministers complained that his interest was only really aroused when Caucasian or artillery affairs came up for discussion. This minister, Polovtsev, referred to Michael as, "My dear, cowardly Grand Duke," because Michael would not stand up to, or contradict, his nephew Alexander III. Although Alexander could indeed intimidate with his huge physical strength and strong will, the reason was rather Michael's ingrained respect for and obedience to the reigning monarch. He took the same attitude toward his great-nephew, Nicholas II, when the latter became Emperor. Nicholas II never intimidated anyone and, to the contrary, suffered from the intimidation of some of his uncles. Polovtsev also complained that Grand Duke Michael had trouble keeping state secrets, because he always kept his wife—known for her sharp and loose tongue—informed of events.[2]

In 1901 Grand Duke Michael went to his beloved Tiflis to preside over the celebrations of the hundredth anniversary of Georgia's incorporation into the empire. There he drank the health of all the numerous Caucasian tribesmen, and was generally received as the Grand Old Man of the Caucasus.

Two years later, at the age of seventy-one, he suffered a stroke which left him in a wheelchair, although he recovered his speech and clarity of mind. Those who remember him before and after the stroke, refer to him as a perfect gentleman, a very elegant grand seigneur of a bygone epoch.

Grand Duke Michael died in Cannes 18 December 1909, the greatest age ever attained by any grand duke. The French authorities paid him all due honors as a Russian battleship came to take the old man home to his final resting place in the Cathedral of the Fortress of St. Peter and Paul.

---

2. *Dnevnik Gos. Sekretarya, 1883-1892*, A. A. Polovtsev

TSESAREVICH NICHOLAS and
PRINCESS DAGMAR of DENMARK

TSESAREVICH NICHOLAS ALEXANDROVICH

CHAPTER VIII

GRAND DUKE NICHOLAS ALEXANDROVICH (1843-1863)

On 20 September 1843, to the general rejoicing of all, Grand Duchess Maria Alexandrovna, wife of the Tsesarevich Alexander (later Alexander II), gave birth to a son at Peterhof, who was named Nicholas after his grandfather. Her first child had been a girl, and the new born infant was the first male Romanov of his generation, and destined to become Emperor of all the Russias after his father and grandfather.

At his birth, his father gave 15,000 rubles to pay the debts of poor people in St. Petersburg and Moscow. The infant was appointed honorary colonel of the Grodno Hussar Regiment of the Guards.

After the accession of his father in 1855, Nicholas became Tsesarevich, the official heir, at the age of twelve. Nicholas possessed the delicate, clear-cut, refined features of his mother, as well as her slender and graceful figure. He was an extremely handsome, intelligent, witty and clever boy, and wrote verses which showed his brilliance. Nicholas was the favorite of his parents, and the Empress neglected her other children in order to attend to Nicholas' needs.

His father saw to it that he was educated as one destined to rule. Most of his training was by foreigners. While still a child and as an adolescent, Nicholas was close to the dramatic reforms his father was introducing in Russia with great difficulty, first and foremost the liberation of the serfs, which was promulgated in 1861, and was very popular with the people.

Nicholas was declared officially of age at sixteen, in 1859. It was not long before a suitable bride was being sought. For many years Germany had had a monopoly on providing brides for the Emperors and Grand Dukes of Russia. Alexander II decided to break this tradition. Alexandra, a daughter of Nicholas I, and sister of Alexander II, had married Frederick of Hesse-Cassel, a brother of Louise, who married the future Christian IX of Denmark. Princess Dagmar, the second daughter of Louise and Christian, was decided upon, and her parents were approached. They agreed, provided that Dagmar also agreed, saying that she was free to make her own choice. Alexander II promptly dispatched the Tsesarevich to Copenhagen.[1]

Dagmar's elder sister, Alexandra, was the Princess of Wales, married to the future Edward VII; her brother, William, would soon ascend the throne of Greece as King George I; and, her father would become King of Denmark, as Christian IX. This alliance with Denmark would strengthen Russian ties with England and Greece, and present no diplomatic problems. It was ideal.

When Nicholas arrived at Bernstorff, his good looks, sophistication, and charm made an immediate impression on Princess Dagmar. She was slim, with large brown eyes, and a smile that appeared like the sun. Her sister, Alexandra, the Princess of Wales, was there to chaperone. The conclusion was foregone—they fell in love at once.

The marriage was never to take place.

Nicholas returned to St. Petersburg in the winter of 1862; he suddenly became ill with some form of paralysis, and had great difficulty in walking. A few years earlier, the Grand Duke had challenged a cousin, Nicholas of Leuchtenberg, to a wrestling match. Nicholas was thrown, and could not move for some minutes. It was now thought that this was the source of his spinal troubles.[2]

The doctors recommended rest in a warm climate, and he was sent by a warship to the Villa Bermont at Nice, on the French Riviera. The ship went from the Baltic to the North Sea, passing near Copenhagen, but Nicholas would not allow Dagmar to see him in his condition. The ship relayed a message by flags to Dagmar.

The inflammation was diagnosed as tuberculosis of the spine, but which may have been spinal meningitis, gradually progressed and went to the brain. Receiving this alarming news, Dagmar could not be restrained. Accompanied by her mother and her brother, Prince Frederick, she crossed Europe as swiftly as trains could carry her. Emperor Alexander, along with his younger sons, was also hurrying to Nice.

Dagmar did not leave Nicholas' side, providing great comfort to his last moments. She was sitting near his bed, when Nicholas sent for his brother, Alexander. He then said that it was his greatest regret that he could not give her [Dagmar] the happiness she deserved. He begged Alexander to take his place, and to make Dagmar happy. Taking Dagmar's hand in his own, Nicholas extended it towards his brother. A few minutes later, on 24 April 1863, Grand Duke Nicholas fell unconscious and died. Nicholas' other two brothers, Vladimir and Alexis, and his fiancée's mother,

---

1. *Alexander II*, Charles Lowe
2. *Mother Dear*, V. Polyakov

Queen Louise of Denmark, were also in the room.[3]

The body of Grand Duke Nicholas was returned to Russia on the frigate *Alexander Nevsky*, and his father bought the house where he had died and turned it into a chapel.

Grand Duke Alexander Alexandrovich now became Tsesarevich. Three years later he married Princess Dagmar, who took the name Maria Feodorovna, and they succeeded to the throne in 1881. Unlike Nicholas, Alexander had reached the age of eighteen with no idea that he would one day be emperor. A man of strong opinions, he developed considerable skepticism and some hostility to the reforms his father was instituting.

It is therefore something more than mere speculation to state that the death of the young Tsesarevich Nicholas had an important effect on Russian and world history. If he had lived long enough to become emperor, he probably would have proceeded in his father's footsteps and at least signed the limited constitution that lay ready on Alexander II's desk the day he was assassinated.

3. *Mother Dear*, V. Polyakov

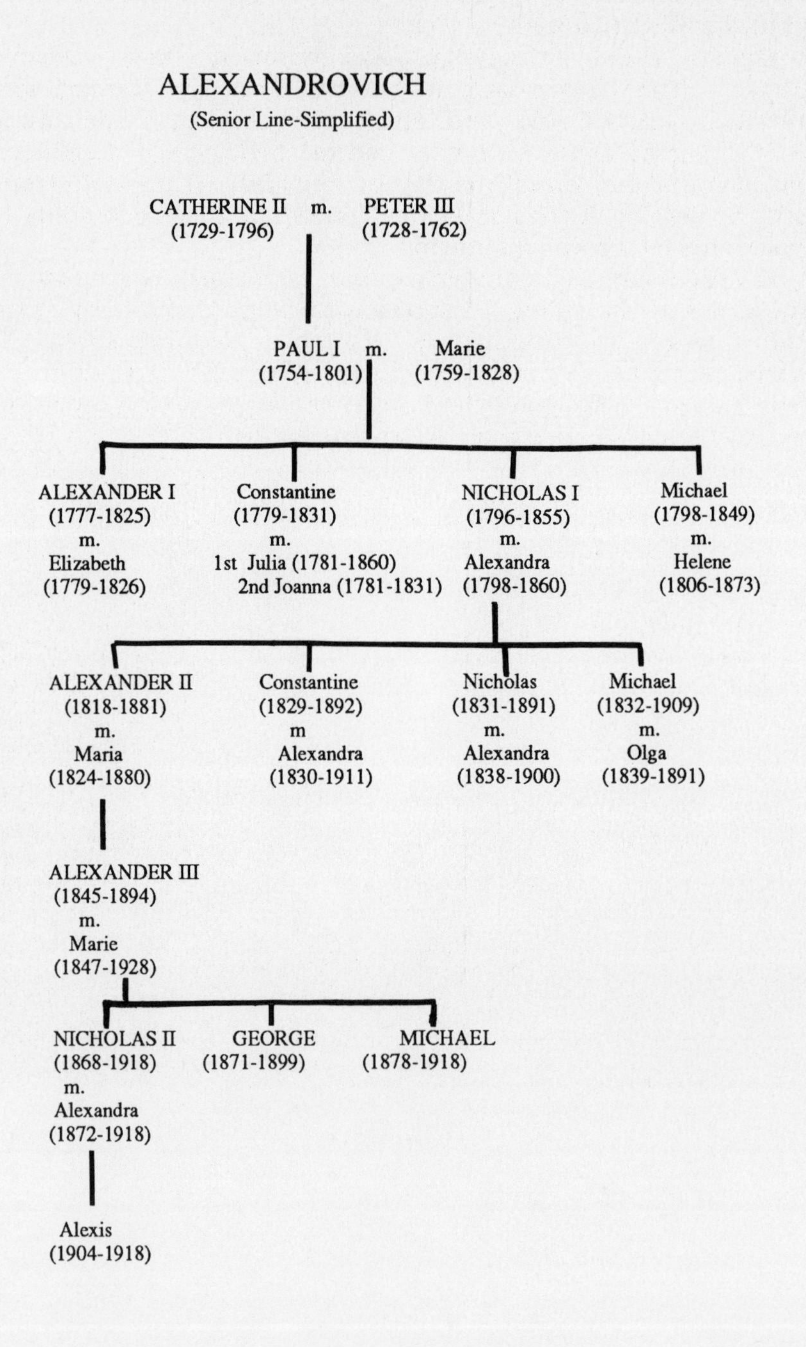
ALEXANDROVICH
(Senior Line-Simplified)
CATHERINE II m. PETER III
(1729-1796) (1728-1762)
PAUL I m. Marie
(1754-1801) (1759-1828)
ALEXANDER I
(1777-1825)
m.
Elizabeth
(1779-1826)
Constantine
(1779-1831)
m.
1st Julia (1781-1860)
2nd Joanna (1781-1831)
NICHOLAS I
(1796-1855)
m.
Alexandra
(1798-1860)
Michael
(1798-1849)
m.
Helene
(1806-1873)
ALEXANDER II
(1818-1881)
m.
Maria
(1824-1880)
Constantine
(1829-1892)
m
Alexandra
(1830-1911)
Nicholas
(1831-1891)
m.
Alexandra
(1838-1900)
Michael
(1832-1909)
m.
Olga
(1839-1891)
ALEXANDER III
(1845-1894)
m.
Marie
(1847-1928)
NICHOLAS II
(1868-1918)
m.
Alexandra
(1872-1918)
GEORGE
(1871-1899)
MICHAEL
(1878-1918)
Alexis
(1904-1918)

GRAND DUKE ALEXANDER
(Alexander III)

ENPRESS MARIE

ALEXANDER III

EMPRESS MARIE

CHAPTER IX

GRAND DUKE ALEXANDER ALEXANDROVICH
(1845 - 1894)

EMPEROR ALEXANDER III
(1881 - 1894)

Grand Duke Alexander Alexandrovich, was born at St. Petersburg 10 March 1845, the second son of Emperor Alexander II and Empress Maria Alexandrovna, and was thus not born to be emperor.

Until 1863, when Alexander was eighteen, there appeared little prospect of his coming to the throne, and he was much in the shadow of his handsome, elegant, studious, and much loved elder brother, Tsesarevich Nicholas, who was already engaged to Princess Dagmar of Denmark. Nicholas became ill, and suddenly died at Nice in 1863. Grand Duke Alexander was at his bedside, and it is reported that the dying boy placed the hand of his intended, Dagmar, into that of his brother, and told him to look after her. Alexander may have already been a little in love with his brother's fiancée, for it is not recorded that he made any objection to this "inheritance."

However the marriage of Alexander and Dagmar—who took the name of Marie Feodorovna on her marriage—came about, they were married at St. Petersburg 9 November 1866, and it was a happy union.

The contrast between Grand Duke Alexander and his brother Nicholas is almost impossible to conceive. While they were extremely fond of each other, they were total opposites. Nicholas was slender, witty, and petted by all; whereas Alexander was uncomely and uncouth, surly tempered, and treated as an ugly duckling by his family. Countess Kleinmichel wrote of him at the age of sixteen, ". . . very tall and broad-shouldered, modelled on the pattern of a Hercules . . . He is kind, frank and honest, but has none of the beauty with distinguishes his brother, and his manners are not pleasant, for he is at the same time shy and noisy; always wrestling with someone, always knocking against something, always upsetting chairs and anything which is in the way."

Describing a visit of Alexander to his uncle, Grand Duke Constantine, in Warsaw, the Countess says, "I remember how the Russians and Poles tried to interest him, attract his attention . . . He would listen to them with an embarrassed look on his face, pulling the while at the collar of his uniform, and quickly dart past them to give a push to his cousin, or to go and devour fruits and cakes."

Alexander was always slighted by court officials in favor of Nicholas, and it came as a disagreeable surprise to these functionaries when suddenly Grand Duke Alexander became the heir and Tsesarevich.

Alexander benefited from the great interest shown by his parents in the upbringing of all their children. In addition to Russian nurses, he and his elder brother were placed into the charge of three English women named Hughes, Isherwood, and Stutton. In 1848, a major general and two colonels also entered the picture as tutors. The tutors had ample praise for Nicholas, but considered Alexander to be ponderous. In the family he was called the "dove" because of his peaceful and innocent disposition. As it was not considered that he would ever come to the throne, he was not trained for this role, but was prepared for the army, and became an officer in the guards, and was finally given a Russian tutor, Pobedonostsev, who later became Procurator-General of the Holy Synod.

In 1856 Nicholas and Alexander, though still children, were allowed to enter Moscow on horseback with their father for his coronation. Later, Alexander studied military science with the cadets of the First Cadet Corps in St. Petersburg.

As children, Alexander and Nicholas made very talented pen-and-ink sketches of a city populated by pug dogs, which they called "Mopsopolis." Alexander collected miniature animals of china and glass, which he loved to show his own children when he grew up. One unusual thing about the future emperor was that while he rode well, he disliked and feared horses, a rare trait in such a horse-loving family! Before he realized that he would become heir to the throne, Alexander fell in love with a Princess Meshchersky, and was ready to abdicate his rights in the succession to marry her. While Alexander was generally considered his elder brother's intellectual inferior, the two were extremely close, and the dying Tsesarevich begged people not to underestimate Alexander's qualities, particularly his strength of character. This he certainly demonstrated when he ascended the throne of all the Russias.

Alexander had an antipathy for mental labor, and early showed a strong determination, and an instinct for insubordination. Once when his father, Alexander II, had proposed a toast to the health of the German Emperor, Alexander had refused to drink, and smashed his glass to the floor. For this he had been placed under arrest.[1]

The cultured court of his father, with its French cuisine, German tutors, and vices did not set at all well with the rather puritan instincts of the Grand Duke. He rebelled early against the German taskmasters provided to tutor him, and eventually acquired the extremely conservative Pobedonostsev as his tutor.

Unlike many other monarchs, Queen Victoria coming to mind, Alexander II was extremely good about grooming his heirs. When Nicholas died, he immediately saw to it that Alexander, the new heir, was also kept abreast of what was going on. He was proclaimed heir in 1863, and being considered already of age, took a solemn oath of allegiance to his father, and was taken by the latter to the old capital of Moscow to be presented to the people. Four years later, after a disastrous harvest, Alexander was appointed chairman of a committee to aid the hungry. In 1872, Alexander II took him along to the meeting of the three emperors in Berlin, and the following year to Vienna on a state visit to Emperor Franz Josef. Grand Duke Alexander participated in the various state discussions which led to the Turkish war of 1877. And, in 1880, he participated in a council discussing the possibility of convening popular representatives to help the government handle revolutionary terrorism. Alexander took a strong stand against this, and after a great battle with his liberal uncle, Grand Duke Constantine Nikolayevich, the idea was abandoned.

During the Turkish War of 1877, the Tsesarevich commanded a group composed of the 12th and 13th Army Corps, the left wing of his uncle, Nicholas Nikolayevich's army. In late November, his group scored a victory over the Turks for which his father awarded him the Order of St. George Second Class. In his bluff way, Alexander thought it was silly to expend blood and treasure to liberate the Bulgarians, who, he said, live much better than the Russian peasants.

Alexander was very close to his mother, Empress Maria Alexandrovna. After she became a virtual invalid, his father took a mistress, Princess Catherine Dolgorukov, with whom he fell in love when she was a young student at the Smolny Institute. Grand Duke Alexander was very displeased with this situation. When Empress Maria died in 1880, Alexander promptly married his mistress, by whom he already had two daughters, Olga and Catherine, and a son, George. She received the morganatic title of Princess Yuryevsky. Afterwards, Alexander appears to have extended every courtesy to his stepmother, and been fond of his halfbrother and sisters.

On 13 March 1881, when Alexander II was brought into the Winter Palace terribly wounded by a terrorist bomb, his heir asked

---

1. *The Court of Russia*, E. A. Hodgetts

the doctors how long the Emperor would live. Fifteen minuets, was the reply. Tsesarevich Alexander burst into tears, hugging his brother Vladimir and his uncle, Michael Nikolayevich, and exclaimed, "See what we have come to!" A few minutes later he became Emperor Alexander III.

Alexander was an enormous man, towering well over six feet, with greyish-blue eyes that could twinkle with merriment or freeze the unwary with a cold glint; he had dark wavy hair which he brushed straight back without a part, until he became bald, and was not unattractive, although perhaps few would have called him handsome. In character, he was a simple, plain, honest man, with no nonsense about him.

Alexander came to love his yearly visits to Denmark. He felt free there, and when it was time to return to Russia, he spoke of 'returning to prison.' He got along well with his father-in-law, and never asked political questions.

He did not care for the arts or literature, unlike most of his relatives; and he had little use for abstract philosophical or political ideas, thinking all these things nonsense. He viewed all of the talk about improving the status of the peasant, of transplanting the spirit of progress and civilization to Russian soil, was but self-deception at best, and absolute humbug in most cases.[2]

Neither as Grand Duke nor as Emperor was Alexander one to deprive himself of the pleasure of the table; in fact, he could be called a gourmand. With his great size also came great strength. He took pleasure in bending horseshoes and heavy silver plates for the amusement of his children. Once, at dinner, the Austrian Ambassador remarked that Austria might mobilize two or three divisions because of some Balkan problem. Alexander picked up a silver spoon and twisted in into a knot, remarking, "That is what I will do to your two or three divisions!"

In his youth, Alexander was great on athletics and physical exercise, going on long walks, hunting and chopping wood. In his later years, however, he became much more sedentary, perhaps because of the injuries sustained when he held up the roof of a railway car after an assassination attempt. Prince Nicholas of Greece, who was present during the last months of the Tsar's life, describes how he had no energy, and wasn't even interested in hunting, and seemed to want to doze in his chair.

Under Alexander III, Russian autocracy worked. The Emperor was decisive; he was the government, and his power was absolute. He was responsible to God only. Even members of the Imperial Family were subject to his will. As under other Emperors, Grand Dukes served as governors of provinces, or as officers in the military,

---

2. *Alexander III*, Charles Lowe; *The Court of Russia*, E. A. Hodgetts

but they served at the pleasure of the Emperor, and with a snap of his finger they stepped aside. Even so, Alexander had a great respect for the established law. Some Russian Emperors were accused of ignoring the laws, which were their own, at will. But Alexander insisted on following what was written, until it was formally changed.[3]

Alexander III and Marie Feodorovna had at least six children, Nicholas (later Emperor Nicholas II) (1868); George (1871); Xenia (1875); Michael (later Emperor Michael II) (1878); and Olga (1881). Some records record the birth of another son, named Alexander, who died in infancy, probably in 1870.[4]

Empress Marie was a short woman, with dark brown hair and large velvety brown eyes. She was almost a twin to her sister, Queen Alexandra of England. Friend and foe of the Romanovs alike attribute to her great personal charm, wit, and good humor. Everyone agrees that she also had considerable personal courage, and was much loved by the Russian people. There the agreement stops. One writer, Hodgetts, states that ". . . . she has no desire to exercise undue influence over the Emperor. Her interest is in maintaining the first place in his affections. In short, she is essentially feminine . . . she is both generous and gentle, but at the same time has a disdain for logic . . ."

Count Vasili, in *Behind the Veil of the Russian Court*, who was usually filled with gossip, not always accurate, wrote, ". . . . She will intrude on behalf of anybody who may have succeeded in appealing to the kindliness which forms the basis of her character, but she is not sufficiently desirous of playing a part in the State to favour seriously and consistently any particular person."

The Count goes on to say that the Empress has passionately embraced the interest of her country, and that while she is very close to her relatives, especially her sister, Alexandra, this is a feeling of family, not of a sovereign.

The death of Alexander II brought great changes in the way of life at court. Alexander and Marie soon moved their residence to Gatchina, which curtailed social functions. The new Emperor was also frugal almost to the point of being stingy. There was soon less gold braid on the clothes of the courtiers; the Circassians in their medieval chain armor went; the thousands of servants were reduced, and strict accountants replaced the gay aides-de-camp of old. Even the kitchens were rationed, to the dismay of the French chief. National dishes were substituted for imported goodies, and Crimean

---

3. *Mother Dear*, V. Polyakov
   Under Three Tsars, Y. Naryshkina
4. The records are not in agreement on the date of birth of this child. Both Grand Duchess Olga (Alexander III's daughter) and Grand Duke Alexander, say the child was born before Nicholas II, whereas Burkes gives the date of birth as 1869.

wines replaced French vintages.

The entire tone of the court changed from elegant and international, to Russian. A story is told that Prince Suvorov, the grandson of the famous Field-Marshal of Catherine II, came onto the balcony of the Winter Palace to announce the news of the death of Alexander II, he said, "*L'Empereur est mort, vive l'Empereur*," and the crowd roared its disapproval of the use of French. The Prince then repeated the message in Russian.

Alexander III was not as friendly with his numerous relatives as his father had been, and quickly took steps to remind them of their place. Alexander had a firm conviction of the rightfulness of his autocratic position, and firmly believed in Pobedonostsev's formula: "Autocracy, Orthodoxy and Nationality." All of the Imperial Family owed their allegiance and reverence to the Emperor, like any other subject. He changed the Fundamental Law so that only the sons and grandsons of an emperor could bear the title of grand duke; and also limited his relatives access to himself. Previously, the grand dukes and their wives and children visited at the palace as they wished; now, they were discouraged from 'dropping by' Gatchina, and had to apply for an audience, unless summoned by the Emperor.

The Emperor also did not encourage the grand dukes engaging in politics; his policy was to keep them out of contact with the people, so that there was no competition with the Autocrat. The elder members of the family were treated coldly, and his uncles, Constantine and Nicholas, were deprived of all influence. Constantine, fuming, withdrew from the court, and Nicholas lived as a private gentleman. He was a little less severe with his two brothers, Vladimir and Alexis.

Vladimir was allowed a certain latitude in public affairs, and was made Chairman of the Council of State. At one council meeting, he exhibited some independence, but was quickly put in his place by a cold stare and the remark, "This is My will." Alexis was in charge of the naval department, and could do pretty much as he pleased, as long as he kept out of politics.[5]

It was said by everyone that only Empress Marie had any influence on the Emperor, and while few implied that she had any political ambitions, there is no doubt that she did exercise considerable influence on public policy, but it was done 'behind the scenes' in private. In the British Foreign Office files, there is a telegram to the Foreign Minister on the death of Alexander II, warning that Russian policy, under the influence of the new Empress, would swing toward Greece in the Balkans, where Marie's brother was king. The British Prime Minister, Salisbury, and Foreign Minister Rosebury, also frequently voiced concerns over the influence of

5. *Mother Dear*, V. Polyakov

Empress Marie. She had a deep seated hatred of Germans, and it was her direct influence which brought about the treaty of friendship between Russia and France. Her son, Nicholas II, said of this, "I heard it at the dinner table twenty times every day."

Robert Massie, in *Nicholas and Alexandra*, wrote that Nicholas relied on Marie for guidance, and quotes Nicholas, "The various affairs you left me, petitions, etc. have all been attended to." Again, Massie cites a letter from Marie, "I am sorry to have still to forward you so many papers, but it is always like that in early summer just before the ministers go on leave."

Clearly, Empress Marie thoroughly understood the workings of the government, and had great influence over policy. Those who faulted her for "caring little for the serious side of life and of giving all her attention to dresses and dancing," simply did not understand that she preferred to remain in the background. Probably had she attempted to compete in public with the Emperor, she would have lost her influence over, and with, Alexander.

A remarkable testimony to her intelligence and personality, is the fact that she remained on excellent terms with all members of the family, including the Grand Duchess Marie Pavlovna, who was liked by few. She had no enemies among the Imperial Family.

Another testament of her influence is that, even with all of the austerity, and Alexander's dislike of society, Marie led the fashion parade of St. Petersburg, her Paris dressmakers bills frequently causing Alexander an unpleasant surprise. She was also an enthusiastic dancer, and an excellent one. Her favorite dance was the Polish mazurka, and all dances and balls which she attended were opened with this dance. As Alexander was not one for dancing, Marie always had a handsome young man as her companion; but her conduct was such that the "serpent's tongue" of St. Petersburg society never touched her.[6]

After Alexander came to the throne, the Empress had a terror of assassination, and they soon virtually withdrew from St. Petersburg, and took up residence at Gatchina where security was much better. Whenever it was necessary to go out, the tiny Empress insisted on being at her husband's side, as if her presence could protect him.

Gatchina was a beautiful place, surrounded by rolling grounds, and fine old timber. The palace itself was enormous, actually, blocks of buildings. One huge square stone edifice occupied the center, and from it branched out on either side were circular wings which served as galleries to connect the main building and the two smaller ones. In the central block were the state and large reception rooms. The wing on the left was occupied by the Imperial

---

6. *Mother Dear*, Ibid.

Family. On the right were the apartments of the household staff.

Arriving visitors were conducted to the central entrance, and except after the most careful examination, were not allowed to even approach the part of the palace occupied by the Tsar. The sitting room of the Tsar, in which he transacted his business, was on the first floor. It was comfortable, but simply furnished with heavy German-style arm chairs, and little ornamentation. A large writing table was used by the Tsar, on which he kept a framed picture of the Empress and her children, the frame of antique Hungarian enamel, and surmounted by the Imperial crown in diamonds.

A typical day of Alexander III commenced at seven in the morning, when he dressed and went to his reception room to receive a report of the chief of his body guards. He then took a long walk in the palace garden. His real labors commenced at nine, and lasted until one o'clock, when he received his ministers. At one o'clock, the Tsar had lunch with his wife and children, and none but their most intimate friends were ever allowed to be present. Afterwards, Alexander went out walking or driving with the Empress and children. At 7:30, the Emperor and Empress dined alone. In the evenings, Alexander liked some music. When he was a boy, it was once suggested that he might like to participate in a musical performance with the palace orchestra. He was delighted, and selected the trombone to play. His performance consisted in a well-sustained effort to drown out the remainder of the orchestra. In his later years, Alexander amused himself by playing a large silver cornet, which could be heard throughout the palace.[7]

Empress Marie was a devotee of cigarettes, and smoked almost continually in an indolent fashion. Her boudoir at Gatchina, which she called her "den," was copied from one of the rooms of the Alhambra, with palms, and diapered gold walls. She also enjoyed caravan tea, brought to her in a service of gold. In her dressing room there was a large swimming bath, entirely built of Carrara marble, in which she delighted in taking cold baths. The bath was surrounded with growing flowers and shrubs.

The Empress' favorite room was her sitting room. It was lighted by three bay-windows; the walls and ceiling were covered with a thick, soft, silken material of a very pale pink, interwoven with threads of silver. A chandelier of pink Venetian glass hung from the ceiling. The sofas, arm-chairs, rockers, and divans were upholstered in pale pink velvet embroidered with silver. The floor was covered with a white Aubusson rug, on which were worked showers of rose petals. In each corner there were pink marble statutes by Kustov, and in the center of the room a pink camelia in full bloom stood on a round console draped with cloth of silver. The mantel was also in

---

7. *Within Royal Palaces*, Countess de Planty

pink marble, crowned by a bank of Neapolitan violets.

The Empress was very fond of jewels, and had one of the finest collections in the world. Ropes of pearls, streams of emeralds green as the jungle, sapphires gleaming like an Oriental sky; diamonds of the finest quality, rare Byzantine jewels, and clusters of rubies. One of the Tsar's presents to her was a necklace of great pearls of perfect form and color. Nine rows of these gems loosely held together by clasps of diamonds in the shape of fleur-de-lis. A favorite parure of the Empress was a long javelin, composed of brilliants to hold up the skirt draperies, and a necklace and tira of emerald shamrocks sprinkled with diamond dewdrops. One of the quaintest of all her possessions was a set of fifteen butterflies to place as epaulets on a low bodice, and to scatter over her skirt. They were made of brilliants—saphires, emeralds, rubies and topazes; their antennae were covered with diamond dust, while as a finishing touch there was a huge moth of pearls and brilliants, with widely outstretched wings, to be placed in the hair. Many other treasures rested in her jewel vault, a tiara of rubies and diamonds, a flat band of diamonds and emeralds to be worn around the neck; a set of twenty pink diamond stars, and a tiara stomacher and collar, composed of hedge roses made of great rubies of the true pigeon blood color, set in a double garland of diamond maidenhair ferns. These, and the many other personal jewels, were brought out of Russia by the Empress in 1919, and most eventually ended up with the British royal family.[8]

As to the crown jewels, the Muscovite regalia included two Imperial crowns, the two collars of the order of St. Andrew, the globe and sceptre. The Imperial crown is that of Catherine, with its fifty large stones and 5,000 brilliants, which was used at all subsequent coronations. The Orloff diamond surmounted the sceptre, and the sphere held the finest sapphire in the world.

Alexander was quite unlike Marie in his taste. He wore his clothes until they were almost in rags; he begrudged the money for keeping his various palaces in repair, and on one occasion when it was pointed out that the furniture in his study needed recovering, he replied, "Yes, it is rather worn, but, never mind, it has lasted so many years, it will last a few more."

Alexander's austerity also extended to his relatives. The extravagance which had prevailed before came to an end. The properties which constituted the Imperial wealth were put on a strictly business footing under one administration. Each Grand Duke and Grand Duchess was provided a yearly income, which was fixed for all time, and could not be exceeded without a humiliating personal appeal to the Emperor. Marie once asked Nicholas II to

---

8. *The Queen's Jewels*, Leslie Fields

grant a loan to a needy princess, to which Nicholas replied, ". . . . as regards a loan of a million roubles from the Bank, I must tell you that this is impossible. I should have liked to see how she would have dared even to hint at such a thing to Papa; and I can certainly hear the answer he would have given her."[9] Even so, this yearly income was not meager. Grand Duchess Olga, Alexander's younger daughter, wrote that her income was "only 800,000 roubles a year," on which she could barely get by [at least $4 million dollars in todays money.]

Alexander's reign was comparatively brief, lasting only thirteen years. He died at Livadia, 2 November 1894, his magnificent physique undermined from his having held up the roof of a railroad car over his family during the 1888 assassination attempt.

Empress Marie lived on, holding her place in the affections of the Russian people, through the abdication of her son Nicholas II, and the revolution that destroyed the Dynasty. She retreated to the Crimea, and was finally persuaded to leave Russia in 1919, when she, along with many of the survivors of the family, were evacuated aboard the *H. M. S. Marlborough.*

Before the *Marlborough* sailed, a costal ship carrying 400 Russian sailors passed, and while the tiny Empress, dressed all in black, stood at attention on the deck of the *Marlborough*, the passing sailors sang *God Save the Tsar*, the last time the Imperial anthem was sung on Russian soil to a member of the Imperial Family.[10]

Empress Marie died in Denmark 13 October 1928.

---

9. *Letters of Nicholas II to Empress Marie*

10. *Prince Felix Yusupov*, Christopher Dobson

GRAND DUKE VLADIMIR ALEXANDROVICH

GRAND DUCHESS VLADIMIR
with two of her children

GRAND DUCHESS VLADIMIR
(Marie Pavlovna)

GRAND DUKE VLADIMIR with
GRAND DUCHESS HELEN

(Seated) Grand Dukes Vladimir and Cyril, Grand Duchess Marie
(Standing) Grand Duke Andrew, Grand Duchess Helen, Grand Duke Boris

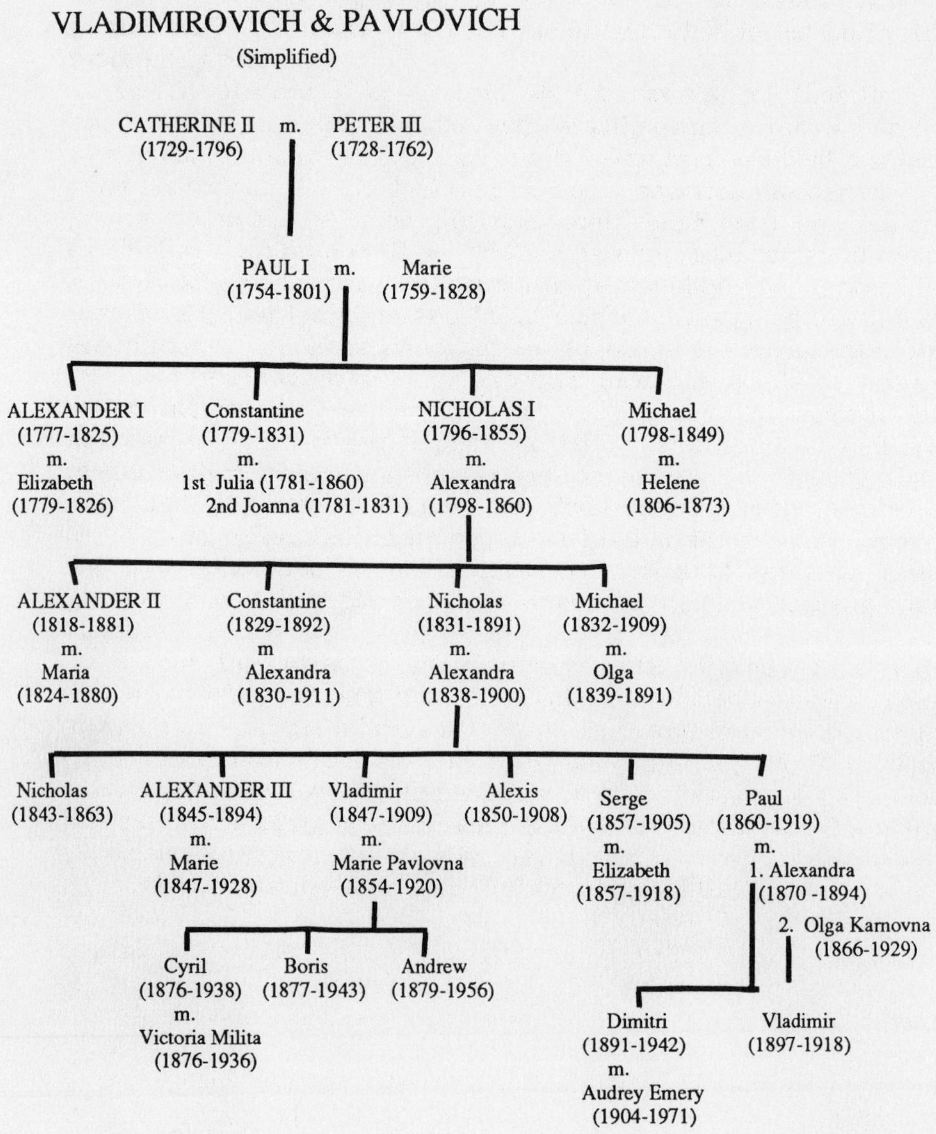
VLADIMIROVICH & PAVLOVICH
(Simplified)
CATHERINE II m. PETER III
(1729-1796) (1728-1762)
PAUL I m. Marie
(1754-1801) (1759-1828)
ALEXANDER I
(1777-1825)
m.
Elizabeth
(1779-1826)
Constantine
(1779-1831)
m.
1st Julia (1781-1860)
2nd Joanna (1781-1831)
NICHOLAS I
(1796-1855)
m.
Alexandra
(1798-1860)
Michael
(1798-1849)
m.
Helene
(1806-1873)
ALEXANDER II
(1818-1881)
m.
Maria
(1824-1880)
Constantine
(1829-1892)
m
Alexandra
(1830-1911)
Nicholas
(1831-1891)
m.
Alexandra
(1838-1900)
Michael
(1832-1909)
m.
Olga
(1839-1891)
Nicholas
(1843-1863)
ALEXANDER III
(1845-1894)
m.
Marie
(1847-1928)
Vladimir
(1847-1909)
m.
Marie Pavlovna
(1854-1920)
Alexis
(1850-1908)
Serge
(1857-1905)
m.
Elizabeth
(1857-1918)
Paul
(1860-1919)
m.
1. Alexandra
(1870 -1894)
2. Olga Karnovna
(1866-1929)
Cyril
(1876-1938)
m.
Victoria Milita
(1876-1936)
Boris
(1877-1943)
Andrew
(1879-1956)
Dimitri
(1891-1942)
m.
Audrey Emery
(1904-1971)
Vladimir
(1897-1918)

CHAPTER X

GRAND DUKE VLADIMIR ALEXANDROVICH (1847-1909)

Grand Duke Vladimir, the first Romanov to bear this historic name, was the third son of Emperor Alexander II and Empress Marie. He was born 22 April 1847 at St. Petersburg, and at birth was appointed honorary colonel of the Dragoon Guards.

From the time of his birth and early youth, there was little possibility of his ever attaining the throne, and thus his upbringing was far less stringent than his elder brothers. But when he was eight years old his grandfather, Emperor Nicholas I, died and his father ascended the throne, then with the death of his older brother, Tsesarevich Nicholas, in 1863, Vladimir suddenly found himself the heir presumptive after his brother Alexander.

During his father's reign Vladimir was made honorary president of the Russian Ethnographical Exhibit, in 1867, and in the same year he accompanied his father and older brother to Napoleon III's Paris World's Fair, where his father was shot at by a Polish nationalist. In 1871 Vladimir again went with his father and brother on a very comprehensive tour, including not only Georgia but the newly conquered regions of Chechnya and Dagestan. The next year he attended the very important meeting of the three emperors (Russia, Germany, and Austria) in Berlin, then went to Vienna for a visit to Emperor Franz Josef. In 1877, Grand Duke Vladimir commanded the XII Corps on the European front of the Russo-Turkish War, receiving the Order of St. George Third Class for his corps' repulse of a serious Turkish attack. In 1880 he was appointed President of the Imperial Academy of Arts. This was far from merely being an honorary appointment, because Vladimir really was a connoisseur of everything concerning the arts. He was a good painter, and a patron of the ballet, particularly helpful to Diaghilev. He was highly intelligent, and better educated than most of his extended family, and was basically a very kind person.[1]

These good qualities were largely canceled out by his rudeness, hot temper, laziness, absent-mindedness, gluttony, and the shady people with whom he surrounded himself. He treated the younger Grand Dukes with contempt, other than his own children, whom he loved.

On August 28, 1874 at St. Petersburg, Vladimir married the twenty-year-old daughter of the Grand Duke of Mecklenburg-Schwerin, known in Russia as Grand Duchess Marie Pavlovna. Marie refused to convert to Orthodoxy from her native Lutheranism. This led to the general belief that she was overly pro-German (specifically denied by Grand Duke Alexander Mikhailovich). There is no doubt that Vladimir himself was an Anglophobe, and both of them loved Paris, where they would go as often as possible.[2]

When his brother Alexander III ascended the throne in 1881, Vladimir became fourth in line to the throne, following Alexander's three sons. The Grand Duchess' refusal to convert to Orthodoxy cast a shadow on Vladimir's own eligibility to the throne, which he could not occupy with a non-Orthodox wife. But if the situation ever came up, Vladimir told his uncle Michael Nikolayevich, Marie would convert immediately for "reasons of state." The situation almost did come up in 1888 when Alexander III and his entire family came close to death in a terrorist-induced train wreck.

Vladimir and his wife were in Paris at the time and did not bother to come back to Russia. This considerably annoyed the Emperor, who supposedly remarked that his brother would have rushed back soon enough if they had all been killed.

There was some conversation on the succession after this near tragedy. Grand Duke Michael Nikolayevich told State Secretary Polovtsev that Alexander had said that if the train wreck had been fatal to all, the throne should have gone to Vladimir's eldest son Cyril, as Vladimir had abdicated his rights when he married. Vladimir himself denied ever having signed anything and his younger brother Alexis backed him up, claiming that the Emperor was wrong on this point. One would think that the Emperor would know what he was talking about, and Empress Marie repeated it after the revolution in connection with Cyril's claim to the throne, but, if so, why was it not made public? It was far from academic in view of the ever-present possibility of assassination. Had Vladimir renounced his rights, it would raise a question as to his children's rights. This minor mystery reminds one of Alexander I's behavior with his brother Constantine's abdication of rights.

Vladimir had come very close to the throne once before he was married, and before the premature death of Alexander II's eldest son

1. *Alexander II*, C. Lowe
2. *Once A Grand Duke*, Grand Duke Alexander

Nicholas, because the future Alexander III almost abdicated his rights to marry Princess Meshchersky. Had this happened, Vladimir would have become Emperor in 1881. Grand Duchess Olga Feodorovna, noted for her sharp tongue and gossipy nature, remarked that Vladimir had never gotten over this. He would hardly be human if he had not suffered some regrets, but there is no evidence that he was ever disloyal. Rather, the intrigues of his wife gave them both the reputation of being extremely ambitious.

During his brother's reign, Vladimir organized what he called a "holy band" to defend the life of the Emperor, for which 250 members of the St. Petersburg Yacht Club volunteered. This effort was so amateurish that Alexander III soon put a stop to it. While there was considerable friction between the two brothers, Alexander III did appreciate Vladimir's good qualities, and utilized them to some advantage. He appointed him commander of the Guards Corps and Chief of the St. Petersburg Military District, a key post that he held from 1884 to 1905. He was also a member of the Council of State. While he was not regular about attending its meetings, he did not, unlike its chairman, Grand Duke Michael Nikolayevich, hesitate to tell the whole truth to his brother, no matter how unpleasant, and the Emperor appreciated this. Vladimir also supported Alexander's measures to limit the number of future grand dukes, which others in the family, particularly those likely to have grandchildren soon, opposed. In 1887 he was sent on a diplomatic mission to Berlin, where he made a very positive impression on Bismarck.

Grand Duke Vladimir and Marie had three sons: Cyril (1876), Boris (1877) and Andrew (1879), all three bearing unprecedented Romanov first names. In 1882 they were followed by a daughter, Helen, who married Prince Nicholas of Greece.

Grand Duke Vladimir also had his bad qualities, which often infuriated Alexander III. At one time he held considerable influence over his brother, but this did not last. Alexander was too strong a personality to "take orders" from anyone, and the Empress had little use for Vladimir or his wife.

Vladimir was disliked in Russia because in St. Petersburg he tried to play the autocrat, which made him many enemies, as did his coarseness, brutality and drunkenness, although he was always popular abroad, mainly because of his high position.[3]

In Paris Vladimir was particularly popular; it was the place where he showed himself to the best advantage, because he could lead there the easy kind of existence that suited him. He was considered a great wit, remarking once when offered a chair by a Montesquieu, "No thank you, in a house like this I prefer to keep my back to the wall." While fussy about his gourmet food, he was an

---

3. *The Court of Russia*, E. A. Hodgetts

extremely lavish tipper.[4]

The Grand Duchess Marie Pavlovna, was a handsome woman who dressed to perfection and tried to play the role, with some success, of the grande dame of St. Petersburg. Empress Marie, who loved the glitter of court functions, and was generally very popular, was forced to spend a good deal of her time off at Gatchina with her rural-minded husband, while her sister-in-law gave huge parties and lavish balls at the Vladimirs' palace, Ropsha, near Peterhof, and the Catherine Palace at Tsarskoye-Selo, all but outshining the official functions in the Winter Palace, in which nobody now lived. The Grand Duchess was a delightful hostess, famous throughout Europe. She was intelligent, well-educated, artistic, sometimes imperious and "grand ducal" in her disposition, at other times very coquettish. She liked to ride around in her carriage with young guards officers while her husband was off on maneuvers. On one occasion, in 1889, she went off to Paris by herself, pretending to be sick. Vladimir, who in addition to his other attributes, was naive and easily taken in, believed her. Both of them tended to be surrounded by sycophants or empty-headed people who happened to amuse them.[5]

After a few years of this it was not only the fun-loving Empress but the strait-laced Emperor who was fed up with Marie Pavlovna, though both of them made special efforts, normally, not to give any sign of this. The Grand Duchess, however, made a lifetime habit of sharp remarks about her husband's relatives, even though so much scandal attached to her own name.

On one occasion friends from abroad came to St. Petersburg, and were received by her and the Grand Duke as guests in their palace. Among them was a prominent clubman of Paris, Mr. Ridgway, of American origin, who it was said was the character described by Paul Bourget in his novels under the name of Raymond Casal. He spent a winter in Russia, shooting with the Grand Duke and playing bridge with the Grand Duchess, who liked to sit up very late at night. He always spent his evenings with her when not otherwise engaged.

Of course this furnished talk for the busybodies, and it was whispered that the Tsar did not approve of his sister-in-law's favorites, but, if such was the case he kept his disapproval to himself, and it was only on two occasions that he let the Grand Duchess know how displeased he was with her. The first time was a few months after the murder of Alexander II. Marie Pavlovna aspired at that time to play a political role and to become the uniting link between her native Germany and Russia. She wrote long letters to Princess Bismarck, who was the all-important personage in Berlin at the time, and in these letters she described everything that was going on at

---

4. *Nicholas and Alexandra,* Robert Massie
5. *Behind the Veil of the Russian Court,* Count Paul Vasili

court in a way that was anything but charitable. One day she accidentally left one of these letters on her writing table, where it was discovered by one of her husband's aides-de-camp, Count Paul Shuvalov, who forthwith carried it to the Emperor. A terrible scene ensued.[6]

Alexander III sent for his brother and gave him to understand that the Grand Duchess must give up her political activities, and that they had both better go abroad. This command was hastily obeyed, and they left for the south of France where they remained for a long time. The Grand Duchess Marie would never speak to Count Shuvalov again, and even after the revolution maintained an attitude of enmity towards Countess Shuvalov, even after the Count died. The Grand Duchess was not of a forgiving nature.

The other scandal was not of a political nature. Grand Duke Vladimir and the Grand Duchess and a small number of their most intimate friends went for supper after the opera to a fashionable restaurant, Cubat, at the time the best restaurant in St. Petersburg. During supper in their *cabinet particulier*, Grand Duchess Marie heard voices in the adjoining *cabinet*, and fancied she recognized amongst them that of a famous French actor, Lucien Guitry, who was performing in the French plays at the Michel Theatre. A waiter was sent for, and asked whether Guitry was indeed present, in which case it was the Grand Duchess's pleasure to see him. This was done.

The actor was entertaining a rather diverse group of friends, male and female Bohemians, including Mademoiselle Agnèle, an actress with whom he was supposed to be on most intimate terms. When the actor presented himself, and the Grand Duchess learned that he had amusing people to supper, she insisted that his party join theirs. Guitry protested that this was impossible, but Marie Pavlovna insisted, demanding to know how these people behaved, and one thing led to another, until the two parties were joined.

Grand Duke Vladimir, who had drunk too many glasses of wine, seized Mademoiselle Angèle and kissed her, which so enraged Guitry that he in turn—egged on by the malicious Grand Duchess, put his arm about her, and it is said, even kissed her. Grand Duke Vladimir now became enraged and grabbed the actor about the throat and attempted to kill him. A general fracas ensued with patrons from other cabinets joining in. The management was unable to restore order, and sent for General Gresser, the Prefect of St. Petersburg. His timely arrival quelled the disturbance, but the next day General Gresser reported the incident to the Emperor.

Alexander III was in such a rage that people who saw him constantly stated that for three days no one—not even the Empress—dared to speak to him. He issued peremptory orders that

---

6. *The Court of Russia*, E. A. Hodgetts

Guitry be sent out of Russia by the next train, and that Vladimir and Marie were to follow as quickly as possible. They were not even allowed to come and take leave of the Sovereign, and were given to understand that if they did not hasten to put the frontier between them and the wrath of the Tsar, they might be asked to repair to some place not quite so pleasant as Paris or the South of France.[7]

When the Grand Ducal couple were at last allowed to return to Russia, Marie Pavlovna was much quieter, and tales of her extravagance and indifference to the opinion of others were not so numerous. She assumed the attitude of the clever woman, desirous of having a salon of her own, patterned after those of Madame Geoggrain or Madame du Deffand in Paris in the eighteenth century. She failed dismally in the attempt, although she did collect around her a most amusing circle of people who repeated every bit of gossip current in the town.

Marie Pavlovna was always eclectic in her tastes and friendships. Provided people had money and were ill-natured, she did not require anything more of them. After the accession of Nicholas II, due to the aversion to society of the new Empress, Alexandra, the Grand Duchess became much more of a social power and, as such, helped more than anyone to bring about the laxity in morals which prevailed in St. Petersburg during the last few years that preceded the great war.

She was a fanatic gambler, and even had her own roulette wheel in her palace. She also received divorced people, something few persons who had been born and bred under the old régime would ever do. No member of the real old Russian aristocracy frequented the Grand Duchess' salon, but you met there a number of *nouveaux riches.* Among her intimate set were to be found ladies like the Princess Cantacuzene, whose father, Mr. Sicard, had been a French hair dresser from Odessa; Madame Serebriakov, whose great wealth was derived from relatives who had been in the timber market; Mr. Benckendorff, whose career had been so adventurous that he had had to bid good-bye to the diplomatic service rather abruptly.

Both the Grand Duke Vladimir and Grand Duchess were overly obsessed with money, in spite of the enormous wealth acquired by the Grand Duke in addition to his allowance from the Imperial appanages, and frequent scandal was attached to their sharp dealings.[8]

Jewelry was a particular passion of Marie Pavlovna, and she assembled a collection of diamonds, emeralds, pearls and rubies that could be matched only by the Crown jewels themselves. When Cartier's set up shop in St. Petersburg, Grand Duchess Vladimir was one of the sponsors. One piece made for her by Cartier was a

---

7. *Secrets of Dethroned Royalty*, Catherine Radziwill
8. *Secrets of Dethroned Royalty*, Catherine Radziwill

kokoshnik made in the form of a diamond bow-knot with drop pearls. This piece is now in the British Royal Family's collection. Their acquisition of jewelry would have bankrupted more than one nation.[9]

With the early accession of Nicholas II in 1894, Grand Duke Vladimir's new sovereign and nephew must have seemed very young and unprepared. Twenty years before, Vladimir had grabbed the new Emperor by the ear to make him behave at a railroad station. In fact, the new Tsar was unprepared and bewildered, and tended to listen to his uncles, particularly Vladimir, Alexis, and Serge, but they terrified him, and he dreaded to be alone with them.

Vladimir, with a certain amount of common sense, told the Emperor that the gentry was undermining the autocracy, while claiming loyalty to it. But when the first Duma met after the semi-constitution of 1905 was granted, Vladimir expressed belief in the patriotism of the newly elected law-makers, and a willingness to go along with them. On the other hand, he opposed the sale of crown lands to help the reforms of Prime Minister Stolypin. Consistency was not the hobgoblin of this far from little mind. In 1894 Grand Duke Vladimir became third in line to the throne; with the death of Grand Duke George Alexandrovich in 1899, he was second, moving back to third with the birth of Alexis in 1904.

Grand Duke Vladimir had lost the respect and affection of his brother, Alexander III, and he fared little better with Nicholas II, who soon learned to stand up to his uncles, and the Vladimirs were rarely received at Court.

Vladimir's last great confrontation with Nicholas II came over the marriage of his son, Grand Duke Cyril to Princess Victoria Melita, the divorced wife of Grand Duke Ernst Ludwig of Hesse, Cyril's first cousin, and former sister-in-law of the Empress! The Emperor deprived Cyril of his official positions, and banished him from Russia. Grand Duke Vladimir went on a rampage, and threatened to resign all of his offices. Eventually, Nicholas relented, and allowed Cyril and his wife to return to Russia, and restored his estates. However, he did not issue a decree recognizing the marriage. After the death of Vladimir, the Grand Duchess continued the bitter quarrel with Empress Alexandra, whom she blamed, even after the banishment was lifted.[10]

Grand Duke Vladimir died at St. Petersburg on 17 February 1909.

Grand Duchess Vladimir continued to carry on her role as the "grand grand duchess," her role as leader of society being made easier by the increasing sequestration at Tsarskoye Selo or in the Crimea of the Empress.

Another source of her anger against the Empress was because

9. *Prince Felix Yusupov*, Christopher Dobson
10. *Nicholas and Alexandra*, Robert Massie

her son, Grand Duke Boris' proposed marriage to Alexandra's daughter, Grand Duchess Olga, had been turned down by the Empress. The Grand Duchess Vladimir had seen a marriage between Boris and the Emperor's daughter as a means of strengthening the claim to the throne of her other son, Cyril, and she took the Empress' refusal as a personal insult.

After the outbreak of World War I, many plots were reported against the Emperor, and the secret police were kept busy running down these stories. There was nothing new in plots against the Romanovs, except that this time the plots were by the Romanovs themselves. Grand Duchess Vladimir was chief among the plotters.

One of her proposals was that the Empress would be sent to the Crimea or a nunnery and Nicholas II would be put on a cruiser for England, and Rasputin would be executed. Another scheme was for the Empress to be sent to England while the Emperor would abdicate in favor of his son Alexis. The British government was well aware of this treachery because Bertie Stopford was a welcome guest at the Grand Duchess' table, and he reported directly to the British Ambassador, Sir George Buchanan. The Grand Duchess, in 1916, went so far as to tell Duma President Michael Rodzianko, that Alexandra had to be removed and destroyed for the good of the country, and that the Duma should do something to this effect. Rodzianko replied that he would pretend the remarks had never been made, otherwise he would be honor bound to report them to the Emperor.[11]

After the revolution, the Grand Duchess fled to the south of Russia; she did not dare to return to St. Petersburg for her jewels, but she was saved by Bertie Stopford, who rescued the jewels and got them to London for her. These jewels were eventually divided among her children. Grand Duke Cyril received the pearls; Andrew the rubies; Boris the emeralds, and Grand Duchess Helen the diamonds.[12]

The Grand Duchess refused to leave Russia aboard any ship that would put in at Constantinople because that city required delousing of all passengers. She somehow managed to commandeer a train for herself from the north Caucasus to the port of Novorossiysk on the Black Sea, arriving in somewhat dilapidated but still grand-ducal style, and this in 1919! Nicholas II's sister, Grand Duchess Olga, who disliked her thoroughly, saw her arrive and had to admire "Aunt Miechen's" style.[13] The Grand Duchess and her son, Grand Duke Andrew Vladimirovich, finally left on a Greek ship in February of 1920. They were the last Romanovs to leave Russia.

Grand Duchess Vladimir died in Switzerland in 1920.

---

11. *Krusheniye Imperii*, M. V. Rodzianko
12. *Prince Felix Yusupov*, Christopher Dobson
13. *The Last Grand Duchess*, Ian Vorres

GRAND DUKE ALEXIS ALEXANDROVICH

GRAND DUKE ALEXIS ALEXANDROVICH

CHAPTER XI

GRAND DUKE ALEXIS ALEXANDROVICH (1850 - 1908)

The four serious, career-minded sons of Emperor Nicholas I produced a new generation of a baker's dozen of tall, strapping Grand Dukes, some as serious as their fathers and others who made the phrase *grand duc russe* legendary in Paris and on the Riviera. The undisputed champion of the latter category was the fourth son of Emperor Alexander II, Grand Duke Alexis Alexandrovich, born at St. Petersburg 14 January 1850.

The three splendid lusty sons of Alexander II—Alexander, Vladimir and Alexis—developed into young ruffians, the stories of their exploits keeping St. Petersburg on its ear. Serge and Paul, younger, did not get themselves talked about so much at that time, only to become the heroes of more tremendous scandals later.

During the reign of Alexander III there was little for most of the grand dukes to do. Samson-Himmelstierna in his *Russia Under Alexander III* says: "Such circles as were to be found thirty years ago in the Michael Palace (Grand Duchess Helen), and at times in the Marble Palace (Grand Duke Constantine), exist no longer, and cannot exist, for the watchword has gone forth from the highest place, that affairs of State concern the Emperor alone and his officials, and that society must confine itself to pastimes. Under Alexander III the Grand Dukes were given to understand that his word of "no nonsense" had special application to them, and that he had no intention to allow any of the members of his family to play a part in politics."[1] So there was not much for these grand dukes, possessing their powerful positions and great wealth, to do besides enjoy themselves, when they were not doing their military service.

Relatives and other contemporaries give similar descriptions of Alexis: "The best looking man in the Imperial Family, but very heavy;" "The Beau Brummell of the family;" "Man of the World, bon vivant, spoiled by women;" "A man of infinite charm and enormous

1. *Russia Under Alexander III*, Samson-Himmelstierna

girth;" "Very Handsome—all the ladies fell in love with him;" "International bon vivant." His own motto, as he told a young cousin, was "You must experience everything in life."[2]

At birth, Grand Duke Alexis was appointed honorary colonel of the Moscow Regiment of the Imperial Guard, but his career, such as it was, was in the navy. In 1871, as a young lieutenant, handsome and not yet fat, serving on the warship *Svetlana*, the Grand Duke arrived in New York where a tremendous reception awaited him. It included a procession up Broadway with bands and national guardsmen, the bells of Trinity Church chiming *God Save the Tsar*, and a huge sign on the Astor House Hotel proclaiming, "Grand Duke Alexis, Son of a Noble Father, Representative of this Nation's Dearly Cherished Ally." It was the administration of President Grant, and fresh in the memory of Americans was the 1863 visit of the Russian Baltic Fleet, showing Russia's solidarity with the Union at a time when Britain and France were leaning toward recognition of the Confederacy.

The first American to see the Grand Duke, however, was disappointed. This was the pilot who guided the *Svetlana* into North River. When a young lieutenant standing watch was pointed out to him, the pilot exclaimed, "He ain't no more royal than I am!" The explanation that the Grand Duke had to take his turn at watch like all the other officers failed to satisfy the pilot. Alexis himself was confused by this sort of attitude. He felt that in a democratic republic he should avoid dressing up, but this never failed to disappoint Americans, who sometimes crowded around a guards hussar aide in a splendid red uniform by mistake.

Alexis went to Washington where President Grant received him, impressing the young Grand Duke as an ill-mannered lout. Then it was back to New York via a stop in Philadelphia, a trip to Boston, a visit to Canada, and out to Cleveland, St. Louis, Chicago and Milwaukee. There were huge receptions everywhere and the young man was shown grain elevators, water works, factories, bridges and everything else his hosts could think of. He could not understand why the Americans were more enthusiastic about royalty than Europeans were. Was democracy a hoax? In St. Louis the Grand Duke killed a bottle of whiskey with Buffalo Bill Cody, a prelude to his trip further west. Early in 1872 Grand Duke Alexis became a proficient buffalo hunter, accompanied by Buffalo Bill and General Custer. In Colorado he was almost charged down by an angry bull, which failed to be stopped by his six revolver bullets. He loved watching Indians bring down buffalo using arrows only. Alexis returned eastward via Topeka, Memphis and New Orleans, and finally rejoined the *Svetlana* at Pensacola, Florida. The ship then went

---

2. *V Mramornom Dvortse*, Prince Gabriel Constantinovich

around the Horn and on to Japan and China, having completely circumnavigated the globe before its return to Russia.[3]

This round-the-world voyage seriously interfered with Alexis's love life. Before the voyage started he had fallen in love with Alexandra Zhukovsky, the daughter of the famous Russian poet who had been in charge of Alexander II's education. There are allegations that Alexis and she were married in Italy in 1870, but, if so, the marriage was annulled and never recognized. Nevertheless, a son was born from the union, Count Alexis Alexeyevich Believskoy-Zhukovsky. Officially, Grand Duke Alexis never married.

In 1877 Grand Duke Alexis returned to the United States, to Norfolk, Virginia, in command of the *Svetlana*, as part of a Russian squadron of four ships which was seeking to avoid the British fleet in European waters. Later that year, when the Turkish War broke out, Alexis commanded the Danube Squadron.

After the forced retirement of Grand Duke Constantine Nikolayevich from naval affairs, Grand Duke Alexis was a Rear Admiral. Six years later in 1888, his brother Alexander III appointed him Grand Admiral of the navy. It was not a good choice. Alexis was more interested in "experiencing everything in life" than in running the Russian Navy. It was said that he preferred to conduct his nautical manoeuvres at Monte Carlo or Paris than aboard a Russian ship.

Unlike his distinguished uncle Constantine, Alexis dragged his feet at any proposed naval reform. His knowledge of naval affairs was stuck in the days of sail, and at every important meeting he would tell interminable stories about his sailing days aboard the *Svetlana*. Yet, he stayed in the job all the way through the disastrous Russo-Japanese War of 1904-1905, when he resigned, dying three years later. He must have felt the Russian naval defeats at Port Arthur and Tsushima deeply, but whether he at least partially blamed his own stewardship of the navy for them is not recorded.

In St. Petersburg he whooped it up among the gypsies with his brother Vladimir, and made frequent visits to Paris. It was a common joke in St. Petersburg that the ladies of Paris cost Russia at least a battleship a year![4] When any Grand Duke traveled abroad it was a major production, which might be compared today to a visit by the President of the United States or the Queen of England. Sometimes they went by ship. Most often, however, the grand ducal party traveled by train. The Imperial trains were something to behold. There could be twenty cars for baggage alone, dining cars with real tables set with crystal and silver, candles and the finest foods and wine. The sleeping car for the Grand Duke had real beds, and there were sitting rooms and parlors for the Imperial party to

3. *Czars and Presidents*, Alexander Tarsaidze
4. *Always A Grand Duke*, Grand Duke Alexander

relax in. The train itself was a marvel, fronted by Imperial and grand ducal standards, the double-headed eagle emblazoned on the sides, and flagged through crossings and way-stops at full speed while all other traffic ground to a halt.

Arrival in Paris or Baden or Copenhagen was a major event. Security from the host country took over the platform and station, while the Imperial body guards swirled about the Imperial person. Dignitaries from the government were always present to greet the Grand Dukes, only a little less formally than they would have for the Emperor; motorcades were ready, and the streets were cleared as the Grand Duke was whisked away to his hotel, usually the Ritz in Paris, where several floors were taken over. Again he would be greeted by the manager and chief of staff, while a whole bevy of servants stood by to serve every whim of the Grand Duke.[5]

Very large sums were always available to the grand dukes [although this was somewhat restricted and a yearly 'allowance' was instituted under Alexander III.] If a grand duke wanted cash, which was rare as most things were simply tabulated and the bill sent to his Comptroller in St. Petersburg, an entire tray of various denominations was presented. There is one story that is of the Grand Duke who had such bad luck at Monte Carlo that the secretary of the company in St. Petersburg from which he kept drawing supplies, telegraphed to the Grand Duke's private secretary imploring him not to wire for any more money, because the entire assets of the company had already been dispatched and there was nothing left, and he could not survive the disgrace of refusing further funds to a Grand Duke![6]

Paris was usually devoted to social events: parties with the titled nobility, expatriate Russians; visits to the restaurants and night clubs, where the Imperial party would take over an establishment for themselves and their entourage. Romance was not the least thing on the minds of the grand dukes.

On the Riveria life was a little more relaxed. The days were spent on the beach or sailing, or perhaps playing golf. Leisurely lunches and late breakfasts, perhaps with a lady of the evening from the night before, and then the preparation for the next night. That was when it really happened, at night in the casino. The Grand Duke would arrive with a beautiful woman on his arm, whom he would then deposit at a gambling table of her choice with a huge stack of 1000 franc chips, while he would go to his own game, which was usually roulette or the crap tables. Bets were not small, or cautious. Vast sums were won and lost with one turn of the wheel or toss of the dice. When the Grand Duke was at table, house limits were suspended without question, because he might suddenly push into

---

5. *Always A Grand Duke*, Grand Duke Alexander
6. *The Court of Russia*, E. A. Hodgetts

play his entire stack of chips, which could be $100,000 or $500,000! While unbelievable sums were lost, equally large sums were won. A Grand Duke was no easy pickings! Grand Duchess Marie records that after a night of winning, presents of jewels were the order of the day.[7]

Besides a general good-natured enjoyment of life, the one consuming passion of Grand Duke Alexis was his love for a relative, Zinaida or Zina Beauharnais, as she was usually called. Zinaida was the wife of the Duke of Leuchtenberg, son of Maximilian, who married the Grand Duchess Marie, daughter of Nicholas I, and the grandson of Eugene Beauharnais, stepson of Napoleon I and vice-King of Italy. Zinaida was described by Count Paul Vasili as "one of the most superb persons who have ever beautified this terrestrial stage. Very much admired, but envied still more as much on account of her charms as for her brilliant marriage, she belongs to the category of women predestined from all eternity to get themselves talked about. Very ambitious, devoid of prejudices and scruples, and possessed of an almost royal indifference to the tittle-tattle of gossip-mongers, she flaunts openly the things which people usually endeavour to keep secret, and in her arrogant pride seems to defy calumny and compel it to be silent. She is a being of intoxicates."

Hodgetts describes one adventure of Grand Duke Alexis and the beautiful Zinaida as follows: "The tale-bearers of the Russian capital relate that on one occasion, when the Duke of Leuchtenberg returned home late from the club where he loved his game of cards, he found the marital chamber locked against him, and proceeded to knock and to insist on being let in, creating quite a disturbance. Thereupon, so runs the legend, the door was opened, and the Herculean Alexis came forth, administered a sound thrashing, and kicked the injured husband downstairs, where he was constrained to spend the rest of the night sleeping on his study sofa. The next day the outraged Duke, smarting from the moral and physical indignities which had been put upon him, went straight to the Emperor to complain. That sapient monarch, whose common sense was only equalled by his aversion to putting himself out, quietly replied that if the Duke of Leuchtenberg was incapable of managing his wife himself he must not expect others to assist him to do so; and that in any case, he, the Emperor, would stand no nonsense and have no scandals, more especially no sensational divorce." So, the Duke of Leuchtenberg returned to his residence and prudently thereafter spent his nights in his study. Whether this story is true or false, to the outside world this grand-ducal *ménage-à-trois* appeared to be happy and harmonious. Grand Duke Alexis died in Paris on 27 November 1908.

---

7. *A Romanov Diary*, Grand Duchess George

GRAND DUKE SERGE ALEXANDROVICH

CHAPTER XII

GRAND DUKE SERGE ALEXANDROVICH
(1857 - 1905)

Grand Duke Serge, the fifth son of Alexander II, was born at Tsarksoye Selo on 11 May 1857. An extremely good looking man, Serge had blond crew cut hair, blue eyes, and a small, closely trimmed beard; he was very tall, with broad shoulders and a slim, erect figure. Yet, Serge was a quiet, withdrawn man, who went about with a sad expression on his face, and his eyes seemed haunted, according to his future wife.

It is safe to say that Grand Duke Serge was the least popular of the Grand Dukes. He was singled out from all the others by the scandal-mongers of St. Petersburg society, and was reputed by some to enjoy unmentionable vices. Current writers have been equally unkind, saying that he raped his wife, and thereafter they had no married life, accounting for the lack of children; that he was homosexual; that he was a sadist, enjoying torturing prisoners; that he indulged in sexual activities with both young girls and boys, particularly Jewish ones. There is undoubtedly an element of truth to these stories, but there is also no doubt that much was exaggerated. His brother, Emperor Alexander III, was very much the strait-laced autocrat, and it is doubtful that he would have appointed Grand Duke Serge Governor of Moscow; nor that Nicholas II would have allowed him to become guardian of the children of Grand Duke Paul, had half of these stories had any foundation in truth.

Grand Duke Serge was appointed Governor-General of Moscow in 1891 by his brother, Alexander III. He ruled the old capital with an iron hand, but with super devotion to duty, reminiscent of his grandfather, Nicholas I. During his years as Governor, he manifested a Haroun al-Rashid kind of activity, going about among the people personally inspecting the bread and other food subject to official examination, and inquiring into and righting abuses. He would spy out fraudulent weights and measures, and generally ferret out grievances. He often went about disguised as a private individual in order to see how things really were. Even with these activities, which should have won him wide approval, he was generally unpopular—at least with the revolutionaries, who did not want efficient governance, and the officials whose cheating and inefficiency came to the Grand Duke's attention. What the common citizen thought of him—there is no record of that.

Some of his general unpopularity can certainly be attributed to his being an unbending, stiff disciplinarian of the old school. Serge's cousin, Grand Duke Alexander Mikhailovich, could not find a single redeeming feature in his character, and called him a poor officer when he was commander of the Preobrazhensky Regiment of the Guards, and an inefficient administrator when he was Governor-General of Moscow. "Obstinate, arrogant, and disagreeable, and responsible for the inefficient arrangements that led to the tragedy of Khodynka Field, when thousands of people were trampled to death trying to get presents handed out on the occasion of Nicholas II's coronation in 1896," he said. Serge insisted that the coronation ball proceed as scheduled, and when Alexander Mikhailovich and his brothers walked out in protest, Serge remarked, "There go the imperial followers of Robbespierre!"[1]

Grand Duke Serge was in charge of Moscow for fourteen years, plenty of time to accumulate unpopularity as embodying the worst features of the old autocracy. When the revolution of 1905 came, he naturally recommended extreme severity in putting it down, and became a target for the revolutionaries. An assassination plot was organized by Boris Savinkov, who was to acquire great notoriety in the post-1917 period, eventually being killed by the Bolsheviks. The Grand Duke was spared death on one occasion because his little wards were with him in his carriage, and Savinkov could not bring himself to give the signal with the children there.

The other side of Grand Duke Serge has been little reported. Other relatives, of very conservative bent, were not quite so hard on him. Grand Duchess Marie Georgievna, wife of Grand Duke George Mikhailovich, admits that he was an unpopular, stern disciplinarian, and carried himself as if he were grand and stuck-up, but she adds that he was a good friend, and loved children, having none of his own.

In 1881, when Tolstoy wrote a letter to Alexander III begging the Emperor to spare the life of his father's assassins, it was the martinet Serge Alexandrovich who agreed to place the letter on his brother Alexander III's desk. The killers were hanged anyway.

The childhood memories of Grand Duchess Marie Pavlovna, the daughter of Grand Duke Paul, give an intimate picture of this enigmatic man. She and her brother Grand Duke Dimitri were made

---

1. *Once A Grand Duke*, Grand Duke Alexander

wards of Grand Duke Serge when their father Paul, Serge's brother, married morganatically and was banned from Russia. They lived with Serge and his wife, Grand Duchess Elizabeth Feodorovna ("Ella"), at the Governor's Palace in Moscow, and at their estate Ilyinskoye, and in the Kremlin during the troubles of 1905. Marie Pavlovna remembers Serge bathing the baby Dimitri with his own hands in the bouillon bath prescribed for him. He developed an almost feminine tenderness toward his two wards, at the same time demanding absolute and exact obedience, and tolerating no back-talk. Serge directed his households down to the last detail, spending much time on Ilyinskoye, its buildings, its horses and cattle. On special feast days he gave presents to the peasants and made sure to patronize all the small merchants around.

Marie Pavlovna describes the relationship between her foster parents as being a state of strained fondness. They rarely met, except at meals, and yet they always slept in one large bed together. Serge Alexandrovich regarded his wife's intense spirituality and piety as immoderate. She always deferred to him in everything, but both of them veiled their true feelings. Ella was tall, slight, blonde, with very fine features—a real beauty. She designed her own dresses, painting water colors of them. Serge Alexandrovich loved jewels and saw that his wife had something special to go with each dress. Ironically, it was Serge Alexandrovich who showed tenderness to the children, while the truly saintly Aunt Ella seemed to be jealous of their presence, was cold, and sometimes actively nasty to them, which she later admitted and apologized for.

Serge had known Ella most of his life. She wrote of once seeing him in tears after being abused by his older brothers, Grand Dukes Alexander and Vladimir. Serge wore a corset, German style, and his brothers teased him about this, imitating the way it made him walk. On the occasion in question, they were holding Serge down, while cutting off the offending garment.

When they became engaged, Serge showed up with a case of jewels, and insisted Ella put on each and every one. She described how he took bracelets, strand after stand of pearls, broaches of rubies and emeralds and diamonds, putting them all over her until she could hardly stand because of their weight, and then standing back to admire the results. "I looked like a Christmas tree!" she wrote, "And we had a terrible time getting them all off, because we couldn't find the clasps."

While Grand Duchess Elizabeth is credited with being saintly, and having great piety, this is primarily based on events after the death of Grand Duke Serge. When she first came to St. Petersburg, Ella was the belle of the ball. She loved beautiful clothes, dancing until dawn, and flirtations with the handsome gentlemen of the guards who served under her husband—both single and married ones. Grand Duke Serge was rarely jealous, it appears, often helping her fill out her dance card, and suggesting which young men she should dance with. Once, noticing how much time she spent with the wives of the officers, he inquired why, saying, "You can't dance with the officers' wives!"

He does appear to have been jealous of his much loved younger brother, Grand Duke Paul, on at least one occasion, according to Princess Radziwill. Apparently Ella, she wrote, had danced too frequently with the young Paul, and Ella's sister-in-law, and arch enemy, Grand Duchess Vladimir, had commented on this starting a rumor that reached Serge's ears. He warned her not to be "too friendly."[2]

When Ella's younger sister, Alix, married Nicholas II, Ella had great influence over the new Empress, and was responsible for introducing her to soothsayers, and other holy men, leading ultimately to Rasputin. Grand Duchess Ella was also interested in politics, and commenced at an early stage to meddle, but had little success with Alexander III on the throne, who listened to no one.[3] She was considerably more influential during the early years of Nicholas II's reign, but then a coolness developed between the two sister, and after Grand Duke Serge's murder in 1905, she withdrew from society and was little heard of after that.

In his later years, Grand Duke Serge grew more and more austere. He had always been a strict and devout member of the Orthodox Church, and was accused toward the end of having inspired the repressive measures which found such favor under Plehve, and the policy of stirring up discontent among the workmen with a view to discovering and arresting the revolutionary ringleaders. Plehve was directly responsible to the Emperor only, and Serge was hardly ever in St. Petersburg, and not in the best of standing with the Imperial Family, so there seems little chance that he could have yielded such a powerful influence on affairs of state.

Grand Duke Serge was also an ardent archaeologist, for which reason he had always wanted to be Governor General of the ancient and historic capital of Russia, Moscow, a wish shared by his wife, who greatly admired the picturesque surroundings of Moscow, and especially the beautiful estate of Archangel, where her brother-in-law, Grand Duke Paul, had at one time resided.

On one occasion, when the Archaeological Congress held a meeting in Moscow, Grand Duke Serge proposed a toast to the city. In the course of his speech he took the opportunity to say that he knew of no town in which he would rather live. This was before his appointment as Governor, and was obviously a hint. The courtly and

---

2. *Secrets of Dethroned Royalty*, Princess Radziwill
3. *Mother Dear*, V. Plyakov

ancient Governor-General, Prince Dolgorukov was so old that it was said that since the days of Methuselah there hadn't been anyone older. He wore an immaculate brown wig, dyed his moustache, roughed his cheeks, was supported by stays, and was one of the most accomplished rogues of a school now as extinct as the dodo. Taking up the Grand Duke's challenge, Dolgorukov replied with irony, that there was also no town which he would not sooner die in. The poor old man, in spite of his many foibles, also had some sterling qualities, and was greatly beloved, but he was not permitted to end his days in the manner he had so tactfully pleaded for in his reply to the Grand Duke. Grand Duke Serge soon superseded him, and the old man died several years later.[4]

One amusing story reported by Hodgetts about Prince Dolgorukov is that once he was recommended a new hair dye for his moustache, but, his valet did not apply it correctly and his moustache became a fierce bright green instead of the intended pleasant brown. Unable to get rid of this horrible verdure, the unfortunate Governor General had to take to his bed and wait until "these calamities had passed." During this time the Emperor visited Moscow, and poor Prince Dolgorukov was unable to receive him, pleading illness. Alexander II discovered the real cause of his indisposition, and very much amused, sent the Prince another hair dye, warranted not to turn green!

On 17 February 1905, Grand Duke Serge's luck ran out. A bomb literally blew him to smithereens. His wife, who dashed from the Kremlin to the scene, picked up several pieces of his body; a finger was later found on a rooftop nearby. Shortly before his death, the Grand Duke had resigned as Governor General, but retained command of the troops, and had moved to the Kremlin from the Governor General's palace. He would have been safe had he stayed behind the walls. So, at the age of forty-eight, ended the life of this strange, unattractive, contradictory Grand Duke, the first Romanov to be assassinated since his father's death in 1881, and the first in the 20th century.

In a gesture of Christian forgiveness, his widow, Grand Duchess Elizabeth, visited the assassin in his cell. After the assassination, Ella devoted herself entirely to her religious vocation. She became a nun and the abbess of a convent. She emerged from seclusion only briefly in 1916 to try, with no success, to make her sister, Empress Alexandra, see the light about Rasputin, and the way things were going. On 17 July 1918, she and several relatives, were thrown down a mine shaft at Alapayevsk by the Bolsheviks, where they died in agony. Her body was somehow smuggled out of Russia, through China, and now rests in Jerusalem. She was separately and

---

4. *At the Court of Russia*, E. A. Hodgetts

individually canonized by the Orthodox Church, not part of the massive "New Martyr" canonization.

GRAND DUKE PAUL ALEXANDROVICH

GRAND DUKE SERGE ALEXANDROVICH, EMPRESS MARIE,
GRAND DUCHESS XENIA, GRAND DUKE PAUL ALEXANDROVICH

CHAPTER XIII

GRAND DUKE PAUL ALEXANDROVICH
(1860-1918)

Grand Duke Paul Alexandrovich was born at Tsarksoye-Selo on 3 October 1860, the youngest son of Alexander II. He was the nicest of the formidable uncles that the young Emperor Nicholas II had to deal with, and was close to him in age. Paul was a very tall, thin, broad shouldered man with a rounded forehead, a long thin nose, a moustache and no beard. At first, Paul enjoyed the life of a carefree young officer, serving first in the Guards Grodno Hussars and later commanding the Horse Guards. He was charming, elegant, humorous, a good dancer and a great favorite among the ladies. In spite of these traits, he was always very close to his next elder brother, Serge Alexandrovich, so different from him in every way, which did not stop Paul from allegedly having a flirtation with Serge's wife shortly after their marriage.

Occasionally suffering from weak lungs, Grand Duke Paul spent several summers in Athens where his first cousin, Olga Constantinovna was Queen. There he fell in love with Princess Alexandra of Greece, the elder daughter of Queen Olga and King George I. Alexandra was a niece of Empress Marie, and she championed the match. Paul and Alexandra were married at St. Petersburg 17 June 1889. They resided in a vast, rectangular palace on the Neva of no particular discernable historical architectural style. In 1890 a daughter, Grand Duchess Marie Pavlovna, was born and seventeen months later a son, Grand Duke Dimitri Pavlovich. His birth cut short this happy marriage. Grand Duchess Alexandra, only twenty-one years old, died at Moscow, 24 September 1891, five days after giving birth, much mourned by all who knew her.

The widower was a loving but not very demonstrative father to his two children, who were largely turned over to nurses and governesses. He went on with his military career for another ten years, and by 1902 commanded a cavalry division stationed at Krasnoye Selo, residing with the children in a suite at the Catherine

Palace in Tsarskoye-Selo.

All of this ended suddenly. In 1902, while in Leghorn, Italy, Grand Duke Paul Alexandrovich married a Russian divorcée, Olga Valerianovna Pistolkors, nèe Karnovich.

Olga and Paul had carried on an affair for a good many years, and had been accepted finally by the whole of St. Petersburg society, where Madame Pistolkors had always been popular on account of her beauty and the excellence of the dinners she was fond of giving. She was extremely clever and had all along played for high stakes, from the first having the firm intention of becoming the consort of Paul Alexandrovich. No one doubted that Grand Duke Paul would marry the lady, provided her husband agreed to grant her a divorce. This, however, he did not seem inclined to do until circumstances forced his hand, which the gossips claimed the lady had skilfully brought about herself.

At one of the balls at the Winter Palace, Madame Pistolkors surprised the guest by wearing some diamonds which had belonged to the late Empress Maria Alexandrovna, and had been bequeathed by her to her youngest son, Paul. Paul had been induced to give them to Olga, who did not hesitate to wear them in the least desirable place possible. They were at once recognized by the Dowager Empress Marie, who, in her indignation, went to seek her daughter-in-law, the young Empress Alexandra, and asked her to exert her authority to have Olga expelled from the Palace. This was done, a chamberlain being given the disagreeable task of asking Olga to leave the ball, thereby creating an unprecedented scandal. The next day the whole town was ringing with the story of her discomfiture, and her husband found himself in the predicament of choosing between divorcing her or sending in his papers and leaving the army.

Olga, upon whom society now turned its back, fled abroad, where she was quickly followed by the Grand Duke, who considered himself obliged to stand by her in her misfortune. He had never thought of marrying her, but now he felt that he could not do otherwise, so as soon as she was free they married. They settled in Italy, for the Emperor notified him that his presence was no longer required in St. Petersburg. Paul was deprived of his military rank, and cut off from all official revenues. Furthermore, the two children, Marie and Dimitri, were made official wards of their Uncle Serge Alexandrovich and his wife, Grand Duchess Elizabeth. They spent the rest of their childhood in and around Moscow, where their uncle was Governor General. In spite of the long-standing affection between the two brothers, Grand Duke Serge made it quite clear in no uncertain terms to his brother that he would have no say whatever in their upbringing.

While upset about the arrangement for the children, Grand Duke Paul settled into a happy second marriage in Paris with his morganatic wife, who was given the title Countess Hohenfelsen. A woman of good looking, if somewhat irregular features, Olga was intelligent and possessed considerable energy and force of character. The couple had had one child, Vladimir (later Paley), who was born in St. Petersburg in 1897 before the marriage and Olga's divorce. In Paris they had two girls, Irina, born in 1903, and Natalia, born in 1905.

It was not long before members of the Imperial family, visiting the French capital, consented to receive Olga, and little by little she won her way back into Russian society; even those she knew had spoken unkindly of her received a warm welcome. She was of the opinion that forgetfulness of the injuries one has received is a great help in life, and this principle, coupled with exquisite tact, carried her triumphantly through. After some years she was allowed to return to Russia for a few weeks, on pretext of being present at the wedding of one of the two daughters of her first marriage. After this visit, much of the prejudice against her vanished, and she returned to St. Petersburg frequently during the winter seasons.

In 1905 Grand Duke Paul asked for, and received, permission to return to Russia for the funeral of his assassinated brother Serge. He made an attempt while there to recover his children, but Serge's widow, Grand Duchess Elizabeth, would not hear of it.

Three years later, in 1908, Paul Alexandrovich was allowed into Russia again, this time with his wife, to attend the wedding of his daughter, Grand Duchess Marie. Paul had been allowed no say about the marriage of Marie to Prince William of Sweden, and it was a miserable marriage annulled in 1914. Paul always held this against Ella.

It was not until 1912, however, that he was fully forgiven and allowed to settle in Russia with his new family. They built a house at Tsarskoye-Selo not far from the Alexander Palace, where Nicholas II and his family resided. In 1915, Emperor Nicholas II relented further: heeding Olga's arguments to be allowed to drop the German name, the Emperor created her Princess Paley in her own right, with the power to transmit her name and title to her children by Grand Duke Paul.

Ten years of exile in Paris, where he met a large circle of new friends, considerably broadened the outlook of Grand Duke Paul. He spent most of World War I at Tsarskoye Selo, but when his health permitted, he commanded the First Imperial Guards Corps at the front, ranking as a full general of cavalry.

These circumstances, plus his status as the last surviving son of Alexander II and brother of Alexander III, and the actions of his own son, Dimitri, conspired to bring Grand Duke Paul, a man never terribly interested in politics, into the center of events in the last few months of the monarchy.

A strange thing happened to him as early as 1915. Empress Alexandra asked the Grand Duke to give a dinner at his Tsarskoye Selo house for the French Ambassador, Maurice Paleologue, to find out his opinion about the idea of Nicholas II taking over personal command of the armies. She did not attend the dinner herself, but sent her loyal but not very bright lady-in-waiting, Vyrubova, to pump Paleologue for his opinion. The ambassador was amazed that such a mission had been entrusted to such an air head, and limited himself to a vague phrase to the effect that it was too late for an outside opinion to count.

Grand Duke Paul happened to be at general headquarters with Nicholas II in December 1916 when the news of Rasputin's murder arrived. There was no information on the identity of the killers, and it was Paul's impression that the emperor seemed rather relieved.[1]

The next day, back at Tsarskoye Selo, Paul learned to his horror that his son, Grand Duke Dimitri, had been one of the three killers, the others being Prince Felix Yusupov and the right wing Duma member, Purishkevich. Dimitri was under house arrest in St. Petersburg. Paul wanted to go to him immediately, but was dissuaded by his wife. Instead, he went to see the Emperor, who had also returned to Tsarskoye Selo. He was rather curt with his uncle, but then sent him a note that he could not lift Dimitri's arrest until completion of the investigation, but prayed that Dimitri would come out clean. Then Paul went to the capital to see his son. Dimitri swore to him on his mother's portrait that there was no blood on his hands.[2]

On 21st December, on the initiative of Grand Duke Paul, a meeting of family members was convened at the house of Grand Duke Andrew Vladimirovich, to inform them of these developments. It was attended by Andrew's mother, Grand Duchess Marie Pavlovna, his brothers Cyril and Boris, and Grand Duke Alexander Mikhailovich. Grand Duke Paul read a draft of a letter to the emperor that he had written, but before sending it, the group decided that Grand Dukes Paul and Alexander would try to talk to Nicholas II personally again. These two interviews took place with no results whatever, and shortly afterwards Dimitri was ordered to the Persian front.

A gloomy Christmas was spent at Grand Duke Paul's house. While Paul thought the murder of Rasputin had been patriotically motivated, he considered it dangerous and thoughtless, a blot on the family, and would make the Empress even more stubborn in granting any reforms. The occasion was made worse by the fact that Princess

---

1. *Memories of Russia*, Princess Paley
2. *Prince Felix Yusupov*, Christopher Dobson

Paley's sister and her son by her first marriage were supporters of Rasputin.

On 29th December, almost all the members of the Imperial Family in St. Petersburg met at the palace of Grand Duchess Marie Pavlovna (the elder), to sign the letter Paul had drafted, adding that sending Dimitri to Persia could, in view of his health, amount to a death sentence because of the epidemics and other rough conditions there. The letter was signed by six Grand Dukes—Paul, Cyril, Boris, Andrew, Nicholas Mikhailovich and Serge Mikhailovich, and by five Grand Duchesses—Olga, Queen of Greece, Marie Pavlovna (the elder), Victoria (Cyril's wife), Elizabeth Mavrikiyevna, Marie Pavlovna, Paul's daughter, and four princes of the blood, all sons of Constantine Constantinovich.

On New Year's Eve came the answer, "Nobody is given the right to be involved in murder. I know that the conscience of many is troubled since not only Dimitri Pavlovich is mixed up in this. I am surprised at your addressing me. Nicholas."

On 13 March 1917, the Empress again unexpectedly sent for Grand Duke Paul, and accused him of heading the whole family in trying to influence the Emperor to grant concessions, meaning a government fully responsible to the Duma. Paul did not have sufficient devotion to the throne, she said. There would be no concessions![3]

The Emperor was expected back from general headquarters the next day. When he did not arrive, Grand Duke Paul composed a manifesto granting a full constitution, obtained the signatures of Grand Duke Michael Alexandrovich and Cyril Vladimirovich, and took it to the Alexander Palace to ask the Empress to sign. She refused, technically correct, since only the Emperor had the right to do so, but she also abhorred the idea. Paul then got in touch with the president of the Duma, Rodzianko. These efforts were too late to do any good. Control over the capital was lost to the government. The provisional government was already forming on 15th March. Soviets of workers and soldiers were coming into being.

On 16th March Grand Duke Paul learned that Emperor Nicholas II had abdicated the throne in favor of his brother, Grand Duke Michael Alexandrovich. Paul immediately went to the Empress and to his astonishment found that she did not know this had happened. Evidently nobody had dared to tell her. She received the news from Paul, and took it with remarkable calm, remarking only "So, now Michael is Emperor," and that she would go to the Crimea with her children, who were sick with the measles.

When Grand Duke Michael refused to take the throne, the commanding officers of the troops at Tsarskoye Selo gathered at

---

3. *Memories of Russia*, Princess Paley

Grand Duke Paul's house and decided the only thing to do was recognize the provisional government.

Some days later the provisional government placed the Empress under house arrest at the Alexander Palace because of rumors that a military unit composed of holders of the Order of St. George was approaching in a rescue attempt. She again asked Grand Duke Paul to come over, not wanting to be alone with the new Minister of War, Guchkov, and the new commander of the Petersburg Military District, General Kornilov, who were coming to see her. She was outwardly calm, and very dignified. She asked for nothing for herself, only that her servants not be penalized for their loyalty and that her hospitals in Tsarksoye Selo continue receiving supplies. Afterwards Grand Duke Paul asked Guchkov and Kornilov to try to control the behavior of the soldiers on guard, but there was little they could do. The soldiers had earlier promised to behave when Grand Duke Paul had made a speech to them, but now they were taking pleasure in making rude remarks and using bad language. They were not, however, violent at this stage.[4]

Now, at the age of fifty-seven, Grand Duke Paul Alexandrovich, who as a youth had visited the victorious Imperial Army in Bulgaria in 1877, had lived to see the monarchy disappear. He was patient and resigned. He continued living at Tsarskoye Selo with his family, seeing fewer people so as not to compromise them.[5]

"There is no country called Russia anymore," he remarked ironically. "Only a country called Revolution, which must be protected at any price."

Paul delighted in his little daughters, but did not quite understand his son, Vladimir Paley, who was extremely talented in poetry, art, and music, but had little interest in the military, although he had attended the Corps des Pages and served as a hussar officer at the front for several months.

In August 1917, the Grand Duke was placed under house arrest by Alexander Kerensky, the head of the provisional government, because Princess Paley and their son Vladimir, had spoken disrespectfully of the government. Indeed, Vladimir had written satirical verses about Kerensky. However, the guards were removed after Paul's daughter, Grand Duchess Marie Pavlovna, obtained an interview with Kerensky in the Winter Palace.

In 1914 Paul had, after some grumbling, supported the efforts of his daughter to divorce the Swedish prince. Now he encouraged her marriage to Prince Serge Putyatin, which took place in September 1917, thinking she would be safer with a good man at her side. Both the Grand Duchess and the Prince survived the revolution.

---

4. *Nicholas and Alexandra*, Robert Massie

5. *Education of A Princess*, Grand Duchess Marie

After the Bolshevik coup in November, Grand Duke Paul was again arrested and taken to Lenin's headquarters at the Smolny Institute, but was released two weeks later and returned to his home. The local Soviet raided Tsarskoye Selo and took over his huge and valuable wine cellar, but everybody got too drunk to do the Grand Duke any harm.

On 18 March 1918 all male Romanovs were ordered to register, and this included Prince Vladimir Paley, although he did not bear the Romanov surname. This led to his death at the age of twenty-one. He was shipped to Vyatka and then to Alapayevsk, where on 17 July 1918 he was thrown down a mine shaft with Grand Duchess Elizabeth Feodorovna, Grand Duke Serge Mikhailovich, and three sons of Grand Duke Constantinovich—Princes John, Constantine, and Igor.

Grand Duke Paul Alexandrovich was excused from the fatal registration for reasons of health, and was the last Grand Duke to be free in the St. Petersburg area. Not for long. On 12 August 1918 he was arrested at his home, taken to Petersburg in a car, and put in jail after a perfunctory interrogation. The order for his arrest had been signed by Uritsky, the chief of the St. Petersburg Cheka, the Bolshevik secret police. The prison also contained his cousins, Grand Dukes Dimitri Constantinovich, Nicholas Mikhailovich and George Mikhailovich[6] The latter three had nobody to try to help them, but the energetic Princess Paley actually managed to see Uritsky to plead for her husband. What were the accusations against him? Nothing, except all Romanovs were enemies of the people and must pay for their 300 years of oppression. Uritsky said that Paul would later be sent to Siberia, and meanwhile gave Princess Paley a pass to visit him in prison and bring him food.

Princess Paley saw everyone she thought could possibly help, at the same time trying to find out what had happened to their son, Vladimir. In September Uritsky was assassinated, and this was followed by wholesale terror. The Grand Duke heard prisoners being taken away at night, expecting his own death at any time.

In December he was at last transferred to a prison hospital, where his wife could talk to him without others present. An escape from there might have been possible, and there were people who wanted to arrange it, but Grand Duke Paul refused for fear of it being taken out on his three cousins.[7]

The last time Princess Paley saw her husband was at Christmas, after which the entire regime in the prison hospital was changed, being considered too lax. She was no longer allowed in, although she continued to go there. In January 1919 she was told

---

6. The authors grandfather.

7. *Memories of Russia*, Princess Paley

that Grand Duke Paul was no longer there. He had been taken to Cheka headquarters.

Princess Paley telephoned the wife of the writer Maxim Gorky, one of the persons she had appealed to for help. She was assured that Gorky himself had obtained a full release for the four Grand Dukes from Lenin in Moscow, and was returning with it. He had indeed done this, especially pleading for the historian Nicholas Mikhailovich, but it was either too late or Lenin had fooled Gorky, the more likely event.

The history of Lenin, and his own words, tell that he was never adverse to using murder, assassination and terror to gain his own ends. While these acts are usually taken in a "political" context, what is overlooked is the fact that he would sanction murder when it served no useful political purpose, and could even be counter-productive. Lenin was without doubt a psychopathic personality with a propensity to violence. Typical of this personality type, he was also a physical coward, and paranoid that someone was going to kill him. While in exile in Switzerland, he cowed before his opponents, and often fled meetings where he suspected members would be hostile; when he emerged victorious, he sought revenge against his opponents. After coming to power in 1917, Lenin spent a great deal of his early time seeking out former opponents and having them murdered. It is clear that Lenin intended to murder every member of the Romanov Family that he could get his hands on—man, woman and child—because no such extensive series of murders could possibly have taken place at that time without his knowledge and consent.

On the night of 29 January 1919, Grand Duke Paul Alexandrovich was taken from the Cheka to the Fortress of St. Peter and Paul, where the other three Grand Dukes were brought directly from prison, and in the early morning of 30 January 1919, the four Grand Dukes, stripped to the waist, were shot in front of a common grave in which other bodies already lay, within sight of the Cathedral where their ancestors and relatives lay buried.

Princess Paley and her daughters escaped through Finland.

GRAND DUKE CONSTANTINE and
GRAND DUKE NICHOLAS

GRAND DUCHESSES VERA and OLGA CONSTANTINOVNA
with their brother GRAND DUKE NICHOLAS CONSTANTINOVICH

CHAPTER XIV

GRAND DUKE NICHOLAS CONSTANTINOVICH (1850 - 1918)

Grand Duke Nicholas Constantinovich was the eldest son of Grand Duke Constantine Nikolayevich. He was born at St. Petersburg 14 September 1850.

Grand Duke Nicholas was a tall, slender youth, exceedingly handsome, and intelligent, but a terror to his instructors. Monsieur Ricard, his tutor was greatly offended by a poem of Nicholas', the last two lines being:

Et sous ce veston civil
Chacun me traitera de manant . . .

Ricard refused to give the Grand Duke further lessons. Grand Duchess Alexandra tried to persuade him to continue, even promising to speak with Grand Duke Constantine. Ricard replied, "No doubt Nicholas has got the military bump."[1]

Grand Duchess Marie overhead Nicholas quoting the Burgraves' song:

Nargue au 'Roi, burgrave,
Burgrave, nargue à 'Dieu.

Being very religious, she took offense and persuaded Grand Duchess Constantine that Monsieur Ricard was a Jacobin, and he was dismissed.

Nicholas' interest ran to the arts, and he became a patron under the direction of Grigorovitch, director of Museums, and spent a great deal on pictures and antiques.

Nicholas achieved rather tragic notoriety because of his love life. He had an obsession with sex, which ruined him. As a very

---

1. *Memories of A Shipwrecked World*, Countess Kleinmichel

young man he was warned by a doctor that his mode of living could lead to insanity, probably meaning through syphilis, but this made little impression on Nicholas. He had a series of lady friends, one of them a maid of honor to his mother, but most of their names have been lost to history.

His mother tried to arrange a marriage between Nicholas and Princess Frederika of Hanover, but she was in love with her father's equerry, Baron Pavel von Rammingen, and married him against her parent's wishes.

The amorous conduct of Nicholas could have been overlooked, except for a scandal that broke in the spring of 1874, when Grand Duke Nicholas was a guards officer.

Nicholas was accused of various thefts of objects from the desk of the Empress Maria Alexandrovna, and from his mother. He even stripped the gold from an icon at his mother's bedside and extracted three large diamonds from it with his teeth.[2] The Ikon had been a gift from Nicholas I. All of this went to support the insatiable needs of an American adventuress who was determined to marry the young Grand Duke, who probably did not have marriage on his mind. As he encountered more and more family and government opposition, he grew obstinate.

The American, Hattie Ely[3], the daughter of a clergyman in Philadelphia, had eloped at the age of sixteen with a drunkard called Blackford, who died an early death. She then became the mistress of various men in Philadelphia, until scandal forced her to flee, and she moved to France. In Paris she became the mistress of a Duke. The Franco-Prussian War made Paris considerably less cozy and Mrs. Blackford moved to St. Petersburg. There she managed to ensnare Grand Duke Nicholas to the point that he was ruining himself with the gifts she insisted on. He wrote her soulful letters, and she smuggled herself into his quarters during summer maneuvers dressed as a man. They ran off to Vienna, but their attempt to marry there did not work out because of the stormy arrival of Nicholas' father, Grand Duke Constantine.[4]

In 1874 the scandal was the talk of St. Petersburg. Count Peter Shuvalov went to Grand Duke Constantine and told him that the police were convinced Nicholas himself had taken the diamonds. He added that the affair could and should be hushed up, that he had a man willing to take the blame in exchange for a large sum of money. The Grand Duke was furious, and accused Schouvalov of making up the entire story, and called Nicholas in and demanded

---

2. *Dnevnik Gos. Sekretarya, 1883-1892*, A. A. Polovtsev
3. While all sources agree that the Grand Duke's American adventuress was called Mrs. Blackford, some give her maiden name as Fanny Lear.
4. *Czars and Presidents*, A. Tarsaidze

that Shuvalov repeated the story.[5]

Shuvalov, now angry himself, accused Grand Duke Nicholas of the theft. Nicholas denied all. Count Verpochovsky, Nicholas' A.D.C. and best friend, was arrested, and after initially denying everything, confessed that Nicholas had given him the diamonds to take to Paris. Alexander II was now informed of these events, and Mrs. Blackford, who may or may not have plotted the thefts with her lover, was arrested, but not before she had stashed her loot at the American Legation. It and the incriminating letters were bought from her by the Crown to avoid further scandal, and she was thrown out of Russia, but considerably richer.[6]

A Commission presided over by Count Adlerberg found that Nicholas was out of his mind. He was deprived of his military rank, the management of his fortune, and was exiled to Orenburg.

Nicholas did not take well to his exile. Under close watch, he wrote, "Am I a madman or a criminal? If I am a criminal, try me and sentence me; if I am a madman put me under treatment, but in any case give me some hope that I may one day come back to life and liberty. What you are doing is cruel and inhuman."[7]

Some of Nicholas' imprudent remarks were repeated to the Emperor as proofs that he was a dangerous revolutionary, and he was transferred to Central Asia.

Nicholas' name was never mentioned again in the St. Petersburg drawing-rooms, where he had been a great favorite before this catastrophe, and people tried to forget him.

In 1881, Alexander II died, and Grand Duchess Alexandra received a letter from Nicholas to be given to the new Emperor, Alexander III. It read:

> "Sire, allow me to come, in chains if need be, and prostrate myself before the ashes of my adored Sovereign, imploring him on my knees to pardon my crime. After that, I shall return into exile without a murmur. I implore Your Majesty to grant this favour to the unhappy Nikola."

Alexander II replied to Nicholas:

"You are not worthy to bow before the ashes of my father whom you so cruelly grieved. Do not forget that you have dishonoured us all. So long as I live, you shall not see Petersburg."

---

5. *Memories of A Shipwrecked World*, Countess Kleinmichel
6. *Czars and Presidents*, Alexander Tarsaidze
7. *Memories of A Shipwrecked World*, Countess Kleinmichel

He attached a note in French to the Grand Duchess, which she showed to Countess Kleinmichel:

> "Chère Tante Sanny, vous me trouvez très dur, je le sais, mais vous ne savez pas pour qui vous intercédez. C'est grâce à vous surtout que j'en veux à Nikola. Je vous baise la main. Votre neveu affectioné: Sasha."

Golovine, the Secretary of State, a great friend of Grand Duke Constantine, told Countess Kleinmichel, that Alexander's anger had been caused by a report from Tashkent, that Nicholas had used some very improper words about his mother.

Years later, Emperor Alexander III told one of his ministers that the 1874 thefts were the culmination of several years of "misdeeds" on the part of the young grand duke. Not only that, but he had denied the thefts and tried to blame members of his entourage.[8]

Grand Duke Nicholas was first exiled to Orenburg, and later to Tashkent in Central Asia, where he spent the rest of his life. Nicholas' position with the Imperial Family was further damaged when eight years later he married a Russian woman, Nadezhda Alexandrovna Dreyer, daughter of a police prefect. It seems, however, that she made him very happy and that he never had occasion to regret having chosen her to enliven his exile.

In Tashkent, Russian officials felt that the Grand Duke was not quite sane. One of his strange actions was to try to enter into some sort of political alliance with a man jailed for revolutionary nihilism, though this episode seems to be missing from the police records there.[9] Grand Duke Nicholas signed his letters "Nicholas Romanoff," and declared to all who wished to hear, that he was a republican by sympathy and a socialist by profession. Some writers report that he renounced his title and rights in the succession, while others deny this.

Nicholas' younger brother, Grand Duke Constantine, visited him in Tashkent and felt, on the first evening that he was quite normal. On the second evening he decided that Nicholas was rather strange, and on the third that he was not entirely sane.[10] Serge Witte, the future prime minister, also saw Nicholas in Tashkent. He impressed Witte as being intelligent and efficient, but local officials, Witte notes, considered him "not normal."[11]

---

8. *Dnevnik Gos. Sekretarya*, A. A. Polovtsev
9. *Dnevnik Gos. Sekretarya*, A. A. Polovtsev
10. Testimony, Princes Vera of Russia
11. *Vospominaniya*, S. Yu. Witte

When Nicholas II came to the throne, the supervision of Grand Duke Nicholas was loosened, and he was allowed the use of his personal fortune

Even so, during the forty-four years of his Tashkent exile, where he received an allowance of 12,000 rubles per month, Grand Duke Nicholas did a lot of useful work in irrigation, a difficult problem in Central Asia, and raising cotton. He also built a theater and an aqueduct.

Grand Duke Nicholas and Nadezhda had two children, Artemi, born in 1883 (he was murdered by the Bolsheviks in 1919), and Alexander, born 15 November 1889 at Tashkent. Both were eventually given the morganatic title of Prince Iskander. Prince Alexander escaped to Paris where he married in 1930; he died at Grasse 26 January 1957, without leaving heirs; but in Tashkent today, there is at least one Soviet citizen who claims descent from Grand Duke Nicholas.

When the Revolution began, Grand Duke Nicholas sent a telegram to Kerensky congratulating him, which was published in all of the newspapers.[12] Nevertheless, he was either murdered by the Bolsheviks in Tashkent in February of 1918, or died of starvation. His wife lived on until 1929.

---

12. *Within Royal Palaces*, Countess dePlanty

GRAND DUKE CONSTANTINE CONSTANTINOVICH

THE CONSTANTINOVICH FAMILY
(Standing) Grand Duke Constantine, Princess Tatiana, Duchess Vera, Queen Olga, Prince John, Grand Duchess Elizabeth, Prince Gabriel;
(Seated) Grand Duke Dimitri, Grand Duchess Alexandra, Prince Christopher of Greece;
(Three boys in front) Prince Constantine, Prince Igor, Prince Oleg

GRAND DUKE CONSTANTINE

in *King of Judea*

CHAPTER XV

GRAND DUKE CONSTANTINE CONSTANTINOVICH (1858-1915)

Grand Duke Constantine, the second son of Grand Duke Constantine Nikolayevich and Grand Duchess Alexandra Iosefovna, née Princess of Saxe-Altenburg, was born at Strelna, 22 August 1858.

Constantine was not a politician, but a dreamer, a man of cultured intellect, and was one of the most talented and accomplished members of the Romanov Dynasty. He followed in the footsteps, and probably outdid, his distinguished father.

The early education of Grand Duke Constantine was typical of the Romanov Family in that it began early, with a heavy concentration on the basics. His father, however, saw to it that he was exposed to the arts and classics as well. He had an excellent musical education, and was an accomplished pianist, and as Chairman of the Russian Musical Society he was in touch with the leading Russian composers of his day, and had a long correspondence with Tchaikovsky.

As was expected of all the grand dukes, Constantine, despite his primarily cultural interest, had to follow a military career. He started off as had his father, in the navy, and stayed with this long enough to make a cruise to Norfolk, Virginia, in 1877 with a Russian squadron, which was attempting to avoid being bottled up in the Baltic in case of war with England. The sea, however, did not agree with Constantine, and he transferred to the Izmailovsky Regiment of the Imperial Guards.

Grand Duke Constantine was a very tall man with a reddish beard and beautiful hands, with long fingers, on which he wore many rings. His was an imposing presence, but unassuming in manner with a knack of putting people completely at their ease. At St. Petersburg, in 1884, Grand Duke Constantine married Princess Elizabeth of Saxe-Altenburg, who was known in Russia as Grand Duchess Elizabeth Mavrikiyevna. Much to her very religious husband's chagrin, she never converted to Orthodoxy, preferring to remain a Lutheran.

It was the prospect of Constantine and his wife producing the first of a new generation of Romanovs, who would be the great-grandchildren—rather than the children or grandchildren—of an emperor, that led to Alexander III changing the Family Law so that only children and grandchildren of an emperor had the title of grand duke or grand duchess. All others would have the title of "prince" or "princess" with the qualification of "highness" rather than "imperial highness." The Emperor wisely thought that the number of grand dukes would get entirely out of hand if this were not done promptly.

Grand Duke Constantine's first son, John, was born in 1886—the first of these "new" princes. There were five other sons and three daughters—Gabriel (1887), Tatiana (1890), Constantine (1891), Oleg (1892), Igor (1894), George (1903), Natalia (1905), and Vera (1906). With this new generation came original names. There had never been a Gabriel, Oleg, or Igor in the Dynasty before, and no John (Ioann) since 1741. Constantine was a fond but strict father with his many children, insisting on strict observance of religious ritual and disliking any foreign words in their Russian, and they all had Russian nannies, rather than British or French.

After transferring from the navy, Constantine was able to pursue his real interest in life—the arts. While skilled in music, the Grand Duke always preferred literature to all other branches of the arts, and was an accomplished poet. His continual aim was to create literary interests in the circles in which he moved. During the years of his military service with the Izmailov Regiment of the Guards, he founded a literary and dramatic society under the name of *Izmailovskie Dossugui* (the leisure hours of the Izmailovsky corps). The society's motto was "Valor, Goodness, Beauty," and the emblem—a sword and a lyre entwined in flowers.

The members of this society assembled once a week in the mess room of the regiment to read the works of Russian authors and poets, and to act detached scenes from native dramas and comedies. They had the privilege of being the first to listen to any new work from the Grand Duke's pen.

When the *Izmailovskie Dossugui* had gained experience, Grand Duke Constantine invited actresses from the Imperial Dramatic Company to take the female parts, and the performances were given in the Hermitage Theatre of the Winter Palace with the flower of St. Petersburg society for an audience. Everyone who was anybody felt eager to be present, and invitations were eagerly sought. One of the best of these performances was that of Shakespeare's *Hamlet*, translated into Russian verse by the Grand Duke. It took him seven years, 1889-1896, to accomplish this. It was considered the best translations of Hamlet up to that time.[1] Salvini, the great tragedian, attended the last rehearsal, and his presence caused a great sensation. Salvini paid a tribute of astonishment and admiration to the acting of his august colleague, praising very highly his conception of Hamlet—the best part in Salvini's own repertory.

Grand Duke Constantine also translated Schiller's tragedy, *The Bride of Messina*, from the German, as well as some of Goethe's works.

As a writer, Grand Duke Constantine wrote poetry, several volumes of which were published under the initials "C.R." [K. P., in Russian), standing for "Constantine Romanov." His original play, called *King of Judea*, was performed in the Hermitage Theatre in 1913, over the objections of the clergy, since Christ appeared in the play. The Grand Duke played the role of Joseph of Arimithea. It was his last public performance.

Unlike his father, Grand Duke Constantine was a great favorite of his cousin, Emperor Alexander III, and of Empress Marie. His sister, Olga, was married to King George of Greece, the favorite brother of the Empress. Alexander III appointed him President of the Academy of Sciences, and, at one time he was the chief of all the Military Colleges in Russia, where he made himself accessible to the boys' parents, and was adored by the cadets. It was a red letter day to them when he visited their college. Constantine also worked for the promotion of sobriety and popular education in Russia, crossing swords with the powerful reactionary minister Pobedonostsev on this point. He also founded the Women's Pedagogical Institute in St. Petersburg.

In 1891 the Grand Duke left the Izmailovsky Regiment to become commander of the senior regiment of the guards, the Preobrazhensky, in which the future Nicholas II served as a battalion commander. Constantine's astounding memory enabled him to address all of the non-commissioned officers of both these regiments by name. Later, when he became inspector general of all the military schools in Russia, this memory stood him in good stead and made him extremely popular among the cadets. The survivors of those schools remember him fondly to the present day, and they have transferred their affection to his daughter, Princess Vera.

The Grand Duke, after the 'renunciation' of his elder brother, Nicholas, became the head of his branch of the Romanovs. Their principal residence was the Marble Palace in St. Petersburg. In the summer the family lived in one of their beautiful country palaces, Pavlovsk, or Strelna.

Pavlovsk had been given by Catherine the Great to her son, Tsesarevich Paul. When the palace was completed, Paul made a gift

---

1. *My 50 Years*, Prince Nicholas of Greece.

of it to his wife, Maria Feodorovna. The estate was raised to the status of an heirloom by Emperor Nicholas I, third son of Emperor Paul, in accordance with his mother's will.

According to a special stipulation the estate was to become the property of Maria's fourth son Michael. In case he should have no male heirs Pavlovsk was to pass over to Emperor Nicholas I's second son and to his descendants by right of primogeniture. As Michael died without male heirs, Grand Duke Constantine Nikolayevich inherited Pavlovsk, and eventually it passed to his son, Constantine.[2]

Pavlovsk was built in the years 1782-4 on plans designed by the Scottish architect Charles Cameron, who also laid out the park in the English style of the 18th century. For forty years Empress Maria continued to enlarge and beautify the palace, using the best Russian and foreign artists of three reigns—Catherine II, Paul I, and Alexander I. The original building was partly destroyed by fire in 1803, and was reconstructed in its present form. The main building is decorated with white columns on both sides, contrasting to a pale yellow background, and surmounted by a flat cupola. Many of the priceless objects contained in Pavlovsk were collected by Paul, when as heir to the throne, he and Maria went to Paris in 1782, using the name *Comte et Comtesse du Nord.*

When Pavlovsk was inherited by Grand Duke Constantine from his father, he devoted himself with the greatest care in restoring every object to the original place it occupied in the days of Empress Maria. He used a detailed inventory drawn up by the Empress herself, detailing to which rooms every object belonged. During World War II, Pavlovsk was dismantled by the Soviets before it could be totally destroyed by the advancing Germans. Even doors and wall coverings were removed, and placed in hiding. After the war, the Soviets reconstructed Pavlovsk, using the same inventory list! Pavlovsk is probably the best restoration work in the entire Soviet Union.

Grand Duke Constantine's favorite residence, however, was their property called Ostashovo. Here all etiquette was abolished, and the Grand Duke and his family led the life of any wealthy landowner. All the children of the grand ducal couple were imbued with the same simple ideas. He was also a very religious man in the true Orthodox spirit, and he inculcated the same strict religious precepts in his children. This was something of a paradox, in that his wife, Grand Duchess Elizabeth, was of a different faith, and never converted to Orthodoxy, but he was too delicate-minded ever to interfere with her religious beliefs.

At the time Kaiser Wilhelm II declared war on Russia, Grand

---

2. *Memories*, Prince Nicholas of Greece

Duke Constantine and his wife Elizabeth were in Wildungen, where Constantine was undergoing a cure. On hearing of the war, he wanted to start instantly for Russia, but the German authorities objected to this, saying he was a prisoner of war. Grand Duchess Elisabeth volunteered to send a telegram to the German Empress, with whom, before her marriage, she had been on intimate terms. The German officials curtly stated that private telegrams could not be despatched.

"This is not a 'private' telegram, but an 'Imperial message'," the Grand Duchess replied.[3]

The Germans used scant ceremony with the Russian Imperials, not even giving them their title, but addressing the Grand Duke as *Mein Herr*, and the Grand Duchess as *Gnädige Frau.* After much parley they were allowed to depart. Several miles before Eydkuhnen, the station on the Prussian frontier, the train stopped and the Grand Duke was told to get out and proceed to Wirballen, the first Russian station, on foot.

The party found themselves in the midst of fields; not a house or human to be seen, and no conveyance to be had. The Grand Duke and his wife were compelled to walk all the way to Wirballen. Considering the state of health of Constantine, he was quite ill when he arrived in St. Petersburg.

Five of Grand Duke Constantine's six sons were old enough for military service in World War I. In October of 1914, his fourth son, Prince Oleg, was mortally wounded in a cavalry charge against the Germans, for which action he was awarded the St. George's Cross. In spite of poor health, Constantine and his wife hastened to Vilna to be at the bedside of their dying son. They delighted the lad by presenting him with the St. George's Cross, won by his grandfather, Grand Duke Constantine Nikolayevich, in 1849.[4]

Prince Oleg died shortly thereafter, and Constantine brought the body of his son back to St. Petersburg, and then to his favourite country seat, Ostashovo, between Petersburg and Moscow, where the young hero was buried. Prince Oleg was the only royal to die in action on the Allied side in World War I.

The grief, excitement and fatigue were too much for Constantine, and he died a few months later at Pavlovsk, on 15 June 1915, but before death claimed him he had to witness the sorrow of his daughter, Princess Tatiana, wife of Prince Constantine Bagration-Mukhransky, who was killed on the Caucasian front in March, 1915. Hers had been a love match.

In 1910, Grand Duke Constantine's eldest daughter, the twenty-year-old Princess Tatiana, fell in love with a handsome Georgian officer of the Chevalier Guards, Prince Constantine

---

3. *Russian Court Memories*, H. Jenkins
4. *V Mramornom Dvortse*, Prince Gabriel Constantinovich

Bagration-Mukhransky, who was equally in love with her and asked Constantine for his daughter's hand. Constantine replied that this was against the law. The prince, though belonging to a branch of the Georgian Bagration dynasty, was a Russian subject and not considered to be of equal birth with Tatiana. The prince was sent off to Persia for a year, where he was awarded decorations by the Shah. Tatiana had something like a nervous breakdown because of her father's refusal. When Prince Bagration-Mukhransky returned he again made his proposal. This time it caused three meetings of the Family Council of the Imperial Family to be held, two under the chairmanship of Grand Duke Constantine, and one chaired by Emperor Nicholas II. The decision was made to change the law, allowing princes and princesses of the blood, but not grand dukes, to marry Russian subjects of suitable families. A manifesto to this effect was issued in 1911. Nicholas II's mother, Dowager Empress Marie, remarked that it was about time.

The Emperor required Princess Tatiana to renounce her and her children's rights in the line of succession.[5] They had been married only three and a half years when the Prince was killed, but the union had been an ideal one. Princess Tatiana, accompanied by one of her brothers, went to Tiflis to be present at her husband's funeral. While in Tiflis she was informed of her father's death.

In the space of six months, at the age of twenty-five, she had lost brother, husband and father, and she was heartbroken, and time did little to assuage her grief. Surrounded by her husband's portraits, she devoted herself to her two fatherless children, Prince Teymuraz and Princess Natalia, and occasionally going to Tiflis to visit the grave of her dead love.

Princess Tatiana lived for a time with her uncle, Grand Duke Dimitri at Strelna, but after his arrest she fled to the south with Dimitri's A.D.C., Colonel A. V. Korotchenzov, whom she later married. They moved to Kiev, then Odessa, and eventually escaped to Roumania at the invitation and intervention of Queen Marie of Roumania. Princess Tatiana eventually became a nun, and then abbess of a convent, and died in Jerusalem in 1979

Grand Duchess Elizabeth, along with her sister-in-law, Queen Olga of Greece, stayed on in the Marble Palace throughout the period of the provisional government, and for a year after the Bolshevik takeover. Queen Olga reported that in order to live, Elizabeth "stole her own possessions" and took them into the street to sell. Queen Olga eventually escaped Russia by train, with the help of the Danish Legation. In October of 1918, Grand Duchess Elizabeth, obtained permission to go to Sweden along with two of her children, Princess Vera and Prince George, and two of her grandchildren, Prince

---

5. *Prince Teymuraz Bagration,* Testimony

Vsevelod and Princess Catherine, the children of Prince John. They sailed aboard the Swedish ship *Angermanland* in November 1918. Grand Duchess Elizabeth died in Leipzig in 1927.

Three of Grand Duke Constantine's children were murdered by the Bolsheviks—John, Constantine and Igor, as well as his brother, Dimitri. Prince Gabriel escaped to Finland with the help of the writer Maxim Gorky. Of the nine children of Grand Duke Constantine, only four survived the war and the Bolsheviks.

Grand Duke Constantine Constantinovich was the last Romanov to be officially buried in the St. Peter and Paul Fortress.

GRAND DUKE DIMITRI CONSTANTINOVICH

CHAPTER XVI

GRAND DUKE DIMITRI CONSTANTINOVICH (1860 - 1919)

Grand Duke Dimitri was the third son of Grand Duke Constantine Nikolayevich, born at Strelna on 13 June 1860. Dimitri was tall—well over six feet, and very thin. He had light hair and blue eyes, and wore a small mustache, slightly turned up at the ends, and kept his hair very short. All in all, he was not unattractive.

Dimitri, like all of Constantine's children, was given a broad education with a solid grounding in the classics, and like the rest of his family, he took part in amateur theatricals, showing considerable acting talent. Like his older brother Constantine, Dimitri was supposed to follow his father into the navy, but he preferred dry land, especially since his passion was horses, which would hardly have been welcome on a battleship! Dimitri served in the Mounted Grenadier Regiment of the Imperial Guards, which he eventually commanded. However, he never made much of a military career, partly because of his increasing nearsightedness, which grew progressively worse. By 1914 he was close to being blind, but he supervised the training of cavalry during World War I, cursing his fate for not being able to play a more active role.

Dimitri took his interest in horses very seriously, and went about it with great energy. He owned a horse breeding station near Poltava, where he raised thoroughbred racers and saddle horses. His stallions were much in demand by officers in the calvary regiments because of their beauty and strength. He also ran a riding academy and a veterinary school, and in 1913 was chairman of the All-Russian Horse Exposition in Kiev.

In her memoirs, my grandmother, Grand Duchess Marie, tells of a pair of special ponies given to her by her Uncle Dimitri. She described them as, ". . . .a pair of lovely fat ponies. . . I believe [they] came from an island in the Baltic provinces called Osel. . . When they were driven they squealed just like pigs! They were rather wild, fat, black ponies, and I was not allowed to drive them that first year, but my sister often drove them down to the sea at Phaleron." They reminded her, she said, of some of the horses sculpted on bas-reliefs on the Parthenon.

Grand Duke Dimitri never married; in fact, he was a confirmed woman-hater. "Beware of skirts," was one of his watchwords. Having no children of his own, he became sort of a second father to the sons and daughters of his brother Constantine, taking them riding, teaching them songs, and giving them presents. He lived very modestly at his ranch and in a small house in the Crimea, staying with his brother's family when in St. Petersburg. He was perhaps one of the most unassuming and unpretentious of the grand dukes, and lived a quiet, almost withdrawn existence devoid of scandal and controversy.

The coming of World War I was no surprise to Dimitri. He had been predicting war with Germany since 1899[1]. After the abdication of Emperor Nicholas II, Grand Duke Dimitri no longer wore military uniform, but could not bear ordinary civilian clothes, and he designed himself a quasi-uniform resembling a chauffeur's.[2] In 1918, after the Bolsheviks seized power, he was exiled to Vologda with his cousins Nicholas and George Mikhailovich. After several months the three Grand Dukes were taken to St. Petersburg and put in prison, where they were joined by Grand Duke Paul Alexandrovich. For a time Dimitri shared a cell with his cousin, George Mikhailovich.

Dimitri's grandnephew, Prince Teymuraz Bagration, then a seven-year-old boy, remembers visiting them twice in their cell, accompanying the wife of Dimitri's aide, Alexander Leiming, who was bringing them baskets of food. "Dimitri was sitting on a stool in the middle of the large cell, while George Mikhailovich stood by the window. Everything happened in total silence. A soldier opened the cell door by lifting the bar with his rifle butt. No words were exchanged," according to Prince Teymuraz.

On 30 January 1919, Grand Dukes Paul Alexandrovich, Nicholas and George Mikhailovich, and Grand Duke Dimitri were taken to the Fortress of St. Peter and Paul where they were shot by firing squad..

A very religious man, Grand Duke Dimitri is supposed to have said just before his death, "Forgive them, for they know not what they do."

---

1. *Once A Grand Duke*, Grand Duke Alexander

2. *V Mramornom Dvortse*, Prince Gabriel Constantinovich

GRAND DUKES - PETERHOF c. 1901

NICHOLAS II, CONSTANTINE, DUCHESS EUGENIA of OLDENBURG, SERGE ALEXANDROVICH, MICHAEL NIKOLAYEVICH, GEORGE MIKHAILOVICH, and SERGE MIKHAILOVICH

PAVLOVSK PALACE

CHAPTER XVII

GRAND DUKE VYACHESLAV CONSTANTINOVICH (1862 -1879)

Grand Duke Vyacheslav was born at Warsaw 13 July 1862, the fourth son of Grand Duke Constantine Nikolayevich. He was born while his father was Viceroy of Poland, and christened with the first of the unusual Slavic names which later appeared here and there among the Romanovs.

His education was entrusted to a Cossack officer, who Countess Kleinmichel says was a very bad influence. While at Lepzig in 1868, this tutor got so drunk in a tavern that students carried him like a corpse into a booth at the Fair, where he was shown for money! A placard bore the inscription, *Der Kosak und das Renntier*, because he was wearing his beautiful national uniform. He was discovered there by Baron Gustav von Gersdorff, a Chamberlain of the King of Saxony.

Vyacheslav was responsible for an incident involving Baron Gersdorff. The Grand Duchess Alexandra came to spend a few days at the Court of King John, and while the party was waiting luncheon, when Vyacheslav asked the Baron something, and he replied, "Anything you order will always suit me—you are master and I am valet. Soon afterwards, as they were sitting down to table, Vyacheslav pointed suddenly at Baron von Gersdorff and shouted, "Mummy, Mummy, look, the valet is sitting at our table."

Everyone stared in astonishment at the little Grand Duke, and his mother, very red in the face, told him to stop talking nonsense.

"It is really true," Vyacheslav insisted, "he told me so himself he was a valet."

Poor Herr von Gersdorff could only give very embarrassed explanations.

Vyacheslav is remembered as being very tall, very amiable, and extremely musical. He joked about his height, predicting that when he died his coffin would get stuck in the door leading to a small stairway in the Marble Palace where he lived with his family. This is exactly what happened.

The very short life of Grand Duke Vyacheslav ended when he was just sixteen years old from a brain tumor. He died at St. Petersburg 27 February 1879.

GRAND DUKE NICHOLAS

GRAND DUKE NICHOLAS NIKOLAYEVICH, JUNIOR.

CHAPTER XVIII

GRAND DUKE NICHOLAS NIKOLAYEVICH, JUNIOR
(1856 - 1929)

It is not often that a son follows so closely in his father's footsteps, particularly a son with the identical name of his father, but this is what happened with Grand Duke Nicholas Nikolayevich, Junior—with certain significant differences.

The eldest of the two sons of Nicholas Nikolayevich, Senior, Nicholas (known in the family as "Nikolasha") was born at St. Petersburg 18 November 1856. He grew up to be the tallest of the Grand Dukes, 6' - 6", very thin with a short pointed beard over a slightly protruding jaw, and a ramrod military bearing. Soldiering was his passion. He disliked social life, loved hunting and shooting, but, curiously, collected old china and was a gourmet, supervising his own chef and cooks in the preparations of fine food. As in the case of his father, war came when Nicholas was a young officer. He served on his father's staff at the beginning of the Turkish war of 1877, collecting a St. George's Cross, Fourth Class, for his participation in the difficult crossing of the Danube in June of that year.

After the war he followed a serious military career, becoming, at the rank of captain, the only Grand Duke on the General Staff. Later, as a general, he commanded a Guards Hussar regiment, and, eventually, the entire Imperial Guard. Unlike his father, Nicholas was not popular in the army. He was too much of an unbending disciplinarian with a one track mind, but he was generally given credit for being an excellent soldier with good intentions, and an honorable man.

For years it seemed Nicholas would remain a bachelor. He formed a liaison with S. I. Burenina, the former wife of a merchant and the daughter of a shopkeeper, which lasted for many years. She already had two children. In 1887 he made an attempt to marry her. In an unusual move, the strict Alexander III was on the point of granting permission after Nicholas told him that his own father had approved the match. "I would do the same thing," said his father, according to Nicholas, "if your mother were not still alive."[1] But when questioned by the Emperor, Nicholas Nikolayevich, Senior, denied having given permission and the marriage fell through. This did not prevent Nicholas Junior from continuing to live openly with Burenina. A reason for Alexander III's near permission, apparently, was that Nicholas, at least, was not promiscuous, but living in a monogamous relationship.

This relationship finally ended, however, and for a long time Nicholas formed a second one, this time with an actress of the St. Petersburg Alexandrine Theatre, Maria Alexandrovna Pototskaya.[2] It was not until Nicholas was already fifty-one, and a very senior general, that he finally married, at Yalta on 12 May 1907.

This time his choice fell not on a shopkeeper's daughter or an actress but on a royal princess, Anastasia Nikolayevna, third daughter of King Nicholas I of Montenegro, a woman twelve years his junior, who for seventeen years had been married to Nicholas cousin, George Maximilianovich, Prince Romanovsky, 6th Duke of Leuchtenburg. She divorced him to marry Nicholas. Furthermore, she was already Nicholas sister-in-law. Her sister, Militsa Nikolayevna, had married Nicholas' younger brother, Grand Duke Peter Nikolayevich in 1889. In spite of these circumstances, Nicholas II granted permission. The bride was Orthodox and one of the daughters of Russia's staunch ally, the King of Montenegro. Another of his daughters was married to King Victor Emmanuel III of Italy. Grand Duke Nicholas' new wife, Anastasia, and her sister Militsa, became known as the "black ladies" because of their dark complexion and because Montenegro means "black mountain." They were of a mystical frame of mind, and some of this rubbed off on Nicholas, or perhaps it was one of the things that attracted him to Anastasia in the first place. Anastasia and her sister Militsa are generally blamed for introducing Rasputin to the Empress in 1905. In his diary Nicholas II wrote, "We have got to know a man of God, Gregory, from Tobolsk Province."

Anastasia died an emigrée in France in 1935, outliving her husband by six years. They had no children.

During the reign of Nicholas II, Nicholas Nikolayevich Junior played not only an important military role, but a political one as well. Nicholas towered over his short sovereign, who was his first cousin once removed, or "secondary nephew" in Russian. In his stiff military way, Grand Duke Nicholas always addressed the Emperor as, "Your Majesty," even *en famille*. What he said when the two of them were alone together nobody knows.

During the revolution of 1905, Grand Duke Nicholas was commander of the St. Petersburg Military District, as well as the

---

1. *Polovtsev Diary*, 1883-1892
2. *Polovtsev Diary*

Imperial Guard, a key position for restoring order, but he utterly refused to accept a military dictatorship for himself, which some people were pushing for. On the contrary, he sided with Prime Minister Witte in getting the Emperor to sign the semi-constitution of 1905, creating a popularly elected parliament, or Duma.

According to Witte, Grand Duke Nicholas threatened to shoot himself if the Emperor did not sign the manifesto. Grand Duke Nicholas had also helped Witte break up the agreement Nicholas II had signed with Emperor William II of Germany at the famous meeting of the two imperial yachts at Björkö. Count Witte considered Grand Duke Nicholas honest and loyal, but overly sure of himself, not particularly logical, and somewhat unbalanced.[3] The Grand Duke played a leading role in the reorganization of the war ministry after the disastrous Russo-Japanese War, but Witte thought he introduced unnecessary confusion in these activities.

With Russia now a semi-constitutional monarchy, there was pressure from the Duma to keep the numerous Grand Dukes out of key command positions, and in 1908 Grand Duke Nicholas, who was by far the most senior general among them, retired from the army. But not for long.

In 1914 war with Germany and Austria-Hungary loomed, after the latter marched on Serbia, whose independence Nicholas' father had helped secure in 1878. Nicholas had always hated the Germans and was delighted with the prospect of war, even ordering the uniforms of the Prussian regiment, of which he was honorary colonel, burned.[4] He encouraged Nicholas II to order general mobilization, after which Germany declared war on Russia.

Just as in his father's case, the outbreak of war found Nicholas in position for high command, and in spite of the fact that he despised Sukhomlinov, the Minister of War, and the Emperor was not enthusiastic for the appointment, Nicholas found himself Supreme Commander of the Russian armies.

The war started badly, with two Russian armies invading East Prussia to take the pressure off their French allies, and being badly beaten at the Battle of the Masurian Lakes. Nicholas was criticized in professional army circles for mounting the attack prematurely, and for favoring General Rennenkampf over Samsonov for command of it. In 1915, however, there was a huge Russian success over the Austrians, resulting in the fall of the great fortress of Przemysl. But the Germans staged a furious counterattack in support of their allies, and the Russians retreated from Galicia with huge losses. This war was way out of scale and very different from the triumphant six month's campaign that Nicholas Nikolayevich Senior had led through the Balkans in 1877.

3. *Vospominaniya*, S. Witte
4. *V Mramornom Dvortse*, Prince Gabriel Constantinovich

Realizing this early, Grand Duke Nicholas, in December 1914, asked the British military observer, Sir George Hanbury-Williams, whether the British could help open the straits in Turkey to help the Russian supply situation. Hanbury-Williams reported this to London, and it later resulted in the disastrous Gallipoli campaign. Hanbury-Williams did not blame Grand Duke Nicholas for Russia's shortage of munitions. He had the highest opinion of the Grand Duke, who was calm, dignified, and at first very reserved, although when the Russians took Lvov (Lemberg) from the Austrians, the Grand Duke hugged the British general, apologizing for his Russian enthusiasm. Hanbury-Williams thought him humorous, very loyal to the allies and to his Emperor.[5]

The last point was a sore one, because reputedly Rasputin was intriguing against the Grand Duke with the Empress, accusing him of having designs on the throne. Grand Duke Nicholas had never made a secret of his loathing of Rasputin, although his wife had been instrumental in introducing this unsavory, hypnotic, and disastrous character to Empress Alexandra.

Emperor Nicholas II had no doubts about the Grand Duke's loyalty. Nevertheless, in August of 1915 he decided to take over supreme command of the armies himself. This was a move that distressed many people. It was not that the Emperor lacked experience—real command would be exercised by the very able chief of staff, General Alexeyev. It was that the Emperor would now be personally blamed for all setbacks and that the Empress, left alone in Tsarskoye-Selo under the influence of Rasputin, would have too much power. This is, of course, exactly what happened.

Grand Duke Nicholas was relieved from command early in September, and transferred to the Caucasus as Viceroy and commander of the Russian forces operating against the Turks there. The Grand Duke claimed to be delighted, as were the Germans who had the highest respect for him as a strategist, particularly Ludendorf.[6]

So Grand Duke Nicholas found himself following the footsteps of his favorite uncle, Grand Duke Michael Nikolayevich, as Viceroy and as commander of troops fighting on much the same terrain as Michael had in 1877. Throughout 1916 Nicholas scored outstanding successes against the Turks. As supreme commander and again as Viceroy, Grand Duke Nicholas achieved great popularity in the army and the country at large, which he had so lacked in peacetime. Hanbury-Williams, observing the Emperor's delighted reaction to the Grand Duke's victories over the Turks, could not see the slightest trace of envy or ill-will.

Grand Duke Nicholas was still in the Caucasus when the

---

5. *The Emperor Nicholas II as I Knew Him*, Sir John Hanbury-Williams
6. *Nicholas and Alexandra*, Robert Massie

February revolution broke out, and the Emperor was at general headquarters. Events moved very quickly. Talk of abdication was in the air, and Nicholas was being pushed in some circles as the best regent for the young Tsesarevich Alexis.

When abdication seemed the only way to save the monarchy, Grand Duke Nicholas joined his generals in the Caucasus in advising his cousin to abdicate. It is highly doubtful that the Grand Duke had any designs on the regency, let alone the throne. Everybody expected the Emperor to abdicate in favor of his son, but he left the throne to his brother Grand Duke Michael.

After the abdication, the general staff received numerous cables urging the reappointment of Grand Duke Nicholas as supreme commander. Even some workers demonstrated in his favor. He arrived at general headquarters on 24 March 1917, greeted by enthusiastically cheering officers and troops. However, Prince Lvov, the first head of the Provisional government, had already written a letter asking for the Grand Duke's resignation. No more Romanovs were wanted. With his usual dignity the Grand Duke complied, asking only that General Alexeyev be appointed, at least temporarily, commander-in-chief.

Grand Duke Nicholas went to the Crimea, his career over. After the Bolshevik coup of October 1917, various White movements started up to oppose Lenin's government, but despite his seniority in the army and his popularity, there was no way Nicholas would be involved in the civil war. While many individual Whites were monarchists, the official position of the White armies was not for restoration of the monarchy, but for a return to the freely elected Constituent Assembly, which Lenin had dissolved at the point of the bayonet after he received only 25% of the vote.

Grand Duke Nicholas was evacuated from the Crimea along with several other Romanovs in April of 1919 aboard the British warship *HMS Nelson.* He spent most of his time thereafter in France, in Choigny, about forty miles from Paris, guarded against possible assassination by the French police and emigré Russian officers. He was certainly the most respected and senior in acquired rank of the eight surviving Grand Dukes.

Grand Duke Nicholas stayed out of emigré politics until 1924 when Grand Duke Cyril Vladimirovich, another "secondary nephew," declared himself Emperor of Russia. Nicholas would have nothing to do with Cyril's claim, and put out his own, very statesman-like program, for the future of Russia, calling for the rule of law and order, without stipulating the form of government, which could not in any case be decided in the emigration.

Grand Duke Nicholas Nikolayevich, Junior, died at Cap d'Antibes 5 January 1929.

GRAND DUKE PETER NIKOLAYEVICH

CHAPTER XIX

GRAND DUKE PETER NIKOLAYEVICH (1864 - 1931)

Grand Duke Peter was the second son of Grand Duke Nicholas Nikolayevich, Sr., who was the third son of Emperor Nicholas I. He was born at St. Petersburg on 22 January 1864, the first and only grand duke since the 18th Century to be given the name of the dynasty's most spectacular ruler, Peter the Great.

Peter was tall, with a high forehead, and a small moustache, and was quite good-looking in a "Douglas Fairbanks" way. He was eight years younger than his brother, the famous Nicholas Nikolayevich Jr., whose military career was so spectacular. Peter moved somewhat in his brother's shadow as an unassuming Guards lancer officer, but he left the service early because of bad health. He suffered from weak lungs, like a number of his relatives, and spent several years in Egypt for his health, where he developed an interest in architecture.

From 1904 to 1909 Peter was chief of the military engineers department and inspector of engineers. Count Witte, the Prime Minister, remembered Peter as being very amiable, but somewhat unbusiness-like. Peter's business manager lost considerable sums in the stock market, and Peter was helped out from the crown lands by Emperor Nicholas II. Others remember Peter as a very nice man with excellent manners, in no way ramrod stiff like his brother. He was also a shy man, who did not talk much, letting his wife lead the conversation.

In 1889 Grand Duke Peter married Princess Militsa, the second daughter of King Nicholas of Montenegro. The marriage was arranged by Emperor Alexander III, but it did not come off smoothly. Princess Militsa refused to go to Russia without her sister, Anastasia. King Nicholas threatened to send her to St. Petersburg clothed in chains, but the Emperor, horrified at the prospect of the bride arriving in chains[1], looked around his relations and found another

1. *Behind the Veil of the Russian Court*, P. Vasili

cousin who was unmarried—the Duke of Leuchtenberg. While the Duke did not like women, he was willing to do anything for the dowry which the Tsar promised to settle on Anastasia, and so the affair was settled.

Militsa and her sister, Anastasia, were known jointly as "the black peril," and both sisters were keen practitioners of the mysticism fashionable in St. Petersburg. They had attended the *Pension de Jeunes Filles* for the daughters of the nobility. Both Militsa and Anastasia were well read and clever, and very ambitious. For many years they were great friends with Empress Alexandra, and very powerful ladies, but not very popular with the family. It was they who first introduced the Frenchman, Dr. Philippe, and then Rasputin, to Empress Alexandra.

When Rasputin replaced the two sisters in Empress Alexandra's confidence, they became his implacable enemies. They went to the Empress with information of how Rasputin had made overtures to themselves. The Empress received them coolly, but their efforts were to no avail. Grand Duke Peter declared that they would not see Rasputin again.

It is doubtful that the kind and intelligent Grand Duke was interested in any of this. Peter built an estate in the Crimea called Dulber. It was totally unlike the other grand ducal villas along the Crimean coast in that it was built something like a fortress. When his cousins joked about this, Peter replied, "You never know what might happen in the distant future."

Grand Duke Peter and Militsa had three children, Prince Roman (1896), Princess Marina (1892), and Princess Nadejda (1898).

Throughout World War I Grand Duke Peter kept a low profile, much in the shadow of his brother Nicholas, the Commander-in-Chief. He lived with Nicholas in the same railroad car at headquarters, making himself useful to him as a trusted set of eyes and ears. When Nicholas was relieved of command and sent to the Caucasus as Viceroy and commander of the front against the Turks, Peter went with him, with the rank of lieutenant-general.

After the fall of the monarchy Grand Dukes Peter and Nicholas, their wives, and Peter's children, went to Dulber. When the Bolsheviks took power, their commissar, belonging to the Sebastopol Soviet, cast a loving eye at the fortress-like Dulber, which the commissar felt could be defended against an attack from his rivals, the Yalta Soviet, so he moved his prisoners there. These included the Dowager Empress Marie and her daughters, Xenia and Olga, the latter's new husband, Colonel Nicholas Kulikovsky, and Xenia's husband, Grand Duke Alexander Mikhailovich with their seven children and son-in-law, Felix Yusupov, and granddaughter, who had all been held at Ay Todor, Alexander's estate. Now they were all gathered at Dulber.

At this time Lenin made peace with the Germans, and this large group of Romanovs were rescued by a detachment of German troops hurrying down from the Ukraine, which was a relief, but also something of a slap in the face. They felt that to be rescued by the German enemy from their own people was a bitter insult. The Germans were amazed when the Romanovs pleaded for the lives of their late jailors, and the Dowager Empress refused to receive the German commander.

In April 1919 many of this group were evacuated in two British warships, the *HMS Marlborough* and *HMS Nelson*. Grand Duchess Olga and her husband had decided to try and reach safety in the White-held north Caucasus.

Grand Duke Peter lived quietly at Cap d'Antibes, France, and he died there 17 June 1931. His widow, Grand Duchess Militsa Nikolayevna, moved to Rome to be with her younger sister Elena, the Queen of Italy [wife of Victor Emmanuel III]. She survived her husband by twenty years, and even the fall of the monarchy in Italy. She died in Alexandria, Egypt, in 1951 at the age of eighty-five.

GRAND DUKE NICHOLAS MIKHAILOVICH
(Uncle Bimbo)

CHAPTER XX

GRAND DUKE NICHOLAS MIKHAILOVICH (1859 - 1919)

Grand Duke Nicholas was the eldest of the six sons of Grand Duke Michael Nikolayevich (the youngest son of Nicholas I), and his wife Olga Feodorovna, née Princess of Baden. He was born at Tsarskoye Selo 26 April 1859, but when he was three his father moved to Tiflis as Viceroy of the Caucasus, and he spent his childhood there. Like all of his brothers, he fell in love with the Caucasus and was somewhat estranged from the cold northern center of the empire. Like his brothers, and most of the grand dukes, he was brought up in the spartan tradition of his grandfather, Nicholas I, sleeping on hard army cots, taking cold baths, and constant lessons by tutors.

Nicholas was also expected to enter the military. To please his mother, he graduated with high honors from the War College, and to please the Empress Marie Feodorovna, to whom he was very close, he served in the Chevalier Guards Regiment, of which she was honorary colonel. But the great passion of his life was historical research and, as soon as he decently could, he retired from the army to devote himself full time to this most un-grand ducal profession. As a hobby, he collected insects. He retained, however, strong opinions on military matters (as in practically everything else) which led to a life-long feud with his namesake and cousin Grand Duke Nicholas Nikolayevich Jr., the future commander-in-chief in 1914-1915, with whom he disagreed on all things military.

As a young man, Grand Duke Nicholas fell in love with his first cousin, Princess Victoria of Baden, but their marriage was not permitted because of the close relationship; she later became Queen of Sweden, as wife of Gustav V. Nicholas remained a bachelor all his life, but he liked children and is said to have fathered several illegitimate ones.[1]

In any contest for sheer intellectual brilliance and depth of

1. Testimony, Princess Nina of Russia

culture within the Romanov dynasty, Grand Duke Nicholas Mikhailovich would be a leading contender for first place, his nearest competition coming from Grand Dukes Constantine Nikolayevich and Constantine Constantinovich. He had a profound knowledge of French culture and Roman civilization, and was elected a member of the French Academy, a rare honor for any foreigner, let alone a foreign prince. He was much in demand as a lecturer on history in Paris, where he lived a great deal of his time, staying at the old Hotel Vendôme, unlike the high style of his cousin Alexis Alexandrovich, and some of the other grand dukes. Nicholas admired the Third Republic and followed its politics with great interest, though he sometimes had to admit in arguments with his brother Alexander that perhaps Russia had not developed to the point of such a regime.

Nicholas did not neglect his native country in his historical studies. He published several seminally important historical works, and, with his access to the imperial and family archives, became an expert on the reign and times of Emperor Alexander I. When his book on Alexander I came out, it was translated and published in France, where it caused much revisionism among scholars of the Napoleonic period. Although Nicholas could not say so officially in print, it is stated by some that he believed that Alexander I did not die in 1825, but lived on as the hermit Fedor Kuzmich into the 1860s. At least Nicholas believed in the psychological plausibility of such a disappearing act on that strange Emperor's part. Nicholas told his brother Alexander that he could find no trace in their grandfather Nicholas I's diary about his alleged visit to Fedor Kuzmich. This in itself, of course, proves nothing.

Grand Duke Nicholas was known as "Bimbo" in the family, a word which has none of the connotations in Russian that it has in English. Like a lot of learned people, he was moody and eccentric. He was once placed under arrest by his cousin, Emperor Alexander III, for riding past the Anichkov Palace in a horse cab driven by an ordinary *izvoshchik* pulled by a scrawny nag, his coat unbuttoned and a cigar clenched in his teeth.[2] Grand Dukes were not supposed to do that, and Alexander III was very strict with his relatives! Bimbo liked to travel that way. Beneath all that culture, said his brother George's wife, there was a mischievous child who enjoyed doing unconventional things. When the emperor and all the grand dukes went to visit the field of the Battle of Borodino on its centenary in 1912, Bimbo refused to sign the French monument (he probably disapproved of Napoleon), and insisted on walking back and chatting with his friends, instead of riding in grand ducal style. In France, he would take a break from his intellectual pursuits by gambling heavily in Monte Carlo or Cannes, distributing princely presents to his

2. *V Mramornom Dvortse*, Prince Gabriel Constantinovich

relatives when he won. His fondness for Cannes resulted in his being the only son to be present at Grand Duke Michael Nikolayevich's death there in 1909.

Grand Duke Nicholas was very tall, bald, had dark eyes and a short, dark, square beard. He grew fat in middle age. Like his uncle Constantine, he was very liberal politically, and even called himself a socialist. In the Chevalier Guards he had been known as "Philippe Egalité" because, among other things, he liked to address the enlisted men as "my friends."[3] He was very outspoken about his ideas. In 1896, after thousands of people had been killed in the crush after the last coronation, he begged Nicholas II to call off the coronation ball, warning him that holding it would remind people of some of the antics of Marie Antoinette. When it proceeded anyway, Bimbo and his brothers arrived in order to depart demonstratively. His liberalism did not prevent his writing to Tolstoy to protest a pamphlet the latter was distributing containing what Bimbo thought was unfair and unhistorical criticism of his grandfather Nicholas I. The great writer thanked the grand duke for the historical data he had provided, said he admired the patriotism of Nicholas I, and went on distributing his pamphlet.[4]

Nicholas Mikhailovich was a pacifist and was horrified by World War I at a time when super-patriotism was the order of the day. He criticized his old enemy Nicholas Nikolayevich's strategy and tactics, particularly the sacrificing of the Imperial Guard and a large part of the regular army in the ill-fated 1914 advance on East Prussia to take the pressure off Paris. Bimbo foresaw that the war could not be won with half trained reservists and draftees. More and more horrified by what was happening in the government, the Grand Duke in 1916 sent Nicholas II a letter begging him to deprive the Empress of power in the government and a sixteen page tract on the misdoings of the prime minister, Stuermer. Always a club man in St. Petersburg, by the end of 1916 Bimbo was sounding off so loudly against the government at his clubs that the very patient Nicholas II ordered him to leave the capital. He returned after the fall of the monarchy a few months later.

Nicholas was still there in 1918. The Bolsheviks, now in power, exiled him to Vologda with his brother George and a cousin, Dimitri Constantinovich, then brought them back to Petrograd and imprisoned them. Bimbo talked and joked with the guards. He also joked with his executioners, holding a kitten in his arms. On 30 January 1919 these three Grand Dukes and Paul Alexandrovich, were taken to the Fortress of St. Peter and Paul and shot. Maxim Gorky, the well-known writer who was on good terms with Lenin, tried to prevent this execution of four men innocent of political

---

3. *Once A Grand Duke*, Grand Duke Alexander
4. *Once A Grand Duke*, Grand Duke Alexander

activity, particularly Nicholas Mikhailovich, who was such an eminent historian and the president of the Russian Historical Society. One version has it that Lenin agreed with Gorky, but the executions were carried out by the Petrograd authorities anyhow; another has it that Lenin said, "The Revolution does not need historians."

If Nicholas Mikhailovich had not been a grand duke, he might have been very valuable to Russia as a diplomat or administrator. His brother, Alexander, thought that Bimbo's life was essentially wasted because he was a grand duke. It also hastened his death.

In 1981 the Russian Orthodox Church in exile, with headquarters in New York, canonized all the members of the Imperial Family and all others whose names it could gather, who had been murdered by the Bolsheviks, as the "new martyrs." There was one exception. Conspicuously missing from the service and the special icon painted, was Grand Duke Nicholas Mikhailovich. Why? Well, the clergy said he was a socialist, atheist, and a Mason. This violated the church's own rules which said that the martyrs were to be forgiven their earthly sins. Nicholas called himself a socialist. He may have been a Mason and perhaps an atheist, although Masons are not generally atheists. Where the church got its information on the latter two points is not known. In any case, sixty-one years after his death, Grand Duke Nicholas Mikhailovich was once again not given what he deserved.

GRAND DUKE MICHAEL MIKHAILOVICH

GRAND DUKE MICHAEL MIKHAILOVICH

CHAPTER XXI

GRAND DUKE MICHAEL MIKHAILOVICH (1861-1929)

Grand Duke Michael was the second son of Grand Duke Michael Nikolayevich and Grand Duchess Olga. Born at Peterhof 16 October 1861, Michael grew up at Tiflis, where his father was Viceroy.

The young Michael was subject to the usual army cots and cold baths upbringing so popular in the Imperial Family for grand dukes. His parents, particularly his mother, were partial to this regime. Michael and his older brother were also required to learn Latin and Greek. These classical languages may have helped make Nicholas an intellectual, but they had no such effect on Michael. His mother referred to him as stupid, and on at least two recorded occasions, Emperor Alexander III referred to him as a fool.[1]

Grand Duke Michael entered the military service, serving in the Chasseur Regiment of the Guards. He adored the military, but was also attracted to the bright lights of St. Petersburg in preference to the rural charms of the Caucasus. By the time he was twenty, he was already building his own palace in the capital. He was known fondly as "Miche-Miche" by his friends, and he enjoyed the clubs, dancing and parties. He was a great favorite with society—tall, handsome, wealthy, and very generous in nature. Miche-Miche seemed to be well on his way to becoming one of those relatively rare "typical" grand dukes, except for one curious detail. Grand Duke Michael wanted very badly to get married!

In 1886 he wanted to marry Irene, daughter of Grand Duke Ludwig IV of Hesse, but this did not work out. In 1887 he proposed to Princess Louise, the eldest daughter of the Prince of Wales (the future Edward VII), but was rejected because he told the princess that, as was natural for people of their position, he had no feelings of love for her.[2] Michael made several attempts to marry commoners, leading to battles with his parents. The most notable of these

1. *Dnevnik Gos. Sekretarya*, A. A. Polovtsev
2. *Dnevnik Gos. Sekretarya*, A. A. Polovtsev

involved Countess Catherine Ignatiev in 1888. Alexander III refused permission and sent Michael abroad to get over it. Michael did not get over it. Instead, he kept sending telegrams to his parents, and finally returned to beg the emperor personally to allow the marriage. Alexander III, feeling some pity for the young man, promised to look into the matter, but later he returned to his original position and even suggested that it would be a good idea to ship Michael off to serve in some remote part of the Empire. Michael eventually gave up on Countess Ignatiev.

Finally, in 1891, Grand Duke Michael took the marriage problem into his own hands. He had fallen in love with Sophia, the morganatic daughter of Prince Nicholas of Nassau, who had the name of Countess Merenberg. Her maternal grandfather was the most famous of Russian poets, Alexander Pushkin. Without permission from the Emperor or his parents, he married the Countess at San Remo 26 February 1891. The telegram informing his parents of this was delivered to his mother, Grand Duchess Olga, at the railroad station at Kharkov. She reportedly had a heart attack, and died.

Alexander III promptly barred Grand Duke Michael from returning to Russia, and stripped him of all military rank. He was allowed to return twenty-one years later at the time of the centenary of the Battle of Borodino, and was restored to the honorary colonelcy of the 49th Brest Regiment.

Michael was not much cramped by his exile. His wife was given the morganatic title of Countess Torby by her relative, the Grand Duke of Luxembourg. For many years the couple lived very well in Cannes in a villa named for the Caucasian mountain, Kazbek. There Michael became an elder of the Russian Orthodox Church, where he passed the plate on Sundays. Eventually, London became the primary residence of Michael and Countess Torby.

Three children were born of this marriage—Anastasia (Zia) in 1892, who married Sir Harold Wernher; Nadejda (Nada), in 1896, who became the Marchioness of Milford Haven when she married George Mountbatten, the second Marquess of Milford Haven; and Michael, born in 1898, known as "Boy Torby," who never married. Through his daughters, Grand Duke Michael has numerous descendants.

At the start of World War I, Michael was made chairman of the commission to consolidate Russian orders abroad. In 1916, he wrote to Emperor Nicholas II that British Intelligence predicted a revolution soon in Russia. Michael had just been to Buckingham Palace and found "Georgie," King George V, to be very upset. He ended his letter by exhorting the Emperor to grant the just demands of the people before it was too late.

The once beautiful Countess Torby became fat, and "Miche-Miche" developed a cantankerous, odd temperament, spending much of his time raving against his Russian relatives. Countess Torby died in 1927; Grand Duke Michael Mikhailovich died at London 26 April 1929.

GRAND DUKE GEORGE MIKHAILOVICH and
GRAND DUCHESS MARIE
(Author's grandparents)

Е. И. В. Вел. Кн. Георгій Михаиловичъ

GRAND DUKE GEORGE MIKHAILOVICH

GRAND DUKE GEORGE c. 1915
(On the back is written "The gate through which I go to Nikolasha's train.")

CHAPTER XXII

GRAND DUKE GEORGE MIKHAILOVICH (1863 - 1919)

Grand Duke George was the third son of Grand Duke Michael Nikolayevich, and was born at Belyy Klyuch near Tiflis 23 August 1863. He was eighteen years old before his family left the Caucasus, and he retained his love for the Caucasus for the rest of his life.

Like his brothers, he had a Georgian nickname—Gogi. After going through the routine upbringing common to his family, he entered the Imperial Guards, his regiment being Her Majesty's Lancers.

Grand Duke George, my grandfather, was a tall man, over six foot four inches, with brown eyes, no beard, and a large moustache. As he aged, he grew bald.

An early leg injury prevented George from making much of a military career, but this was probably not much of a disappointment, since he did not have a military temperament, and had a scholarly bent. His mother, Grand Duchess Olga Feodorovna, was always frank in her assessment of her six sons. She considered George intelligent, unlike his older brother Michael, but he was not one of her favorites. This role fell to the eldest, Nicholas, the historian, and to her fourth son, Alexander. George was a good friend of the future Nicholas II, who was five years younger than he was, and participated in some youthful escapades with him.

Unable to be active militarily, George, for many years, held the post of curator of the Alexander III Museum in St. Petersburg, an institution which is still one of Russia's finest museums, now called the Russian Museum. His passion was neumismatics, and his coin collection included practically every coin ever used in what was then the Russian Empire, going back to ancient times. He wrote a number of monographs on coins, which can still be found in libraries, and one of them was recently reissued in facsimile in the United States. After the revolution his coin collection was somehow brought out of Russia, badly pilfered along the way, and was finally returned to his widow. It is now in the Smithsonian Institution in Washington.

As a young man, Grand Duke George fell in love with a Georgian girl, Princess Nina Chavchavadze. This marriage would not have been permitted under the Romanov Family laws, although he could have married her morganatically and been exiled abroad. However, it never came to this, because the girl's mother, a direct descendent of the Kings of Georgia, would not hear of an arrangement in which her daughter would have to take a back seat to minor German princesses who had become grand duchesses. Nina Chavchavadze was heartbroken, and did not marry until she was thirty-seven. As it happened, Grand Duke George was also thirty-seven when he finally married. In 1892, he wanted to marry Marie, the eldest daughter of Queen Victoria's second son, Alfred, Duke of Edinburgh, and his wife Marie, daughter of Emperor Alexander II. Alexander III made a big fuss about this, assuming that the girl, his niece, would not convert to Orthodoxy, and the Emperor was very strict on this point. Grand Duke George and his father would not give up. This led to a family council at which Alexander III exclaimed that he would rather have grand dukes marry Orthodox women morganatically than to marry royal women who would not convert. He probably had in mind his brother Vladimir and his cousin, Constantine Constantinovich, whose wives steadfastly remained Lutheran. Finally, it was decided to send Grand Duke George with a letter from the Emperor to his sister, asking her to talk her daughter into converting. George delivered the letter to the Duchess of Edinburgh (who was his first cousin) in Munich. She would not even let him see her daughter, but promised to reply to her brother.[1] Whether she did, or what she said, is not known, but the marriage did not take place. Princess Marie later became the Queen of Roumania.

After this disaster, another eight years would pass before George married. This time he fell in love with another Princess Marie, the youngest daughter of King George I of the Hellenes. She was Orthodox, and also a Romanov on her mother's side, her mother having been born Grand Duchess Olga Constantinovna. Marie, however, was in no hurry to be married, and was particularly loath to leave her beloved Greece. Besides, she was not in love with George. Nevertheless, the marriage took place in Corfu in 1900, and George became the only one of the six sons of Michael Nikolayevich to marry a foreign princess. Three of them never married at all.

After six years of residence in St. Petersburg in an apartment in the palace of Grand Duke Michael, and at the huge summer residence of Mikhailovskoye, George and Marie bought land in the Crimea, calling the estate by the Greek name of Harax. Marie was delighted at the thought that the Crimea had in ancient times been

1. *Dnevnik Gos. Sekretarya*, A. A. Polovtsev

settled by Greeks. Meanwhile, they had two daughters, Princess Nina (1901) and Xenia (1903). Both had the title of Princess of Russia, with the style of Highness, because of the law of 1886 restricting the title of grand duke and grand duchess. At birth, they received a twenty-one gun salute.

In June of 1914, Marie, known in Russia as Grand Duchess Marie Georgievna, and abroad as Grand Duchess George, took her two daughters for an extended visit to England, perhaps a trial separation. The visit turned out to be extended indeed. With the outbreak of World War I, Marie was unable to return to Russia, and she spent the entire war in England. They never saw Grand Duke George again.

George went back into the army as a lieutenant-general, and was used by Nicholas II as sort of a roving inspector general to report on conditions and morale in various parts of the army, confident that George would tell him the truth. This he did, making a number of enemies in the process. In 1915 he was sent on a mission to Japan, then allied in the war against Germany, and on the way back inspected various places in the Far East, where grand dukes were a rarity. He found the general mood in the Far East to be much healthier than in European Russia. In 1916 George, convinced that revolution was inevitable, was one of the grand dukes who urged the Emperor to grant a full constitution.

George arrived at Gatchina shortly before Nicholas II abdicated, and was present when word came that Grand Duke Michael had been named Emperor. He did not remain long at Gatchina, primarily because he did not like Michael's wife, Countess Brasova.

Three months after the fall of the monarchy, Grand Duke George was allowed by the provisional government to go to Finland, from where he hoped to be able to rejoin his family in England. The British were not helpful. George would probably have been safe in Finland, had he kept a low profile. Instead, in 1918, he naively applied to the local Soviet for a passport to leave the country. This resulted in his arrest and he was escorted back to St. Petersburg by Red guards in April 1918. There, after an interview with the Cheka chief, Uritsky, he was exiled to Vologda, where he found his eldest brother Nicholas, and his cousin Dimitri Constantinovich. In July the three grand dukes were jailed in Vologda, and three weeks later taken to a prison in St. Petersburg, Shpalernaya, where they were joined by Grand Duke Paul Alexandrovich. Uritsky told them that they were being held hostage against the release of the German communists, Liebknecht and Adler. Actually, the four grand dukes outlived Uritsky, who was assassinated in August 1918. During the months of imprisonment, Grand Duke George managed to smuggle out frequent letters to his wife, who received many of them.[2] The last one was dated 27 November 1918. An attempt to buy out the four grand dukes for 50,000 pounds sterling was made by Grand Duchess Marie through the Danish minister in St. Petersburg, but the effort failed. Maxim Gorky pleaded for their lives with Lenin, but nothing worked.

On 30 January 1919, Grand Duke George Mikhailovich, his brother Nicholas, and his cousins Paul Alexandrovich and Dimitri Constantinovich, were taken to the Fortress of St. Peter and Paul and shot, the last Romanovs to be executed.

---

2. There are many quotations from these letters in Grand Duchess George's autobiography, *A Romanov Diary*, Atlantic International Publications, New York, 1988.

GRAND DUKE ALEXANDER MIKHAILOVICH

GRAND DUKE ALEXANDER MIKHAILOVICH,
GRAND DUCHESS XENIA and daughter IRENE

CHAPTER XXIII

GRAND DUKE ALEXANDER MIKHAILOVICH (1866 - 1933)

Grand Duke Alexander Mikhailovich was the fourth son of Grand Duke Michael Nikolayevich and Grand Duchess Olga Feodorovna. Alexander was born at Tiflis 13 April 1866. His father was the youngest brother of the ruling emperor, Alexander II. Alexander grew up to become one of the best known and most controversial of the grand dukes of his generation. He spent most of his childhood in the Caucasus, developing a distaste for the cold plains of Russia proper, and especially for the capital, St. Petersburg. At the age of seven he was taken from the care of nurses and subjected to the same spartan upbringing as his older brothers, with endless lessons by tutors, whom he hated, with one exception—a well-traveled officer who developed in the young Alexander a wanderlust that never left him.

At the age of nine, during a trip to the Crimea, Alexander met his first cousin once removed, the future Emperor Nicholas II, who was a year younger than himself. The two boys took an immediate liking to each other, which was to last for forty-two years. Nineteen years after this first meeting, Alexander would become Nicholas II's brother-in-law by marrying his sister Xenia.

In 1877 when Alexander was eleven, war broke out with Turkey, and Tiflis was suddenly full of troops on their way to the Caucasian front, of which Alexander's father became commander-in-chief. The boy's biggest thrill was to be allowed to put on the uniform of, and review, the 73rd Krymsky Infantry Regiment, of which he had been honorary colonel since birth. The bearded giants of the Regiment, 4000 strong, barked, "We wish health to Your Imperial Highness," as they passed in review. Alexander was the envy of his brothers, whose regiments served far away in the Balkans.[1]

In 1881 he was present with the rest of his family at the

1. *Once A Grand Duke*, Grand Duke Alexander

Winter Palace in St. Petersburg when the bomb-battered, barely living form of his uncle and namesake, Emperor Alexander II, was brought in to die. This was a never-to-be-forgotten scene of horror.

Since no civilian occupation was thinkable for a grand duke, Alexander early developed a desire to enter the navy, a thought quite shocking to his father, who not only did not take the navy seriously, but within the army favored the artillery above all other branches. Alexander persevered, and by the time he was old enough to become a naval cadet, he was supported by the new Emperor, Alexander III, who was interested in building up the navy's prestige.

In that same year, Alexander's father, the favorite uncle of the new Emperor, left the Caucasus and was appointed President of the State Council. The family now resided in the Mikhailovskoye palace, outside St. Petersburg. In 1882, Alexander got his wish and became a naval cadet. Although tutored separately, he took his exams at the academy. On cruises in the Baltic, he had a separate cabin and ate with the admiral, but went through the same rigorous training as his fellow cadets, was criticized for mistakes in the same way, and did his best to make friends with them. The cadets seemed, to his surprise, to be honored to have him in their midst, and fascinated to find out that all the grand dukes, even the heir to the throne, were subjected in their youth to spartan discipline.

In 1895 Grand Duke Alexander was commissioned as ensign, and the following year, becoming of age, he received an income of 210,000 rubles yearly [$110,000 in 1885 dollars], a tremendous increase over his previous allowance of fifty rubles per month!

We get a glimpse of Alexander at that age through the eyes of State Secretary A. A. Polovtsev, who thought him a splendid youth, full of charm, and obviously one of his mother's two favorites. Polovtsev was shocked, however, to observe Alexander and his brothers tossing bread at each other at dinner with their parents and guests present.

Grand Duke Alexander was then scheduled for a cruise on the warship *Rynda*. His mother was horrified at the thought that young Sandro, as he was known, Georgian-style, in the family, was to be subjected to a cruise of almost three years. Alexander was touched, but remarks in his autobiography, *Once a Grand Duke*, that she had shown him very little love when he needed it in his childhood. Fortunately for him, his mother liked the honest eyes of the first lieutenant of the *Rynda*, and made him promise to take care of her boy and guard him from the fleshpots of the orient. Lt. Eberline, unknown to the Grand Duchess, was one of the biggest rakes in the fleet, and he managed to arrange for Alexander to lose his virginity to an American girl working in a very high class bordello in Hong Kong.

Aboard ship the young Grand Duke was treated like any

other junior officer, but ashore ship's captain had to salute him. Before heading to the Far East, the *Rynda* stopped in Rio de Janeiro, where Alexander made an official call on the aging Emperor of Brazil, Dom Pedro II, who predicted that Brazil would soon become a republic, and was not in the least upset about it.

After Brazil, it was on to South Africa, Singapore, Hong Kong, and Japan, where the *Rynda* was based for a long time in Nagasaki, while making side trips to the Philippines, India, Ceylon, Australia, and various Pacific Islands. At Nagasaki Alexander, like all the other naval officers, acquired a Japanese temporary "wife." Known there as the "Russian Samurai," Alexander had the choice of sixty girls. Since they all looked more or less alike, he picked the one with the prettiest kimono. From her he picked up quite a bit of Japanese, which he thought would come in handy when he was ordered to pay an official visit to the Emperor of Japan. Seated next to the Empress at dinner, Alexander tried out his Nagasaki Japanese, and was somewhat chagrined when she and all the other Japanese present laughed until they cried; they recognized immediately the milieu in which the young Grand Duke had learned their language.

The *Rynda* returned to Europe through the Suez Canal in 1889, stopping in England. Alexander was not happy at having to call on Queen Victoria, whom he considered an enemy of Russia, but he found her charming, very intelligent, and well-informed. In England, Alexander bought a yacht from an American millionaire for 19,000 pounds sterling, rechristening it *Tamara*. Having up to that time had little to spend his income on, Alexander began to collect rare naval books, eventually accumulating 20,000 in what was to be called the best naval library in the world.

Returning to St. Petersburg in 1889, this very atypical grand duke could not wait to leave again, this time with his younger brother Serge on the *Tamara* to Egypt and India, taking along some botanists and zoologists. Then Alexander spent two years in the Black Sea fleet, and in 1892 was in command of a torpedo boat squadron in the Baltic. His mother, who died in 1891, left him an estate in the Crimea called Ay Todor.

For several years Alexander and Grand Duchess Xenia, daughter of Alexander III, had been interested in each other. She was only eighteen, but in 1893 Alexander steeled himself to ask Alexander III for Xenia's hand in marriage. The Emperor, upon learning that Xenia herself had encouraged Sandro to ask him, agreed in principle, but said they should wait a year at least. Her mother would never agree to such an early marriage for Xenia. Sandro's second request was granted immediately—a transfer to the cruiser *Dimitri Donskoy* for a trip to the United States, which he had longed to visit all his life. Alexander III thought it would be a good idea for a member of the Imperial Family to thank President

Cleveland for American aid during the previous year's famine. These two requests were linked, Grand Duke Alexander states, because without the promise of Xenia he was afraid that he would fall for some American girl and never return!

Grand Duke Alexander spent several months in the United States, including a visit to the Chicago World's Fair, and was tremendously impressed, in spite of the financial crash then in progress. He determined to work on the "Americanization" of Russia, particularly by getting rid of the Russian, and European, class system. Curiously, Alexander does not mention seeing President Cleveland in his memoirs.

Back in St. Petersburg, he found an unexpected ally in his father on the question of Xenia. Uncharacteristically, the old Grand Duke, whose reverence for sovereigns was proverbial, took the initiative in facing the diminutive Empress Marie Feodorovna, and after a tremendous scene in which she accused him of stealing her daughter, he obtained final permission for the marriage of Sandro and Xenia. The marriage took place at Peterhof in July 1894. This was the first and only marriage between two Romanovs. There were seven children from the marriage—Irina, the future Princess Yusupov (1895); Andrew (1896); Theodore (1898); Nikita (1900); Dimitri (1901); Rostislav (1902), and Vasily (1907), all of them Princes of the Blood, but not grand dukes, under the new law, even though through their mother they were grandchildren of an emperor, Alexander III.

At the time of his marriage, Alexander was twenty-eight, a strapping 6'-3", extremely handsome, with brown eyes, dark hair, and a neatly trimmed beard very much in the style of his new brother-in-law and great friend, the Tsesarevich Nicholas. Xenia was nineteen, short, blue-eyed, with prominent Romanov eyebrows, and her dark hair upswept in the style of the 1890s. Nobody suspected at this happy event that Grand Duke Alexander's cousin and new father-in-law, Alexander III, would not live out the year. His magnificent frame was still intact, but his kidneys were damaged by the train wreck in which he had held up the roof of the coach over his family's head.

There is no doubt that Grand Duke Alexander adulated Alexander III, and considered his death at the age of forty-nine to be Russia's greatest tragedy, and the beginning of the end. There is some doubt, however, that Alexander III trusted the young Grand Duke. The future Prime Minister Witte, writing long afterwards, claimed that Alexander III disliked Sandro and considered him a bad influence, but Witte had reasons to dislike the Grand Duke. Polovtsev, writing in 1891, states that Alexander III suspected Sandro of wanting a spy on the imperial yacht because he pushed for a boatswain from the *Tamara* to be transferred there, and Polovtsev had nothing but praise for Alexander. No explanation was offered as to why Alexander would want a spy anywhere.

Whatever the truth, at Livadia on 2 November 1894, Grand Duke Alexander witnessed the death of another Emperor, and the horror of the new Emperor at the thought of inheriting the crown so prematurely. Nicholas II, not yet twenty-eight, cried on Sandro's shoulder and begged for his help. As the years went by, Sandro was not stingy with advice, but it was not often heeded.

There was the matter of the uncles. The inexperienced young Emperor was showered with advice, and even orders, from his father's brothers, Grand Dukes Vladimir, Alexis, and Serge. Sandro begged the Emperor to assert himself and not be overwhelmed by them. Alexander himself, however, immediately got into trouble with one of them, Grand Duke Alexis, Grand Admiral of the navy. Alexis suspected his young cousin of wanting to replace him in his job, of being a dishonest intriguer and meddler, with too much influence on Nicholas II.[2] Grand Duke Alexander, who was pushing for a larger battle fleet, thought Alexis ran the navy in a style suitable for the 18th century. This ended in 1896 in Alexander's being pushed out of the navy for four years, during which time he retired with his young bride to Ay Todor in the Crimea. In the same year there was the Khodynka Field tragedy in Moscow after the Emperor's coronation. Thousands died running for the Imperial presents, which Alexander attributed to inadequate police measures, and blamed Grand Duke Serge, the Moscow Governor General. Grand Duke Serge also insisted that the coronation ball, scheduled for the evening of the tragedy, not be called off. Alexander and three of his "wild Caucasian" brothers left the ball in protest before the dancing started.

In 1900, after four years of relative idleness, Grand Duke Alexander was promoted to captain and given command of the new battleship *Rostislav* in the Black Sea, which probably inspired him to give his fifth son this ancient Slavic name. Shortly afterwards, Nicholas II asked him to be chairman of a government supported venture to develop resources in Korea by Vladivostok businessmen. Alexander quit this job in 1902, believing, he states, that Russian intrigues in Korea and Manchuria would lead to war with Japan, whose armed forces he had viewed at first hand. The resignation was not publicized until Soviet times, however, and a lot of blame for the subsequent Russo-Japanese War rubbed off on Alexander in political circles.

In 1902 Grand Duke Alexander, still only thirty-six, was promoted to rear admiral and actually became a member of the cabinet, being appointed to a new Ministry of Merchant Marine and

---

2. *Vospominaniya*, S. Yu. Witte

Ports, carved out of the Ministry of Finance. This earned him the enmity of Witte, then Minister of Finance, who attributed it to Alexander's undue influence on his Imperial brother-in-law. No grand duke of that age had ever before advanced to ministerial rank.

When war did break out with the Japanese attack on Port Arthur in 1904, Alexander begged to be sent, but Nicholas II refused, Alexander believed, under pressure from his mother not to expose her daughter's husband to danger. He was allowed to organize a squadron of armed passenger ships (several Russian ones and four brought in Germany) to intercept foreign ships bound for Japan with military contraband. They managed to seize twelve ships in the Red Sea. This action, a preview of similar ones in World War I, aroused great indignation in London and Berlin, and the intercepted ships were ultimately released.

As even Witte agreed, Grand Duke Alexander was adamant against sending the Baltic Fleet to the Far East. In this he actually found support from Grand Duke Alexis, and from the designated commander of the ill-fated expedition, Admiral Rozhestvensky, who gave himself no chance of success, but was suicidally resigned to making the effort. The Emperor agreed that the expedition was a bad idea, but finally bowed to the pressures of a press howling for Japanese blood. In a logistical nightmare admired to this day, the fleet rounded Africa and Southeast Asia only to meet its doom in the straits of Tsushima.

With all of his talk of "Americanization," Grand Duke Alexander was furious when the 1905 revolution led to a semi-constitutional monarchy and an elected Duma. He believed in a fight to the end to preserve the autocracy. He resigned as Minister of Merchant Marine, refusing to work with the new Duma and his old enemy, Prime Minister Witte, and took over the torpedo boats on the Baltic. This assignment was cut short when it was learned that sailors of his flagship were waiting to seize him as a hostage before starting a mutiny. He was ashore at the time, and was not permitted to return. Obviously, no member of the Imperial Family could be risked as a hostage to revolutionary forces.

Grand Duke Alexander, who had always considered himself the enlisted men's friend, was personally terribly hurt. All these events led to a breakdown in his psyche, and he admits to having developed a hatred for Russia, and that his only desire was to get away. Taking his family to Biarritz in 1906, it was not long before he fell in love with a woman of Spanish-Italian background, (whom he does not name). He told all to his wife, who, he says, behaved like an angel, and they remained friends, closer than before perhaps. Of course, there could be no question of divorce. In 1910 the Grand Duke actually asked his lady friend to go off to Australia with him, but she had the good sense to refuse.

Despite his periods of despair, Grand Duke Alexander was not the type of man to remain inactive. During his exile from the navy he invented a naval war game, which was adopted by the Naval College. This time he was excited with the possibilities of aviation, particularly the accomplishments of the French aviator Blériot. In 1908 he returned to Russia, demanding that planes be bought for the military. He was laughed at by Sukhomlinov, the Minister of War, but Nicholas II took his advice and authorized a group of Russian pilots to be trained in France. They finished their course in 1909, after which Grand Duke Alexander formed the first Russian aviation school outside of Sebastopol, a far-sighted move leading to an effective Russian air force in World War I.

In 1913 Alexander made his second trip to the United States to consult with the Curtiss-Wright company and look at its factories. Between 1908 and 1914, he made frequent trips to Russia in connection with his new passion for aviation, but basically he lived abroad. After returning from the trip to the U.S., he found a flourishing economy with a stock market that even interested guards officers, complete with American style robber-baron capitalists. This was not, evidently, they type of Americanization he had had in mind. He mentions that these robber barons were financing revolutionary parties, but nowhere does he allude to the Imperial government's very advanced, for the time, labor legislation of 1912, which put a brake on the laissez-faire activities of the capitalists.

In 1914 Grand Duke Alexander barely made it back to Russia from Paris, going via Austria and Roumania. His family, then in England, as was the Dowager Empress, also returned in the nick of time through Scandinavia. Alexander found Russia boiling with patriotic fervor, to which he reacted with skepticism.

Grand Duke Alexander was assigned to general headquarters, where his cousin, Grand Duke Nicholas Nikolayevich, ruled as supreme commander. The two had had a running antipathy for forty years, and hence were extra polite to each other. Alexander ascribes the antipathy to the long-standing feud between Nicholas Nikolayevich and Alexander's eldest brother, Nicholas Mikhailovich. Nicholas Nikolayevich packed Alexander off to the staff of the 4th Army, operating against the Austrians, but then recalled him and put him in charge of all Russian military aviation, a very sensible assignment. Alexander remained in charge of the air force until the fall of the monarchy.

Thanks to the designing genius of Igor Sikorsky, Russia was producing the first two engine and four engine bombers in history, and thanks to Alexander, Russian pilots had been trained since 1909. By 1916 there were hundreds of planes, and three Russian factories turning them out, plus deliveries from Britain and France. A Duma commission, however, blamed the Grand Duke for having aircraft purchased from the Allies sent to the front without proper inspection, and for mysteriously cancelling some orders from France.[3]

In 1915 Grand Duke Alexander welcomed the Emperor's assumption of supreme command, unlike most of his relatives, provided that Nicholas II kept a strict eye on the doings in St. Petersburg. This was a difficult thing to do, even if the will to do it had been present.

From his headquarters in Kiev, Alexander made frequent trips to the capital. In contrast to the front, which was well supplied and ready for an offensive, he found St. Petersburg very unhealthy, the talk being exclusively about the intrigues surrounding Rasputin and his influence on the Empress' appointments. Alexander had had many talks with Nicholas II about Rasputin, starting long before the war. The Emperor was not Rasputin's admirer, Alexander says, but could not bring himself to deprive his wife of this "miracle man" who could alleviate the young Alexis' pain and whom she believed to be the true voice of the people. In 1916 Alexander had a huge scene with the Empress at Tsarskoye Selo, but it produced no result whatever. Alexander had now come to the same conclusion as most of the family, that the only solution to imminent revolution was a government fully responsible to the Duma. He wrote at length from Kiev to the Emperor about this.

There was general rejoicing when news reached Kiev that Rasputin had been murdered. The rejoicing was not shared by Grand Duke Alexander, first of all because it had occurred at the house of his son-in-law, Prince Felix Yusupov, with both the latter and Grand Duke Dimitri Pavlovich directly involved. Alexander learned of the news when his aide-de-camp entered with a broad smile, "Your Imperial Highness," he said, "Rasputin was assassinated last night."

The Grand Duke, more politically astute than his aide, immediately set out for St. Petersburg, like the Emperor. He was afraid that the Empress, in her grief, would exact vengeance on Felix and Dimitri; and he was also convinced that it was a poor idea for members of the Imperial Family to take the law into their own hands. In fact, when Dimitri had attempted to leave the night after the murder for the Crimea, guarded by Captain Rayner, he had been stopped by the police, who told him that he was forbidden to leave St. Petersburg 'by order of Her Majesty the Empress.' Alexander, knowing the Empress as well as he did, also knew that the murder would harden her resistance to any change. The Dowager Empress, also residing in Kiev, agreed.

Back in St. Petersburg, Alexander attended a family

---

3. *Krusheniye Imperii*, M. V. Rodzianko

conference consisting of Grand Dukes Paul (Dimitri's father), Cyril, Boris, Andrew and their mother, the widowed Grand Duchess Maria Pavlovna. They acted, as Alexander says, as if they expected Dimitri and Felix to be decorated for their patriotic act, and wrote Nicholas II what he calls a "silly" letter, which he refused to sign. Nevertheless, he did visit Nicholas II to plead for light punishment for the misguided, but patriotic young men.

"Nice speech, Sandro," the Emperor replied. "Are you aware, however, that nobody has the right to murder, be it a Grand Duke or a peasant?"

The Emperor did promise to be moderate in his punishment. The punishment was light indeed. Grand Duke Alexander was one of those who saw the young Grand Duke Dimitri off to his life-saving exile in Persia, and rode the train with Felix, who was exiled to one of his estates.

Grand Duke Alexander was in Kiev when news of the abdication reached him. Unlike others in the family, who were amazed that Nicholas II abdicated in favor of his brother rather than his son, an arrangement politically impossible at that point, Alexander could see no point to abdication at all. How could his friend "Nicky" abdicate because of a little rioting, when he commanded an army of 15,000,000 men? It does not seem to have occurred to him that with all the generals, including Grand Duke Nicholas Nikolayevich, advising him to abdicate, there was no way the poor Emperor could cause a single battalion to move anywhere, even if he had wanted to, and he had a horror of causing a civil war.

After the abdication, Alexander accompanied the Dowager Empress Marie to headquarters to watch her son take leave of his staff. The only other Romanov present was Alexander's brother Serge. The nobility, modesty, and total lack of self-pity in the ex-Emperor's address, as well as his plea for them to continue serving Russia, were extremely moving. It was the last time that mother saw son, and Alexander saw the boy he had met in Livadia so long before. It was also the last time he was to see his brother Serge, who accompanied Nicholas II back to Tsarskoye Selo, while Alexander and Empress Marie returned to Kiev.

For a couple of weeks Kiev was very pleasant, officers still saluting the Grand Duke on the street, and cheering the Empress. Then the press and public mood turned ugly. The provisional government insisted that they go to the Crimea. The old Empress absolutely refused to budge, not wanting to be further away from her sons. Finally persuaded, she, her daughter Grand Duchess Olga and the latter's husband, Colonel Kulikovsky, and Alexander were taken by train to Alexander's estate, Ay Todor. According to Alexander they were guarded by revolutionary sailors during the trip; Olga's version was that Alexander had shown great energy in finding a loyal group of engineer troops to guard them. Grand Duchess Xenia and her children arrived shortly afterwards from the north.

There followed a short, pleasant period of "house" arrest for the Romanovs at Ay Todor, which included 175 acres of land along the coast. When the Bolsheviks came to power, the family was transferred to Dulber, the near-by estate of Grand Duke Peter Nikolayevich, where they remained until liberated by the Germans.

With the November 1918 armistice, the Germans left the Crimea. Allied ships were in Sebastopol, but there was danger to the Crimea from advancing Red armies in the Ukraine. In December 1918, Grand Duke Alexander Mikhailovich departed the Crimea with his eldest son, Prince Andrew, and the latter's wife, on the British warship *HMS Forsythe.* The reason for Alexander's early departure was to represent the dynasty and, somehow, Russia, at the peace conference in Paris that was to end with the Treaty of Versailles. It would seem that Grand Duke Nicholas Nikolayevich, whose troops had sacrificed themselves to save Paris in 1914, would have carried more clout, but he apparently preferred to stay in the Crimea at that time.

In any case, Grand Duke Alexander got nowhere. Clemenceau refused to see him. President Wilson and his Secretary of State, Lansing, brushed him off. British Foreign Secretary Balfour fled down the fire escape of a hotel to avoid him.

Grand Duke Alexander was furious at the allied statesmen's disregard of all of Russia's sacrifices in the war, just because the Bolsheviks had made a separate peace; and at their ignorance of what was really happening in Russia, and of the Bolshevik menace to the rest of the world. He had to endure another slap from his former allies—the British refused to grant him a three day visa to see his wife's aunt, Queen Alexandra!

Furthermore, Alexander was broke. He only had enough to live in Paris for two months. His immediate solution was to sell the fine collection of ancient coins he had accumulated before the revolution, fortunately stored in Paris. He had found some of them by participating in archaeological digs before the revolution. They brought a small percentage of what they had cost him, but solved his problems for a while. Considering his interest in neumismatics, it is odd that in his books Alexander never once mentions that his brother, Grand Duke George, was one of the most prominent coin collectors in the world, with several publications to his credit.

The Grand Duke's sense of irony was tickled when one day, at a Paris cafe, he saw two fellow Russian exiles sitting at separate tables and glaring at each other with hatred. One was Alexander Kerensky, who had run Russia under the provisional government, and the other was Boris Savinkov, the terrorist responsible for the 1905 assassination of Grand Duke Serge Alexandrovich, and a minister in Kerensky's government. Savinkov would later die in a Bolshevik jail. They both looked with displeasure at the Grand Duke. The proprietor apologized, saying, "This is a public establishment, Your Imperial Highness."

It was from a Paris newspaper that Grand Duke Alexander learned of the death of his brothers Nicholas and George, and cousins Paul and Dimitri, in January 1919 at the hands of a Bolshevik firing squad.

Alexander's own immediate family all got out safely. The Dowager Empress returned to her native Denmark with Xenia, who soon returned to England where she settled in a grace and favor cottage near Windsor Castle, lent to her by King George V. Grand Duke Alexander stayed in Paris. He benefited for three years from the sale of his wife's pearls at 20% of their original value. According to his sister-in-law, Grand Duchess Olga, who managed to join her mother in Denmark, Alexander encouraged the Empress to sell or pawn her jewels so the Romanovs could open a paper factory and become solvent. She did not go along with the idea.

Another of Alexander's suggestions was that the entire family should move to Fiji, which he remembered fondly from that cruise on the good ship *Rynda*. They thought he was losing his mind. The only ones quite well off were Alexander's daughter Irene and her husband, Prince Felix Yusupov, who had brought out two Rembrandts and sold them for $450,000. Much later they were to augment their income by successfully suing the American movie studio that made *Rasputin and the Empress*, in which Princess Irene was libeled. The case was ultimately settled for the total sum of 100,000 pounds sterling, equivalent today of about $5,000,000.

The Fiji idea was only part of Grand Duke Alexander's search for lost youth. He haunted the golf links at Biarritz, hoping to run into his old love of 1907-1910. For a moment, in 1919, he thought he had found her. It was an illusion—a young British girl who drove a blue Rolls Royce. The fact that he was thirty-one years older than she did not stop him from pursuing her for three years, with some success. He asked Xenia for a divorce, which she refused. The British girl, in a repetition of the first episode, refused to run off to Australia with him.

Throughout the 1920s Grand Duke Alexander made visits to reigning relatives, but was uncomfortable with them. They acted, he thought, as if the Romanovs had an incurable disease which they prayed was not catching.

Life held one more exotic journey for the Grand Duke. In 1925, while in Monte Carlo, he was approached by a dark gentleman he took to be a jewel salesman. He was very far off the mark. The gentleman turned out to be an Ethiopian statesman whom Grand Duke Alexander had introduced to Nicholas II in 1902, a man called

Abuna Matheus. Matheus enlisted Alexander in a scheme to help recover twelve plots of land, including a convent and some churches, that the Ethiopians laid claim to in Jerusalem. This property, which was close to the Church of the Holy Sepulcher, was in the hands of Armenians and Copts. The Imperial Russian Government had helped the Ethiopians uncover proofs of their claims in Turkey in the form of some 7th century firman from an early caliph, the expenses of this effort being covered by Grand Duchess Elizabeth Feodorovna. Now the vital papers were in the hand of a former Russian official in Constantinople, who would only surrender them to a member of the Imperial Family. Hence the approach to the Grand Duke. Alexander managed to acquire the desired papers, and this resulted in a six month visit to Addis Ababa as a guest of the new Emperor Ras Tafari, later to be known as Haile Selassie.

Arriving in the Ethiopian capital, Grand Duke Alexander was received with Imperial honors, and presented with two twelve-year-old concubines whom, he says, he rejected. There turned out to be a colony of seventy-five Russians in Ethiopia. Alexander saw the Emperor almost daily, but it was three months before his host mentioned the Jerusalem matter. After three more months, Alexander returned to France. The Ethiopian claims in Jerusalem were not yet settled, and were still being discussed in the League of Nations in 1932.[4] It is doubtful that they ever were settled.

Alexander had long ago parted ways with official Christianity. Instead, he found spiritualism. He wrote several books on the subject, published at his own expense, the first one called *Union of Souls*. By his own admission, hardly anybody read them. Beginning at the end of 1928, he spent three years in the United States, lecturing on spiritualism, a total of sixty-seven lectures, the first in Grand Rapids, Michigan. He did write three other books which were not about spiritualism, and which sold very well. These were *Once A Grand Duke*, *Twilight of Royalty*, and *Always A Grand Duke*. The last two were finished in the last fifteen months of his life. They contain much of interest, and also numerous mistakes, which raises the suspicion that they were at least partially ghost-written, with Alexander himself not caring much about details. He was also working on a novel based on the life of Catherine the Great, and a book on the two Danish sisters, Queen Alexandra of England and Empress Marie of Russia.

During the last sixteen months of his life, Alexander fell ill, suffering severe pains in his spine. He had never been ill in his life before, and he kept right on working on his various projects, and reading a wide variety of literature and non-fiction.

Grand Duke Alexander Mikhailovich died at Roquebrune,

---

4. *Always A Grand Duke*, Grand Duke Alexander

France, 26 February 1933.

An anonymous American friend, in the preface of *Always A Grand Duke*, summed up the character of this most unusual Grand Duke as follows, "Opinionated and tolerant, belligerent and kind, sarcastic and romantic. . . .an arch-foe of bunkum in all its forms and disguises."

GRAND DUKE SERGE MIKHAILOVICH

CHAPTER XXIV

GRAND DUKE SERGE MIKHAILOVICH (1869 - 1918)

The fifth son of Grand Duke Michael Nikolayevich, Serge was born at Borjom, Georgia, 7 October 1869.

He had a tutor called Colonel Helmerson, who brought him up in a very pessimist vein. Serge had one quality which delighted his father—he was interested in the military, and particularly the artillery, which was a passion with his father.

Grand Duke Serge Mikhailovich was the only one of the "Caucasian" Mikhailovichi to have blue eyes like his father. Serge was 6'-3", and prematurely bald. His sister-in-law, Grand Duchess George, thought he was ugly, unlike the rest of the family, and she once asked him why this was so. "It is my charm," said Serge, seemingly undisturbed by his appearance. She also thought him attractive and clever, with a great sense of the ridiculous. His jokes could sometimes be cruel, however, and he tended to be moody and a sloppy dresser. Serge had a mathematical, analytical mind, which suited him for the artillery.

Only two years younger than the future Emperor Nicholas II, he and Serge were great friends, especially during the period when the Tsesarevich was having an affair with the famous ballerina, Mathilde Ksheshinska. After Nicholas broke up with her, Serge bought her a dacha and may possibly have been the father of her son, but who was officially recognized by Grand Duke Andrew as his son.

Grand Duke Serge Mikhailovich was close to his brother Alexander, with whom he traveled to India on the latter's yacht, *Tamara*. Relations cooled between the two, however, after Alexander had succeeded in wooing and winning Grand Duchess Xenia Alexandrovna, one of the two sisters of Nicholas II. Serge was also in love with her, and lost out. He remained a bachelor.

Living in his own apartment in his father's palace, Mikhailovskoye, outside St. Petersburg, Serge used to bicycle through the lengthy halls to visit his relatives.

Like his father before him, Grand Duke Serge obtained the rank of Inspector-General of the Artillery. With his ingrained pessimism, he was certain that war with Germany would come sooner or later. During a trip to Vienna in 1913 he became convinced that the Austrian and German munitions factories were feverishly preparing for war. His warnings went unheeded by the Russian ministers.

During the war he was attached to general headquarters, once making a trip to Archangel to check on the munitions being sent there by the Allies. As chief of the Artillery Department, Serge came under the fire of the President of the Duma, Michael Rodzianko, who thought that the Grand Duke made an unwitting cover for a gang of thieves. There were also rumors that the Grand Duke's former mistress, Ksheshinska, was getting preferential orders for certain firms. All this, Rodzianko feared, would rub off on the Imperial Family if it became known. Serge resigned as head of the Artillery Department, but was appointed Inspector of Artillery at General Headquarters.[1]

In 1916 Serge was the only grand duke in a position to see his old friend Nicholas II every day, living in the same headquarters train with him. Serge grew more and more pessimistic about the future, and told his brother Alexander that there was no way to open the Emperor's eyes. He was mesmerized by his wife. Serge predicted a revolution in the near future. If it did not come, Serge said, the army would be in a very good shape for a decisive offensive in 1917. Serge tried to calm his premonitions by growing a small vegetable garden. Unfortunately, his pessimism turned out to be correct.

After the February 1917 revolution had started, Grand Duke Serge asked the British observer, Sir John Hanbury-Williams to write a letter to the Emperor begging him to grant a full constitutional government with ministers responsible to the Duma. Nicholas II never received the letter, which probably would not have had an effect in any case.[2]

Grand Duke Serge remained in St. Petersburg throughout the period of the Provisional Government, and through the seizure of power by the Bolsheviks. He was still there in March 1918, when all the Romanovs were ordered to register, and found himself in the same net with many of his relatives. Three sons of Grand Duke Constantine Constantinovich—Princes John, Constantine and Igor; Vladimir Paley, the morganatic son of Grand Duke Paul Alexandrovich; Grand Duchess Elizabeth Feodorovna, the widow of Grand Duke Serge Alexandrovich, were all arrested and sent to Vyatka and then to Alapayevsk where, on 18 July 1918, they were

---

1. *Krusheniye Imperii*, M. V. Rodzianko
2. *The Emperor Nicholas II As I Knew Him*, Sir John Hanbury-Williams

thrown down a mine shaft and left to die in agony. Thus perished Grand Duke Serge Mikhailovich, the most junior of all the grand dukes from the point of view of primogeniture at that time.

GRAND DUKE ALEXIS MIKHAILOVICH

CHAPTER XXV

GRAND DUKE ALEXIS MIKHAILOVICH
(1875 - 1895)

Grand Duke Alexis was the only grand duke to have both the name and patronymic of a Muscovite Tsar. He was the sixth son and youngest of the "Caucasian" brood of Grand Duke Michael Nikolayevich. Alexis was born in Tiflis 28 December 1875.

Little is known of Grand Duke Alexis, owing to his short life. We do have a few glimpses of him from comments of his brothers and other family members. He was educated like all of his brothers, and was intelligent and lively. At the age of eight he attended a function at the Winter Palace, and was terribly interested to see all of the foreign uniforms, particularly those of the exotic oriental envoys.

As a child he was solemnly toasted in the presence of his mother and his brothers on occasions such as his birthday and nameday, but he was brought up strictly, and was overwhelmed by his older brothers. One visitor, State Secretary A. A. Polovtsev, complained that Alexis' older brothers were ruining his character. "Particularly the eldest one," said Emperor Alexander III when this was repeated to him. Perhaps Alexis' brother, Nicholas ["Bimbo"] was already annoying the conservative Emperor with his liberal ideas.

At the age of eighteen, Alexis was a tall, thin, young man, quite good-looking dressed in his uniform.

Alexander III liked little Alexis, and at least on one occasion, when the child was thirteen, delivered through him an order to Alexis' father. The Emperor told Alexis that his brother Michael was a cretin and that Alexis should come to him, Alexander III, for good advice when it was time for him to marry. The Emperor was upset over Michael Mikhailovich's marital problems.[1]

Alexis yearned for the company of children his own age, and frequently played with Alexander III's younger children, Michael, Xenia. and Olga.

---

1. *Dnevnik Gos. Sekretarya*, A. A. Polovtsev

With this brief glimpse of Alexis' childhood, the page closes on this young Grand Duke. All his brother Alexander has to say about him is, "Although attached to him stronger than to any other member of my family, I never regretted his passing away. A brilliant boy of liberal heart and absolute sincerity, he suffered acutely in the atmosphere of the palace." And perhaps he was spared a worse death.

Grand Duke Alexis Mikhailovich died of tuberculosis, at age twenty, at San Remo 2 March 1895.

TSESAREVICH NICHOLAS
(Nicholas II)

THE CATHERINE PALACE

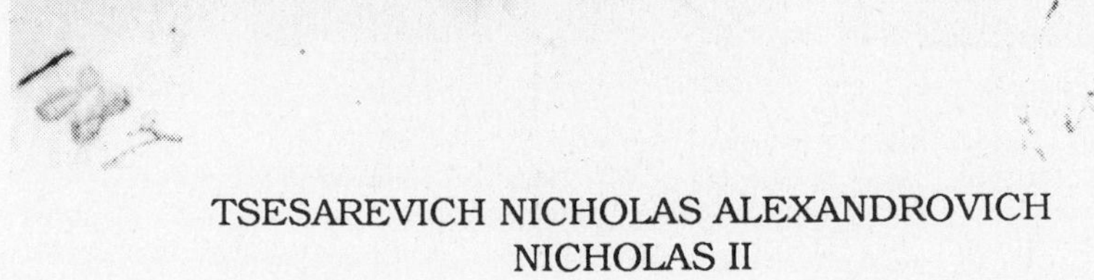

TSESAREVICH NICHOLAS ALEXANDROVICH
NICHOLAS II

THE IMPERIAL FAMILY

(Back row) 1. Serge Mikhailovich, 2. Prince Alexander of Oldenburg, 3.Constantine Constantinovich, 4. Serge Mikhailovich, 5. Nicholas Nikolayevich, 6, Duke George Mecklenburg Strelitz, 7. Dimitri Constantinovich, 8. Prince Peter Alexandrovich of Oldenburg, 9. Duke George of Leutchtenberg;
(second row) 10. Xenia Alexandrovna, 11. Marie Pavlovna, Sr., 12. Helen Vladimirovna 13. Alexandra Iosifovna, 14. Queen Olga of Greece, 15. Tsesarevich Nicholas, 16. Vladimir Alexandrovich, 17. Empress Marie, 18. Emperor Alexander III, 19. Michael Nikolayevich, 20. Paul Alexandrovich
(Front) 21. Alexis Mikhailovich; 22. Michael Alexandrovich; 23. Andrew Vladimirovich; 24. Boris Vladimirovich

EMPRESS ALEXANDRA C. 1896

EMPRESS ALEXANDRA C. 1896

CHAPTER XXVI

GRAND DUKE NICHOLAS ALEXANDROVICH
(1868 - 1918)

EMPEROR NICHOLAS II
(1894 - 1918)

Grand Duke Nicholas Alexandrovich was born at St. Petersburg on 18 May 1868, the son of Tsesarevich Alexander. At the time of Nicholas' birth, his grandfather, Emperor Alexander II was still alive, and his father, the future Alexander III and been Tsesarevich and Heir Apparent for five years.

According to some sources, a son had been born prior to Nicholas, but had died. This is mentioned in the biography of Grand Duchess Olga, Nicholas' sister, and in the autobiography of Grand Duke Alexander, although it is not mentioned in *Burkes*.

Through his mother, Marie Feodorovna, who was born Princess Dagmar of Denmark, he came into a very close relationship with several other European reigning houses—King George V of Great Britain was his first cousin; King George I of Greece his uncle, and King Christian IX of Denmark his grandfather.

In 1881, with the accession of his father to the throne, Nicholas himself became Tsesarevich and Heir Apparent, as well as Grand Duke. He accepted the burdens of his birth as something coming from God, though lacking any desire for power himself. Thus, to his horror, he became Emperor of Russia only thirteen years later, when his father died at the unlikely age of forty-nine on 2 November 1894. Nicholas was only twenty-six.

Nicholas had grown up in a warm, close family atmosphere, but his father had, surprisingly, done little to prepare Nicholas to rule.

During his youth, Nicholas was a playboy, and quite rowdy, getting drunk and rolling in the grass with his army buddies.[1] During one period in January 1880 he attended twenty stage

1. *Diary of Nicholas II*

performances, sometimes two a day. He loved everything, from *The Merchant of Venice* to *Sleeping Beauty*. Nicholas was a sought after guest at late night parties, and attended two or three balls a week. "We danced to exhaustion . . . went to bed at 3:30 a.m." Another time he wrote, ". . . skating with Xenia [his sister] and Aunt Ella [Grand Duchess Elizabeth]. Put on skates and played ball." The Tsesarevich also had had several not very serious affairs. He met, and fell in love with the Polish ballerina, Mathilde Ksheshinska. This affairs was not taken lightly by the Empress, although his father seemed unconcerned. Nicholas set her up in a house, and he and three of his cousins, Grand Dukes Alexander, George and Serge Mikhailovich, would visit her. It is clear that Nicholas considered this establishment as a "home," because he would almost always appear in time for dinner, riding up on his horse, and would frequently stay the night. The affair officially broke up in 1894, just before Nicholas became engaged to Princess Alix of Hesse and By Rhine. Writers of the period, however, uniformly state that Nicholas continued to visit Mathilde frequently throughout his life, talking with her, and accepting her advice on political matters. Whether the affair continued or not is uncertain, but most observers said not.

Mathilde had at least one recognized son named Vladimir. Vladimir claimed in later life that he did not know who was his father, Grand Duke Serge or Andrew, although Andrew recognized Vladimir as his after the revolution.

Nicholas was a man of great personal charm, considerable intelligence, and a phenomenal memory, but he was indecisive, and weak-willed. He could be stubborn, however, but usually at the wrong times. His kindly and gentle disposition, and unassuming personality, simply made him unsuited for absolute power. His tragedy was that he would have made a first class private citizen, or constitutional monarch, or even an autocrat in calmer times, but he was destined, like a Greek tragedy, to rule in a historical maelstrom.

It is not within the purview of this work to say more about Russia's last reigning Emperor. He is frequently mentioned in these biographies of the grand dukes, where their lives touched his. His reign is also extremely well-known from many other sources. Suffice it to say, he was a good man, often misjudged by history, who did not deserve the fate he received.

Emperor Nicholas II abdicated on 2 March 1917[2] in favor of his brother, Grand Duke Michael Alexandrovich, who became the last Emperor of all the Russias. Nicholas and his family were then exiled to Tobolsk by the provisional government, and were later moved to Ekaterinburg by the Bolsheviks, where they were murdered on the orders of Lenin on 17 July 1918.

---

2. Old style

GRAND DUKE GEORGE ALEXANDROVICH

TSESAREVICH NICHOLAS and
GRAND DUKE GEORGE c. 1875

CHAPTER XXVII

GRAND DUKE GEORGE ALEXANDROVICH (1871-1899)

The second of Emperor Alexander III's three sons, George, was born at Tsarkoye-Selo on 8 May 1871. He was probably the cleverest of the three. He certainly had the most sparkling personality. George grew up very close to his older brother, the future Emperor Nicholas II, and benefited, as did the rest of Alexander III's children, from the totally unstuffy, happy and largely rural life the family lived at Gatchina. George had an outstanding sense of humor. In fact, his brother Nicholas found him so funny that he would take notes on what George had said, filing them in a little box, which even when he was Emperor he would take out and read, laughing aloud. George was also a great tease. He had a parrot called "Popka," a rather typical Russian name for a parrot. He trained the bird to imitate the accent of his English tutor, much to the latter's discomfiture.

His cousin, Grand Duchess George, tells a story of George's courage. As children, they were visiting their grandfather, King Christian, who dressed in a sheet, holding it well above his head with a stick as he approached the children in the darkened palace grounds. Seeing what appeared to be a very tall ghost, the children fled—all but George, who pounced on the figure, beating it with his fists until he recognized his grandfather's cries. King Christian pronounced Grand Duke George a very brave young man, and the rest of them cowards!

As a child George, with the rest of his immediate family, lived through the train wreck caused by revolutionary terrorists. It was on that occasion that Emperor Alexander III, with his enormous physical strength, saved his family's lives by holding up the roof of the coach until help came, undermining his health in the process.

At the unexpectedly early death of his father and the ascent of his brother to the throne, Grand Duke George Alexandrovich was declared heir to the throne. In England this would have been called "heir presumptive," as the newly married Nicholas II was expected to produce children of his own.

George's tragedy was that he was plagued with bad health—weak lungs. In 1892 he accompanied his brother the Tsesarevich on a long trip to the Far East on the battleship *Pamayt Azova.* The trip was to end in Japan where Nicholas was almost killed by a berserk policeman. George, however, did not make it that far. He developed a bad, lingering fever, and at Bombay had to be sent back to Russia in a destroyer. His father, Alexander III, spent hours by his bedside.

In time George developed tuberculosis in both lungs and was sent to Abbas Tuman in the Caucasus, where the climate was deemed healthful. In the opinion of his younger sister Olga, George need not have died. The doctors bungled his case. On 9 August 1899, at Abbas Tuman, the young Grand Duke, not yet twenty-eight, was found dead by a peasant woman by the side of a road, next to his overturned motorcycle. He was still the heir to the throne when he died, his brother having only had two daughters by the time of the accident. George's younger brother Michael then became the next in line to the throne until the birth of Nicholas II's son Alexis in 1904.

Their sister, Grand Duchess Olga Alexandrovna, was of the opinion that had George lived, he would have accepted the crown upon the abdication of Nicholas II, instead of turning it down as Michael did, and would have had a good chance of saving the monarchy.

These "ifs" can lead to endless speculations. If Nicholas, as Tsesarevich, had been killed by the Japanese policeman, Grand Duke George would have become emperor in 1894, only to be succeeded by Michael in 1899 if George, in the meantime, had not married and had a son of his own. Or, if George's life had been saved by more competent doctors, he would have continued on the throne until—? In this useless exercise, the only thing one can say is that history would have been very different if any of these "ifs" had become reality.

Е. И. В. Вел. Кн. Кириллъ Владимiровичъ.

Grand Duke Cyrille

GRAND DUKE CYRIL and GRAND DUCHESS VICTORIA

CHAPTER XXVIII

GRAND DUKE CYRIL VLADIMIROVICH (1876 - 1938)

Grand Duke Cyril [English for the Russian *Kirill*] was the eldest of the three sons of Grand Duke Vladimir Alexandrovich, brother of Alexander III. He was born 12 October 1876 at Tsarskoye Selo. Cyril, his brothers Boris and Andrew, and sister Helen, made up a sub-branch of the Imperial Family known as the Vladimirovichi. In age, they were among the youngest of the grand dukes, but by primogeniture they were very close to the throne.

Cyril's father, Grand Duke Vladimir, came within a hair-breadth of becoming emperor in 1888 when Alexander III and his entire family were nearly killed in a train wreck. Had this happened, Cyril would have become Tsesarevich and heir at the age of twelve. After his father's death in 1909, Cyril became third in line to the throne, behind Tsesarevich Alexis and Grand Duke Michael Alexandrovich.

In his early years Grand Duke Cyril was put in the care of an English nanny, Miss Milicent Crofts, and English was his first language. When he was old enough, there was the inevitable procession of tutors. His childhood and youth were mostly spent in the country, at the Catherine Palace at Tsarskoye Selo, or the Vladimir Palace in St. Petersburg, which he remembered as a sombre, Florentine-style place on the Neva embankment.

Cyril was designated to have a career in the navy. It is difficult to determine now whether this was his own choice, as in the case of his cousin Alexander Mikhailovich, or whether it was something he was told he had to do. His intelligent and cultured father, so gruff and rude to most of the outside world, was a loving parent and probably would not have forced Cyril to go to sea against his will.

In 1892 Cyril went on the first of several training cruises, his first time to be away from his immediate family. The training ship was the *Moryak*, an old hulk that ended its life as a restaurant on the Neva River in St. Petersburg. The other training ships were not much better. While the Grand Duke had separate quarters on them, he was treated equal with his fellow midshipmen in every other respect, except that he did not have to take his final oral exams with them. The examiners came to the Vladimir Palace, which was even worse because Cyril had to perform in the presence of his father. Fortunately, he passed. Also, before being commissioned, he was detached for a cruise on the new battleship *Ryurik*, for the opening of the Kiel Canal in Germany. The Kaiser invited him aboard his yacht and decorated him with an order. A year later, at the 1896 coronation, Cyril was commissioned sub-lieutenant, and had to take the double ceremonial oath of allegiance obligatory to all members of the dynasty.

The Grand Duke was a tall, fine-looking man, with an elongated face, heavy moustache and dark hair, and he was an elegant dresser..

Grand Duke Nicholas Mikhailovich, in a letter to a friend in Paris, described Cyril as ". . . . a pompous fool, but with a charming wife. . . ."[1]

Some insight into Grand Duke Cyril's character can be obtained from his memoirs, *My Life in Russia's Service, Then and Now*, published in 1939. In describing the coronation of Nicholas II in 1896, Cyril does not mention the tragedy at Khodynka Field, in which thousands were trampled to death through poor planning, except as the sole glitch in an otherwise perfectly organized event. The reader has no clue as to what happened. Not having mentioned it, he could hardly blame his uncle, Grand Duke Serge Alexandrovich, the Governor General of Moscow, for it. In fact, he calls Serge (the most universally disliked grand duke) his favorite uncle, a man of "the loftiest principles" and a character of "the rarest nobility." Were they kindred souls? Or, perhaps, has Serge been misjudged? It is interesting to note that Grand Duchess George, a cousin and a very straitlaced lady, was also not unkind to Grand Duke Serge.

Cyril, in his book, also failed to mention the revolution of 1905, except in a short aside when writing about 1914. Finally, while he has plenty of sharp remarks about the deficiencies of the Russian navy from 1892 through the Russo-Japanese War, it never seems to occur to him that another uncle whom he loved, the genial Alexis Alexandrovich, was grand admiral of the navy for this entire period. Of course, Uncle Alexis did his nephew a couple of important favors.

After being commissioned, Cyril went through some infantry training in the Guards, and was assigned to the Naval Guards, a curious unit, not marines, but sailors, some of whom were organized

---

1. *Secrets of Dethroned Royalty*, Princess Radziwill

as infantry battalions and others as crews for certain ships and the imperial yachts. In 1897 Cyril sailed in the new and well-designed battleship *Rossiya* to the naval review honoring the diamond jubilee of Queen Victoria. It was at this time, in England, that he met his future wife, Victoria Melita, daughter of Queen Victoria's second son Alfred, Duke of Edinburgh and Alexander II's daughter Marie. Victoria Melita was thus Cyril's first cousin, and was at that time married to the Grand Duke of Hesse, the brother of Empress Alexandra.

From this Spithead Review, the *Rossiya*, with Cyril aboard sailed for the Far East, through the Suez Canal, arriving at the new Russian base at Port Arthur in 1898. Cyril remarks that it was a very poor harbor from a naval point of view. Relations with Japan were already strained, but the ship stopped at Nagasaki on its way to Vladivostok. This was a splendid harbor, but coal had to be imported from Wales by the agents of the tycoon, Baron Ginzburg, even though it was available everywhere in the area, and could be picked up by hand. The trans-Siberian railroad was just being finished, and Cyril took the opportunity for seeing something of Siberia. He was then sent back to Japan as a good will gesture to see the Emperor. Cyril was a great success there, according to the Russian ambassador, and he was charmed by the country.

Leaving Japan, Cyril was ordered to return to Russia via the United States, which he breezed through very quickly, in a hurry to get back to Europe. He spent two days in Chicago and a week in New York. Unlike Japan, the United States made little impression on him, other than the theaters and night clubs of New York, and the fact that reporters pestered him all the time.

In 1901 Cyril served for a time in the Black Sea fleet aboard the *Rostislav*, commanded by his father's cousin, Grand Duke Alexander Mikhailovich. Here was a unique situation—two grand dukes serving aboard the same ship. Both survived the revolution, and were the only grand dukes to write autobiographies. The two books differ so widely in describing the same people and the same events, that one has to wonder how the two of them got on confined to one ship together. Neither book gives any hint about this. They got on well enough, apparently, as Cyril was invited to Alexander's Crimean estate, Ay Todor, and he also stayed with Alexander's brother, Nicholas Mikhailovich, at Borjomi in Georgia. From there he made a trip to Tiflis, the capital of the Caucasian vice-royalty, with its kaleidoscope of fascinating nationalities and tribes.

Cyril also attended gunnery school, another collection of old hulks, but with modern guns and commanded by the brilliant Admiral Rozhestvensky, who was fated to lead the Baltic Fleet to its doom at Tsushima in 1905. By way of relief from gunnery training, Cyril was taken to a family gathering at Wolfsgarten, near Darmstadt, the country estate of the Hesse and by Rhine family. Nicholas II and Alexandra were both there. It was Alexandra's childhood home, and Cyril writes that he had never seen her so gay and carefree. The hostess was none other than Victoria Melita, then still Grand Duchess of Hesse and by Rhine, who was known in the family as "Ducky." It was here that she and Cyril supposedly fell in love.

Once, while visiting Russia with her husband, Ducky was observed dancing frequently with Cyril, and vanished from the party with him. It is strongly hinted that at least one of her children born during her marriage with the Grand Duke of Hesse was in fact fathered by Cyril (a son was stillborn, a daughter died as a child). Cyril's father, Grand Duke Vladimir, argued with the Tsar that his son "had been seduced by a married woman."[2]

Grand Duke Cyril had a season in St. Petersburg after this, serving again with the Naval Guards. He comments that the Imperial Court was the best organized thing in Russia, run by a special ministry, really a state within a state, managing, however, to be charming without excess show.

A transfer to the *Peresvyet*, a new ship just being fitted in the Baltic, gave Cyril the chance to see quite a bit of Ducky on motoring trips in Europe. He was an enthusiastic motorist in those embryonic days of the automobile. Obviously, marriage was being discussed between them. According to Cyril, Ducky's mother's Orthodox chaplain assured them that nothing in Canon Law would prevent their marriage. If this is true, he was a curious priest, because marriage between first cousins is strictly forbidden in the church. Cyril conveniently omits mentioning that they were first cousins, although it is easy enough to figure out by the information provided, i. e., that Ducky was the daughter of Cyril's aunt.

In 1902 the *Peresvyet* set out for Port Arthur with Grand Duke Cyril aboard, and promptly ran aground off Jutland. The *Peresvyet* was a cross between a cruiser and a battleship, with the disadvantages of both and the advantages of neither, and it was staffed with a complement of bad officers and an amiable but totally incompetent captain. In France, Ducky came aboard. She was newly divorced from her husband, and hence exiled from Hesse. Both were aware that there would be many troubles ahead of them before any marriage was possible.

After more disasters, the *Peresvyet* made it to Port Arthur, where it was greeted by the admiral who administered a tongue lashing to the captain in front of his officers. Port Arthur had changed dramatically since Cyril's earlier visit. A town had grown up, and feverish work was in progress on formidable fortifications.

---

2. *Alexander III*, C. Lowe

Secrets of Dethroned Royalty, Princess Radziwill

Cyril called on the Empress of China in Beijing, as a good will gesture after the troubles of the Boxer Rebellion. In a most complicated court ritual, he was carried to the inner court in a sedan chair. There was none of the Europeanized procedures in China such as Japan had adopted for visiting foreign royalty.

A telegram arrived from the Emperor ordering Cyril to remain in the Far East. To Cyril it was obvious that this was a move to keep him and Ducky from seeing each other. However, Grand Admiral Grand Duke Alexis came to the rescue, assigning Cyril as lieutenant-commander aboard the *Nakhimov*, a ship which had been in the Far East for five years and was due to return to Europe. Cyril made another official call, this time to the Emperor of Korea, a potentate whose throne would be abolished by the Japanese a few years later.

The *Nakhimov* was manned by Naval Guards, many of them known to Cyril. Her captain was excellent, but after a visit to Hanoi, the captain had a stroke and Grand Duke Cyril found himself in command. The captain was removed to Saigon, a "wretched hole," and died there.

All of this took three weeks, during which time Cyril would not grant shore leave to the crew because of a dysentery epidemic, which could be fatal to a ship. It is not clear why it was all right for the officers to go ashore. The crew was in a state of near mutiny, kept in line, luckily, by a very good chief petty officer. Things were better at Singapore, where the *Nakhimov* was very popular for providing the town with its excellent civilian orchestra, made up of hopeless drunks who were made to sleep in empty coal bunkers so they would not disturb the rest of the ship. When the *Nakhimov* stopped at Naples, Cyril's father was there to try to talk his son into giving up Ducky. Grand Duke Valdimir's heart wasn't in it, however, and when Cyril insisted, he became very supportive. There was a reunion with Ducky at Nice.

After a stop at Lisbon, where Cyril called on King Carlos, the *Nakhimov* steamed back to Kronstadt. With the Emperor's permission, Cyril then spent a summer with Ducky in Coburg, where her mother lived, leaving to hurry back to Russia in 1904 when the Japanese attacked Port Arthur.

Grand Duke Cyril was assigned to the staff of Admiral Makarov, Russia's finest and most energetic admiral, who flew his flag on the *Petropavlovsk*. Cyril reached Port Arthur via the Trans-Siberian railroad, still a single track line. It was a long journey, as the line was overloaded with troop trains. The track around Lake Baikal was still incomplete, so the passengers rode troikas over the ice to a temporary tavern. After warming up with vodka, coaches were hauled by horses over the tracks the rest of the way, the ice not being firm enough for locomotives.

Admiral Makarov's strategy was to break out of Port Arthur

and join his ships to those in Vladivostok. Together they might have formed a powerful enough force which, while unable to knock out the superior Japanese fleet in a general engagement, could have seriously interfered with their land operations on the Asian continent. This would have altered the course of the war, but luck was not with the Russians. In April 1904, as the Port Arthur squadron made its way out of the harbor one by one to engage the Japanese squadron, the flagship *Petropavlovsk* hit a mine and sank immediately, rolling over on its port side. Cyril, standing on the bridge, was able to jump down onto one turret, then another, and dive off the starboard side where there was much less suction. He was one of only eighty persons, out of 631 aboard, to survive. Admiral Makarov perished, as did one of Russia's most famous artists, Vereshchagin, who was aboard as a war correspondent, to sketch the action.

One of Grand Duke Cyril's fellow officers who survived, Lt. (later Captain) Vladimir Petrovich Shmitt, a staunch monarchist until he died in New York in 1965, could not stand Grand Duke Cyril and considered him a poor officer who did not take care of his men. Cyril had managed to make himself generally unpopular by this time, and there were even rumors that he had offered sailors gold to save him while he was in the water. Whatever the truth, Cyril was the only grand duke ever to be wounded in action. His face was burned, some muscles pulled, and he suffered, according to his own account, from shell shock. Grand Duke Alexander thought that Cyril became a changed man after this experience. He began to believe in his "star of destiny."

Cyril returned to European Russia via the Trans-Siberian, on which he had a special car with its own galley. In St. Petersburg, he had an interview with the Emperor. Curiously, Nicholas II did not ask him about the *Petropavlovsk* or even the war, but allowed him to go to Coburg for another summer with Ducky. This was followed by some boring staff work at the Admiralty in St. Petersburg. The disasters on sea and land in the Far East were followed by the ill-conceived dispatch of the Baltic Fleet to the Far East, around Africa, which ended in its destruction in the Straits of Tsushima. Cyril, like almost everybody in the navy, opposed the plan, stating that the Admiralty was "unusually negligent" in allowing it to go through, but the press forced the issue, and, of course, made good reading for the Japanese. Cyril states that he wanted to go back to Vladivostok, but there was no point to it after the battle of Tsushima (which occurred thirteen months after the sinking of the *Petropavlovsk*). Cyril needed treatment for "nerves," as he states, in Germany.

On 8 October 1905, without permission of the Emperor, mandatory for all members of the imperial family, or of his father, Grand Duke Cyril married Victoria Melita at Tegernsee in Germany. Returning to St. Petersburg, Cyril was "dumbfounded" at the suddenness and severity of his punishment. He was stripped of all his military rank and ordered to leave Russia within forty-eight hours; Ducky was not recognized as a Grand Duchess, and, in fact, the marriage was illegal under Romanov law for purposes of the succession statutes. The punishment was perhaps severe and unexpected in that the Emperor had twice allowed him to go to Coburg, but Cyril knew the rules—he had not asked permission. Furthermore, Victoria Melita was his first cousin, a degree of consanguinity strictly prohibited by the Orthodox Church; and, a divorcée—and from the brother of Empress Alexandra, of all people!

Grand Duke Vladimir stormed into the presence of Emperor Nicholas II, where he created a terrific row, threatening to resign all of his own positions if the ban was not lifted, and the marriage recognized. By this time, Nicholas II had learned to say no to his formidable uncles. Nicholas' sister, Grand Duchess Olga wrote that "Nicky was adamant, and would not yield . . . calling the marriage 'semi-legal,' although he did later allow Cyril to return." While Grand Duke Cyril was restored to military rank and Ducky was recognized as a Grand Duchess, there is no known record that Nicholas II granted retroactive permission changing the status of the marriage from "semi-legitimate" to "legitimate." The two daughters of Cyril were listed as members of the Imperial Family.

It was a pleasant exile for Cyril. They were very happy wintering at Cannes and motoring about Europe visiting people. In 1907 Ducky converted to Orthodoxy just in time for the birth of their first child, Princess Marie, at Coburg. A second child, Princess Kira, was born in Paris in 1909. The exile ended in 1909, and Grand Duke Cyril was allowed to return to Russia just in time for his father's funeral. He had been allowed to return briefly the year before to attend another funeral, that of his Uncle Alexis.

Cyril was now appointed executive officer of the cruiser *Oleg*, and promoted to captain in 1910. He then spent two years at the higher naval school. Finally, in 1910, the family were united on Russian soil, and were given use of the Cavalier's House at Tsarskoye Selo.

In 1912 Cyril was given command of the *Oleg*, but soon had to leave, overcome by what he calls the "devils" and "holy terrors" of the sea from his experiences in the sinking of the *Petropavlovsk*. Even so, he ordered a yacht made for himself in England. While the "holy terrors" prevented him from crossing the Channel to England to see the yacht, they did not prevent him from later cruising on it in the Baltic!

With the outbreak of war in 1914, Ducky organized an ambulance service while Cyril joined the naval detachment on the staff of the supreme commander, Grand Duke Nicholas Nikolayevich. In 1916 he was promoted to rear admiral and put in command of some naval sappers who were mining lakes, and later the same year was given command of the Naval Guards in St. Petersburg.

After the murder of Rasputin, Cyril was one of the members of the Imperial Family to see Grand Duke Dimitri Pavlovich and express solidarity with him, an episode that he totally omits from his memoirs. In fact, he tries to play down the importance of Rasputin's influence.

The most notorious episode in Cyril's life occurred after the start of the February Revolution of 1917. On 14 March he led his Naval Guards, which he commanded, to the Tauride Palace to pledge allegiance to the Duma. He marched at the head of this force, many of whom had served as crew of the Emperor's yacht, and were one of the last effective military bodies in the capital on whom the Emperor might have relied. This was the day before the abdication of Emperor Nicholas II. After this act, breaking his oath to the Tsar, Grand Duke Cyril returned to his palace and raised the red flag above it. He was the only member of the Imperial Family to betray his oath and go over to the revolution.

His justification for his action was as follows: The call of the already formed provisional government for troops to declare themselves in favor of it put him in a difficult position. As the commander of the only remaining well-organized troops in the capital, he decided to lead them himself to do this, in the hopes of restoring law and order in St. Petersburg, and to give the Emperor time to return with loyal troops from the front.

What Grand Duke Cyril fails to say is that he wore a big red bow on his uniform. The daughter of the future White hero, General Wrangel, watched Cyril march with the naval guards and remembers this clearly, as she recently told Princess Vera Constantinovna. She was by no means the only witness. He also hoisted a red flag on the roof of his palace, and later, during Kerensky's short period of power, Princess Vera, who played with Cyril's little girls, remembers his wearing a uniform without shoulder boards (which were still worn until the Bolshevik takeover) with some sort of sleeve insignia instead. Princess Vera, then eleven years old, recalls how unpleasantly this struck her.

Grand Duke Cyril went home from the Duma episode in his car, without the Naval Guards. He says that the abdication of the Emperor was the saddest day of his life. At this point he resigned his command and was lifted on the shoulders of his enthusiastic men. Again, what Grand Duke Cyril does not tell us in his memoirs, is that he was deeply involved, along with his mother, in a plot to overthrow the Tsar and force him to abdicate many months earlier. His mother, Grand Duchess Marie Pavlovna, even approached Rodzianko, the President of the Duma, with the proposition that Empress Alexandra "had to be annihilated."[3]

In his Political Memoirs, the French Ambassador, Paléologue, wrote on 9 January 1917, "Prince Gabriel Constantinovich gave a supper for his mistress, formerly an actress. The guests included the Grand Duke Boris . . . a few officers and a squad of elegant courtesans. During the evening the only topic was the conspiracy—the regiments of the Guard which can be relied on, the most favorable moment for the outbreak, etc. And all this with the servants moving about, harlots looking on and listening, gypsies singing and the whole company bathed in the aroma of Moët and Chandon Brut Impérial which flowed in streams." The forced abdication was to be in favor of the Emperor's son, Alexis, with Grand Duke Nicholas as regent. As the Grand Duchess said, the Tsesarevich was ill, and would not live long . . . leaving her son, Cyril, the heir and future Emperor.

In June of 1917, Kerensky allowed Cyril and his family to leave by train for Finland along with two English nurses and some servants, crates of personal possessions and jewels. They went to an estate near Borgo, where they had often stayed. On 30 August 1917 Cyril's only son, Prince Vladimir Kirillovich, was born in Finland. Later there were some rough moments as the Finnish civil war raged around them, but then came German troops and the eventual victory of the Finnish Whites under Mannerheim, and they were safe again.

In 1920 Cyril, his wife, and their three children left Finland to go to the south of France through Germany. They still had an apartment in Paris that they had maintained throughout the war. There was also a villa in Coburg left to them by Ducky's mother, their own jewels, and those of his mother. The Cyril family was well set. Cyril resumed his hobby of motoring, became an avid golfer, and bought a villa in Brittany at St. Briac, where the family settled permanently in 1928.

There was an unwritten agreement among the surviving Romanovs that while the Dowager Empress still lived, nobody would make claims on the throne, one reason being that the Empress would not acknowledge the murder of her sons. In violation of this understanding, in August 1924, Grand Duke Cyril issued a 'manifesto' proclaiming himself "Guardian of the Throne," which he followed up a month later with another manifesto naming himself Emperor of all the Russias, and his son, Prince Vladimir Kirillovich as Tsesarevich, Heir, and Grand Duke. It followed, of course, that Victoria Melita became Empress and their two daughters grand duchesses.

By 1924 there were thousands of Russian emigrés all over Europe, particularly in Paris, Yugoslavia, Berlin, and Prague. The

---

3. *Krusheniye Imperii*, M. V. Rodzianko

survivors of General Wrangel's White Army still retained their organizations. Numerous other organizations had sprung up, including a Supreme Monarchist Council. To Cyril's chagrin he got very little support. General Goleyevsky, the head of a monarchist movement in Russia, in 1917, had already recognized Grand Duke Dimitri as heir after Nicholas II and Tsesarevich Alexis, and the General stated in doing so that "Vladimir, Boris, and Andrew (Cyril's father and brothers) had "no claim to the throne because their mother was not Orthodox as required by the Pauline Law."[4] General Wrangel refused to recognize him also, which was hardly surprising, for whatever the Baron's personal feelings about monarchy, he was the last head of a movement that was not restorationist. All White armies had fought against the Bolsheviks usurpation of power, and for a return to the popularly elected Constituent Assembly which the Bolsheviks' had crushed.

More surprising was the fact that the Supreme Monarchist Council also did not support Cyril. Of the seven other surviving grand dukes, Cyril was naturally supported by his brothers Boris and Andrew, and surprisingly, by Alexander Mikhailovich. The grand duke with the greatest seniority in age, the greatest personal accomplishments, and the greatest respect in the emigration was the former commander-in-chief, Nicholas Nikolayevich, who also lived in France. He would not give Cyril the time of day, and rejected all of Cyril's approaches to him. The Empress Marie ridiculed Cyril's claim, and stated that his father, Grand Duke Vladimir, had renounced his and his descendants rights to the throne, although Vladimir had always denied this.

Even so, why all of this opposition to Cyril's proclamation? In 1924 the emigration still hoped for the fall of the Soviet regime, and many were actively working for this; there was a White army still capable of being reassembled to take advantage of any suitable situation. Among these people, unified by little else than their hatred of the Bolsheviks, there was a strong feeling that it was politically disastrous to be tarred by a restorationist brush; a great opportunity for the Bolsheviks to represent them all as working under the banner of a shadow emperor at St. Briac, which would also have scared off help from foreign governments; and a feeling that the emigration must not pre-support any specific form of government, a question that must be decided in Russia itself. The future of monarchy, if any, must be decided there, as well as the identity of the monarch. This was the prevailing view.

In addition to all this, there was the odium attached to the figure of Grand Duke Cyril himself, particularly his defection to the Duma before the Emperor's abdication. Whatever his inner

---

4. Br. F.O. W38, No. 3350, #151453

motivation, this was perceived as a deeply dishonorable and self-serving act. Hence, at that stage, Cyril got support only from die-hard legitimist monarchists, and not all of those. Having made his proclamation, the St. Briac "emperor" did not gain any respect by passing out military promotions and noble titles, some of the latter for money.

In 1928 the Dowager Empress Marie died in Denmark. Cyril attended her funeral, being granted honors as head of the family by the King of Denmark, at least according to his memoirs. In 1929 she was followed to the grave by Grand Duke Nicholas Nikolayevich. These deaths, Cyril's son Vladimir has stated, strengthened Cyril's position.

Perhaps they did. Slightly. With the passage of time and the fading of hope that the Bolsheviks were a temporary phenomenon, the minority of emigrés who belonged to monarchist organizations did tend to center on Cyril and, later, his son Vladimir, who was only twenty-one when his father died. Vladimir, at least, could hardly be blamed for his father's past, and had the good sense not to call himself "emperor." He also never gave out any promotions or titles, except for promoting Prince Gabriel Constantinovich to grand ducal status.

Through the late 1920s and until 1938, Cyril put out a number of manifestos addressed to the Russian people which contained sound accounts of what the Bolshevik regime was doing in Russia and promised that a monarchical restoration would not simply be replay of the old monarchy, but would guarantee various rights and privileges such as peasant ownership of land and the rights of national minorities, as well as representative government. He also rejected the idea of freeing Russia with the aid of foreign troops.

In 1934 Cyril and his family went to London to attend the wedding of Cyril's niece, Princess Marina of Greece to George V's son, the Duke of Kent. They stayed at Buckingham Palace. In 1936 Victoria Milita died at the age of sixty. Her death hit Cyril very hard. He himself was not in good health, suffering from arteriosclerosis. As a sick man, he managed to attend the wedding of his daughter Kira to Prince Louis Ferdinand of Prussia, who was to become the head of the House of Hohenzollern and the pretender to the thrones of Prussia and the German Empire. Cyril's other daughter, Princess Marie, had married the Prince of Leinigen in 1925.

Grand Duke Cyril Vladimirovich died at the age of sixty-three on 13 October 1938 at the American Hospital in Paris, and is buried at the Russian cemetery.

GRAND DUKE BORIS VLADIMIROVICH

CHAPTER XXIX

GRAND DUKE BORIS VLADIMIROVICH
(1877 - 1943)

Grand Duke Boris, the second son of Grand Duke Vladimir, was born at St. Petersburg 24 November 1877.

Grand Duke Boris was a handsome, sociable man, who liked to drink and have fun. He was also a world class womanizer, equalled in the Imperial Family perhaps only by his uncle, Grand Duke Alexis. Boris seems to have been born for the express purpose of getting into trouble. He was absolutely unscrupulous, and soon became the terror of jealous husbands as well as of watchful mothers, who were always anxious when he invited one of the daughters to dance.

Thanks to him, the engagement of a young girl very prominent in society, Mademoiselle Demidov, was broken off almost on the eve of her wedding day. Fortunately for her, this did not permanently destroy her happiness because she ultimately married one of the richest men in Russia.

Boris did not mind what the world thought of him and his doings, including the Imperial Family. He had an English country house built for himself at Tsarskoye-Selo, complete with a British butler and coachman. English had been his first language, learned from British nannies in childhood. On some occasions, according to Prince Gabriel Constantinovich, he would be calmly taking a bath when his relatives were all dressed and ready to call on the Emperor.

Another story has Boris courting a married lady which caused much heartburn in the family when this romance nearly got the Grand Duke and the lady into serious trouble. Boris used to meet the lady in the apartment of one of his friends. The janitor was suspicious of these two people stealing into the house with their faces buried in their furs, and he thought it his duty to notify the police of these mysterious visits.

A detective appeared and insisted upon being admitted to the apartment. Grand Duke Boris did not care to disclose his identity to this underling, so he telephoned to the Prefect of the town, General von Wahl. The General was terribly inquisitive, and he insisted upon learning the lady's name, which the Grand Duke was obliged to reveal. Von Wahl was not discreet, and a few days later the whole of St. Petersburg became aware of the adventure.[1]

Boris attempted to win the hand of his cousin, Grand Duchess Olga, the eldest daughter of Nicholas II. The Empress angrily turned him down, expressing her distaste for the proposed marriage in one of her letters to the Emperor. She wrote in September 1916 of: ". . . .giving a pure fresh girl of eighteen years his junior, to a half-worn, blasé . . . man of thirty-eight to live in a house in which many a woman had shared his life!! An inexperienced girl would suffer terribly to have her husband 4th, 5th hand—or more!" This rebuff further strained the relations between the Vladimirs and Nicholas and Alexandra.

When war broke out in 1914, Grand Duke Boris became a Major General, and was at the front in command of the Ataman Cossacks of the Guard, doing a creditable job leading them into action. Thereafter he was attached to general headquarters. Boris had followed a military career of sorts in the Guards before the war. In 1904 he was at Port Arthur watching with horror as Admiral Makarov's flagship *Petropavlovsk* struck a mine and went down with what appeared to be all hands. Boris' brother, Cyril, was aboard, but he was one of the few to be saved. It is not clear what Boris was doing at Port Arthur, other than accompanying a Serbian prince. The prince had proposed boarding the ship, saying it would be fun to watch a naval battle, something one did not see very often. Luckily, Boris was less adventurous than his companion and vetoed the idea.

Boris was as much an anglophobe as his father, Grand Duke Vladimir, had been. On one occasion he got drunk at a regimental mess in the presence of several officers of the British Military Mission and accused the British Army of sitting in its trenches while the French were being massacred. This was not taken kindly by the British officers, and an angry scene took place. The incident was reported to London and Boris was called on the carpet by the Emperor and by General Sir Alfred Knox, commander of the British mission. Sober and chastened, Boris apologized, but no one had doubts about his true feelings.[2]

In the final days of the monarchy, Boris was one of the Grand Dukes who met with his formidable mother, Grand Duchess Marie Pavlovna, to send a letter to Nicholas II asking for lenient treatment for Grand Duke Dimitri Pavlovich and Prince Felix Yusupov after Rasputin's murder. Boris was also heavily involved in the conspiracy

---

1. *At the Russia Court*, E. A. Hodgetts
2. *Prince Felix Yusupov*, Christopher Dobson

of his mother to bring Cyril to the throne. On learning that Grand Duke Michael was planning to accept the Regency for Tsesarevich Alexis, Boris furiously wrote to Grand Duke Paul, "Misha has gone sneaking off to secretly negotiate with Kerensky!"[3]

When Nicholas II abdicated on 2 March 1917, Boris was at Gatchina, and the new Emperor Michael hurried to consult with him, and with Grand Duke George Mikhailovich.

The Grand Duke, along with his brother Andrew, was imprisoned briefly at Kislovodsk in the summer of 1918. By a strange coincidence, the Bolshevik commander sent to execute them had once been a struggling artist in Paris before the war, and Boris had taken pity on him, buying a few pieces so that the artist could eat and buy paints. The Bolshevik recognized his benefactor, and risking his own life, he put the Grand Dukes aboard a Red train from which they somehow made their way to White territory.

In 1919 Boris and his mistress succeeded in leaving Russia from Anapa in the Caucasus by boat through the Black Sea. His mistress, a divorcée named Zinaida ("Zina") Yeliseyeva, was the daughter of General Serge Rashchevsky, who had commanded the fortifications of Port Arthur during the Japanese siege.

Grand Duke Boris sought permission to go to England, but like many of the Romanovs, found himself on a "prohibited list." On 7 January 1919, General Frederick Poole, the British representative in Constantinople, sent a dispatch to the Foreign Office for permission to grant a visa to Boris. This request received a lot of attention. In the margins it is noted, "Ought not Lord Stamfordham [the King's private secretary] be consulted before we reply?"[4]

"We know H.M.'s wishes on the subject. Reply that it is regretted that permission cannot be granted at the present moment."

"I agree. He is no good," are some of the comments.

Boris was refused permission to come to England with impeccable politeness by the Foreign Secretary, Lord Curzon. Because of his and his father's notorious dislike of the British, as well as his sexual adventures, Boris was very unpopular with the British Royal Family. This unpopularity was caused in part by Sir Basil Thomson, Commissioner of Police and head of the Special Branch. Sir Basil had become Director of Intelligence at the Home Office, charged with finding subversives. He prepared weekly reports to the Cabinet on revolutionary organizations, and to him anything less than blind support for England was unacceptable. Both he and Buchanan kept the Cabinet and King fully informed.

Grand Duke Boris and Zinaida went to Italy, were they were married at Genoa on 12 July 1919. There were no children. They

---

3. *Memories of Russia*, Princess Paley

4. *Prince Felix Yusupov*, Christopher Dobson

settled in Paris, where Boris acquired a reputation of being very sociable, a man with "a Russian soul." He liked to drink with the great writer and Nobel Prize winner, Ivan Bunin, at the meetings of General Wrangel's White veterans.[5] He was also a great friend of King Alfonso XIII of Spain, and for a time, before settling in Paris, Boris went to Spain as his guest.

Boris died at Paris, 9 November 1943.

---

5. Testimony, Dr. Nina Bouroff

GRAND DUKE BORIS VLADIMIROVICH

GRAND DUKE ANDREW VLADIMIROVICH

CHAPTER XXX

GRAND DUKE ANDREW VLADIMIROVICH (1879 - 1956)

Grand Duke Andrew was born at Tsarskoye Selo on 14 May 1879, the third and youngest son of Grand Duke Vladimir Alexandrovich. Like his older brother, Boris, he was something of a cut-up in his youth, to the extent that Count Witte, the prime minister, saw fit to complain about this to Grand Duke Michael Alexandrovich, who was a great friend of Andrew. They were almost the same age.

Andrew soon settled down and followed a military career, of no particular distinction. He served in the Guards horse artillery, although he went through courses of military law. In 1907 he and his father went on an official mission to Bulgaria. Andrew, who was quite a joker, succeeded in teasing the Coburg Prince Ferdinand of Bulgaria (later King or Tsar) into a frenzy by appearing in his presence wearing a Turkish decoration. The reason Ferdinand was so furious was because officially he was still a vassal of the Sultan. Ferdinand recovered his composure and became very friendly with Andrew. However, during a second trip to Sofia in 1911, Andrew succeeded in getting Ferdinand's goat again. Andrew recorded these incidents in his diary, fondly remembering them because Ferdinand was joining Germany and Austria in the war against Russia. Andrew's diaries fell into Soviet hands and some of them were published in the Soviet Union in the 1920s.[1]

Grand Duke Andrew was the third grand duke to fall in love with the famous Polish ballerina, Mathilde (Maria Felixovna) Ksheshinska. Her first grand duke had been none other than Tsesarevich Nicholas. Nicholas had been deeply in love with her, and she soon was moved into a house of her own. Nicholas usually arrived, riding horseback, and bringing three of his cousins with him—Grand Dukes Serge, George and Alexander Mikhailovich. Mathilde served them champagne while they sang songs from Georgia.

---

1. *Dnevnik Andreya Vladimirovicha Romanova*

Nicholas and Mathilde parted in 1894, when he became engaged to Princess Alix. Mathilde was not left alone, however, as Grand Duke Serge Mikhailovich remained to console her. Serge bought her a dacha with a garden by the sea, and showered her with jewels.

At the height of her success—she has been ranked with the great Anna Pavlova and Tamara Karsavina—Mathilde met another cousin of Nicholas II, Grand Duke Andrew. Andrew was seven years her junior, and he was following in Nicholas II's footsteps, as well as taking her away from his cousin, Serge. This seemed not to bother Andrew. They went to Biarritz and Venice together, and Andrew bought her a St. Petersburg mansion, showering her with jewels. In 1902, Mathilde gave birth to a son who was named Vladimir. In later life, Vladimir said he was not sure whether his father was Andrew, or Grand Duke Serge Mikhailovich. Nicholas continued to visit Mathilde after he was Tsar, supposedly on a friendly basis, and received "good advice" from her.

In 1914 Grand Duke Andrew joined General Ruzsky's staff at the headquarters of the Northwest Front, later transferring to General Headquarters. In 1915 he was appointed to the command of the Guards horse artillery. This did not mean very much, since its batteries were scattered in various places, and were not a united command.

As the revolution neared in 1916, it was at Andrew's palace on the Admiralty Embankment that a meeting was called, at the initiative of Grand Duke Paul Alexandrovich, attended by Andrew's mother, Grand Duchess Vladimir, his brothers, and Grand Duke Alexander Mikhailovich. The purpose of the meeting was to try to get the Emperor not to be too harsh on Paul's son, Grand Duke Dimitri, and Alexander's son-in-law, Prince Felix Yusupov, for their part in Rasputin's murder.

After the revolution and abdication, Andrew was arrested briefly in 1918, and imprisoned by the Bolsheviks in Kislovodsk along with his brother Boris. Later, Andrew made his way to the White controlled territory in the south, where he was reunited with Mathilde and their son. Eventually, he left Russia with his mother, Grand Duchess Marie Pavlovna, on an Italian ship from Novorosiysk. This was February 1920, and Andrew was thus the last grand duke to leave Russian soil.

In January 1921, Andrew and Mathilde were married at Cannes, France. At the age of forty-nine, Mathilde finally had her grand duke, the one who had been faithful to her throughout, and their son, Vladimir, who had left Russia with them, was finally legitimized at the age of nineteen. Thereafter he was known as Prince Romanovsky-Krasinsky, though he later called himself Prince Vladimir Romanov. He died unmarried in 1972.

The family lived modestly in Paris, where Andrew was remembered shopping in the food market with his shopping bag and enjoying games of bridge, as long as they were for small stakes.

Mathilde, whose house in St. Petersburg had once been Lenin's headquarters, now taught dancing in Paris, and, among many others, instructed Margot Fonteyn. In 1936, at the age of sixty-three she danced in a jubilee performance at Covent Garden. She died in Paris in 1971, eight months short of her one hundredth birthday.

Grand Duke Andrew was the only grand duke to support the claim of Anna Anderson to be Nicholas II's youngest daughter Anastasia. For doing so, he got into trouble with other members of the family, including his brother Cyril, who had declared himself emperor. Andrew was very persistent about this, conducting a wide correspondence and trying to raise money for her hospital bills. He was particularly surprised at the virulence with which some relatives, particularly the Hesse-Darmstadt family, opposed this claim. In spite of his activity in her behalf, Andrew did not actually meet Anna Anderson until 1928, and then declared himself absolutely convinced that she was Anastasia. "Dear Olga," he wrote to Nicholas II's sister, ". . . . I spent two days with her. I observed her closely . . . I must acknowledge that Anastasia Tschaikovsky is no one other than my niece, Grand Duchess Anastasia Nicolaievna. I recognized her at once. . ."

Grand Duke Andrew implied that there was far more to the story than merely the escape of one grand duchess. He declared in 1956, before his death, that his dossier on the "Anastasia" affair should not be opened to the public until the Kremlin, the estate of Kaiser Wilhelm, and the German War Office released their papers. "There is no doubt, Andrew wrote, "that there exists a vital basic relationship between the tragic events of March 1917 and the present circumstances . . . I am convinced that this investigation will lead us steadily back to Ekaterinburg, Tobolsk, the events of 1917 and even further." There is no hint of what Andrew knew, and upon his death his papers were immediately seized by his brother, Grand Duke Cyril.

Grand Duke Andrew died in Paris on 30 October 1956. He was one of the two longest living Romanov males at the time of his death, equaled only by his great uncle, Michael Nikolayevich, who was almost exactly the same age when he died, seventy-seven.

GRAND DUKE DIMITRI PAVLOVICH

GRAND DUKE DIMITRI PAVLOVICH

GRAND DUKE DIMITRI and GRAND DUCHESS MARIE

CHAPTER XXXI

GRAND DUKE DIMITRI PAVLOVICH
(1891 - 1942)

Grand Duke Dimitri was the youngest of the Grand Dukes, with the exception of Nicholas II's son, Alexis. He was born at Ilyinskoye, near Moscow, 18 September 1891, the second child of Grand Duke Paul Alexandrovich and Grand Duchess Alexandra. Sixteen months earlier, his mother had given birth to a daughter, Marie Pavlovna, but this time Alexandra went into a coma when she was seven months pregnant, and died three days after Dimitri's birth. She was only twenty-one years old.

In the efforts to save Alexandra's life, the feeble infant, delivered by a midwife, was forgotten for a while, and his life was almost lost. Despite this inauspicious entry into the world, the boy grew up well-formed, tall, and handsome. From photographs, it is arguable that he was the best looking of all the Grand Dukes. At the opening of the first Duma at the Winter Palace when Dimitri was fourteen, Grand Duke Serge Mikhailovich remarked that Dimitri looked as if he had been made by Fabergé.[1]

Circumstances conspired to deprive the two children of a normal family life, and made Dimitri and his sister Marie extraordinarily close for their entire lives. Until 1902 they lived with their widowed father, who was very affectionate, but leading a military and social life, he had little time to devote to them. Their early lives were entirely controlled by two Englishwomen, "Nanny" Fry and her assistant, Lizzie Grove, and they spoke nothing but English for several years. Their winters were spent in St. Petersburg in their father's large, rather non-descript palace on the Neva. In the spring, for the maneuvers of the Guards, they would move to an apartment in the Catherine, or "large" palace at Tsarskoye Selo, and then spend their summers at Ilyinskoye with their uncle and aunt, Grand Duke Serge and Elizabeth, sister of the Empress. Ilyinskoye was a 2400

---

1. *V Mramornom Dvortse,* Prince Gabriel Constantinovich

acre estate about forty miles from Moscow on the Moscow River. Dimitri occasionally played with a somewhat older boy from a neighboring estate, Prince Felix Yusupov, but most of his games were played with his sister, who, fortunately, preferred Dimitri's toy soldiers to dolls. He was a lively, humorous boy. During the springs at Tsarskoye Selo, Emperor Nicholas II and his family, were extremely hospitable to the two semi-orphans, and, as time went by, the Emperor became deeply attached to Dimitri, and treated him more like a son than a cousin. In 1901, Dimitri acquired a tutor, General Laiming, a most fortunate choice, since his warm and close family provided some company and attention to Marie and Dimitri. This routine was suddenly cut short in 1902 when their father, Grand Duke Paul, married morganatically without the Emperor's permission, and was exiled from Russia. Both children took this very hard, and, as if it wasn't enough in itself, they were officially made wards of their uncle, Grand Duke Serge Alexandrovich and his wife. They now moved to Moscow, where Serge was governor-general. Their father was not allowed the slightest say in their upbringing. In the next three years, they only saw him once while on a trip abroad.

Their life in Moscow was spent at the familiar Ilyinskoye, and two other estates, but also in the Governor General's palace in Moscow, and, during the revolutionary troubles of 1905, in the Kremlin. While their uncle and foster-father really loved the children, he insisted on prompt, unquestioning obedience, and they were scared of him. Their Aunt Elizabeth, called Ella, was childless herself, and was cold and snappy to them, as if resenting their presence, a strange reaction on the part of a deeply religious woman who would one day be canonized by the church.

This new life was again cut short by the revolution of 1905. They moved into the Kremlin for greater safety, which did not prevent their hearing shooting and explosions, giving them a feeling of danger and dread. On one occasion, unknown to themselves at the time, Dimitri and Marie came very close to death. They were riding in a carriage with their uncle, and it was this fact that stopped a revolutionary terrorist from giving the signal to throw a bomb. Later, their uncle was not so lucky. A bomb was thrown, and he was blown to bits. Marie and Dimitri had to attend the church service immediately afterwards, and they saw their Aunt Ella with her dress soaked in Serge's blood. For the official funeral, their father was allowed to return to Russia, and he made an attempt to recover the children, but Ella would have none of it. She did, however, change her attitude toward the children, but with limited impression on them, particularly Marie. It is interesting to note that immediately after the assassination, as Dimitri and Marie sat together wondering about their future, Dimitri remarked, "Will we be happier now?"

In view of Ella's religious inclinations, as well as the devout nature of his Uncle Serge, Dimitri had a curious lack of knowledge of church ritual.[2]

For awhile, they were sent to Tsarskoye Selo for greater safety, and again the Emperor took them under his wing. They took their meals together at the Alexander Palace, and Nicholas frequently kept Dimitri at his side.

Back in Moscow, Ella was determined to retire to a religious life, which she could not do with the two children to care for. Dimitri was no problem, as he was soon to be off to military training, but Marie was. Ella decided that the solution was marriage, and she set out without delay to arrange this. The candidate selected was Prince William of Sweden, the second son of King Gustav V. William soon arrived in Moscow, and Dimitri took an immediate dislike to the extremely tall, thin, and humorless youth. Marie was not more impressed. William, however, was quite taken with Marie, and he proposed.

Grand Duchess Marie refused to make a commitment, insisting that she would not consent without her father's approval. Ella informed her coldly that her father had no say in the matter. Marie was having none of this, and continued in her refusal, and finally Ella had to write to Grand Duke Paul. He was not in favor of the marriage, but would not stand in the way provided that Marie agreed, and that the marriage did not take place until she was eighteen.

With this conditional approval, Marie consented. The marriage took place in 1908, and one son was born, the present Count Lennart Bernadotte.

Grand Duke Paul was allowed to return to Russia for the wedding, and brought with him his morganatic wife,

Marie and William spent their honeymoon in Venice and Biarritz, stopping in Paris on the way home to see Grand Duke Paul. There they found Dimitri, being somewhat mysterious about his plans. The reason soon became clear. When the couple reached Stockholm, there was Dimitri again. It was the first of several visits. He still could not stand to be long parted from Marie.

It soon was time for Dimitri to enter the cavalry school, where he worked very hard, which somewhat affected his health, as he was never too robust. But he was a first rate horseman, and was commissioned in the Horse Guards. The young guards officer was described as tall, elegant, well-built, with thoughtful, somewhat mystical eyes, and always ready for escapades.

He and his childhood friend Felix Yusupov did the usual St. Petersburg routine of ballerinas, including the famous Anna Pavlova, and Gypsies until Dimitri was told to stop seeing so much of Felix,

---

2. *V. Mramornom Dvortse*, Prince Gabriel Constantinovich

whose reputation was rather unsavory.

In 1912, Dimitri's father was forgiven his transgressions and allowed to return to Russia with his new family—a boy and two girls. They built a house for themselves at Tsarskoye Selo. Meanwhile Dimitri, for greater independence from not only his father, but his doting sovereign, moved into a palace of his own at the Anichkov Bridge in St. Petersburg.

Dimitri rode with the Russian Horse team at the 1912 Stockholm Olympics, and the following year he was chairman of the first Russian Olympiad, held in Kiev, where, as one relative put it, he conducted himself as an old professional at the age of twenty-two.

The world was Dimitri's oyster at this time. He was young, handsome, charming, leading an independent life, driving 100-horsepower automobiles, a national hero because of the Olympics, great wealth, the favorite of the Tsar—almost a second son—who, with his children, was often reduced to tears laughing at Dimitri's jokes. There was hardly another prince in Europe who could compare with him. Yet, Dimitri had a serious side. When Stolypin, Russia's last great statesman, was assassinated in 1911, Dimitri was shocked at the apparent indifference of the Emperor and Empress to this tragic event.

In 1914, Dimitri's fabulously rich friend Felix Yusupov married the beautiful Princess Irina, the daughter of Grand Duke Alexander Mikhailovich and Grand Duchess Xenia Alexandrovna, the Emperor's sister. According to Felix, Grand Duke Dimitri was also in love with Irina, but she preferred Felix, and this caused a cooling off in their relations.[3]

Another historical event put an end to this short, ideal period in Dimitri's life. World War I. Unlike many other officers who could not restrain their enthusiasm, Dimitri took the outbreak of war gravely. On 4 August 1914, he left for East Prussia with the Horse Guards, and was in action within a few days. He took part in a charge in which the regiment captured a German battery, and he rescued a wounded corporal, took him to the rear on his horse, and then returned to action. For this gallantry under fire, Dimitri received the Cross of St. George. Half of the regiment's officers were killed.

Dimitri then became a liaison officer with Rennenkampf's ill-fated army, and by 1915 was at General Headquarters where his father's cousin, Grand Duke Nicholas Nikolayevich was in command. When Dimitri heard that the Emperor intended to relieve the Grand Duke and take over personal command of the army, Dimitri made a dash for Tsarskoye Selo, unknown to Grand Duke Nicholas, to attempt to persuade the Emperor not to do so. Dimitri was not unaware of the special position he held with the Emperor, and was

---

3. *Lost Splendour*, Prince Felix Yusupov

not averse to taking decisive action. This time, apparently the Emperor realized what was afoot, and Dimitri experienced some difficulty in seeing Nicholas. Finally, he was received and made his plea. The Emperor thanked him for his frankness, and embraced him. Dimitri was sure that he had carried the day, but two days later, Nicholas II took personal command, a fact which Dimitri learned from the newspapers. Nevertheless, Nicholas II sent for Dimitri and made him an aide-de-camp at General Headquarters.

In 1916, the Emperor gave Dimitri a telegram to send, in which he refused to meet with a delegation of the rural and town councils, who were pleading for the Duma to be reconvened. Dimitri, on his own, deliberately failed to send the telegram. He was kicked out of General Headquarters for this, but later was more or less forgiven and called back.[4]

How could a Grand Duke, and a very young one at that, take such steps which would have landed any other in exile? It was obvious that Dimitri was deeply involved in thinking about politics by this time, and he could see, as most people could, that things were going from bad to worse. Unlike some of the grand dukes, who intrigued only in their own little circles, and tended to their assigned fiefs, Dimitri was capable of seeing the big picture, and was unafraid to take action.

One of the most serious problems of the day, and which Dimitri was seriously concerned about, was Rasputin.

This "holy man," a Siberian peasant with hypnotic eyes, had been around the court since 1907, though Dimitri had never met him. He exercised a tremendous influence over Empress Alexandra, because he seemed to be able to alleviate the pain caused by the Tsesarevich's hemophilia. She came to look upon him as a holy prophet, and a true voice of the common people. While acting the holy man at Tsarskoye Selo, Rasputin indulged his sexual appetites freely in other places. The Emperor was always skeptical of Rasputin, but knew how much he meant to the Empress, and so did not have the heart or the strength to get rid of him. All this was not so threatening until the Emperor took command of the armies in 1915, leaving the Empress in charge in the capital. At this point she took Rasputin's advice in political matters, appointing and relieving ministers at his whim. By mid-1916, this whole state of affairs had become a national scandal.

So it was not difficult for Prince Felix Yusupov to recruit Grand Duke Dimitri into a plot to murder Rasputin. According to Felix, Dimitri said, in December 1916, that he had thought of killing Rasputin for months. The plot also included a well-known right-wing member of the Duma, Purishkevich, an officer called Sukhotin, and a

---

4. *Education of a Princess*, Grand Duchess Marie Pavlovna, New York 1930.

Doctor Lazovert. Cyanide was decided upon as the method of murder, the doctor obtaining enough to kill a dozen men. The bait was to be Felix's beautiful wife, whom Rasputin wanted to meet, and who was actually in the Crimea at the time.

The bait worked. Late on the night of 29 December 1916, Felix went to fetch Rasputin and brought him back to his house on the Moika Canal. There, in a downstairs room, Felix spent two hours getting Rasputin to eat and drink, feeding him poisoned cakes and wine. Meanwhile, Dimitri and the other conspirators were upstairs pretending to have a party, playing *Yankee Doodle* on the gramophone. The cyanide merely made Rasputin sleepy and groggy, so Felix dashed upstairs, grabbed Dimitri's revolver, descended again and shot Rasputin through the heart. Dr. Lazovert came down, felt Rasputin's pulse, and pronounced him dead. Then, according to the plan, Dimitri, Dr. Lazovert, and Sukhotin drove off in the direction of Rasputin's house in a car, Sukhotin wearing Rasputin's coat to establish evidence that Rasputin had left the house.

Meanwhile, Felix and Purishkevich stayed with the corpse. To their horror and amazement, the corpse staggered to its feet and lurched outside. Purishkevich fired twice, and twice again, and Rasputin fell in the courtyard. The shots attracted a policemen, to whom Purishkevich unwisely identified himself as a member of the Duma who had just shot Rasputin. The policeman promised to keep his mouth shut at this patriotic deed.

Dimitri and the others returned, under the impression that Rasputin had been dead since before their departure. They loaded the body into the car, took it to Petrovsky Island, and dumped it from a bridge into the river. Later, an autopsy stated that Rasputin had died from drowning! The shots had been heard at the police station and the policeman told his superiors what Purishkevich had said.

The next morning the chief of police called on Felix, who was unpleasantly surprised that the affair of the shots had been so quickly connected with Rasputin. He told the chief of police that Purishkevich had been drunk, had fired at a dog, and may have mentioned Rasputin's name to the policeman as deserving a dog's death, or something of the sort, and the policeman had misunderstood the statement. The chief appeared to accept the statement. He also established that one of the guests had been Grand Duke Dimitri Pavlovich.[5]

Yusupov, Dimitri, and Purishkevich then had lunch and agreed to stick by Felix's dog story. The had previously sworn never to reveal what happened to anyone. By nightfall the whole town knew not only of Rasputin's death, but who had killed him. For one thing, that afternoon, Felix Yusupov broke his oath by telling a brief

---

5. *Lost Splendour*, Prince Felix Yusupov

version of the true facts to the President of the Duma, Michael Rodzianko. For another, he had told the police when they wanted to search the house that they could not do so because his wife, a member of the Imperial Family, was there. It was easy to establish that she was in the Crimea. For a third, two servants had cleaned up the mess. It was not, to say the least, an air-tight conspiracy, though it might have worked if Rasputin had had the mortality of an ordinary man and died from the poison.

That night Grand Duke Dimitri went to the theater, and had to leave in embarrassment because he received a standing ovation from the audience. In Moscow the people were soon talking about "our Grand Duke," and there was general rejoicing.

There was no rejoicing at Tsarskoye Selo. The Empress refused to receive Dimitri, and considered him one of the prime movers of the killing. She ordered him placed under house arrest. Strictly speaking, she had no right to do this, but Dimitri agreed not to leave his palace. Much to his surprise, Felix Yusupov arrived, having been prevented by the police from taking a train to the Crimea. He moved in with Dimitri. Most of the members of the Imperial Family who were in St. Petersburg came to express their approval, and there was even talk of Dimitri leading a coup to force the Emperor to abdicate in favor of his son, with Grand Duke Nicholas as regent. This Dimitri flatly refused to do.

Not among the rejoicers, however, was Dimitri's father, Grand Duke Paul, who arrived from Tsarskoye Selo. To him Dimitri swore that he did not have blood on his hands. Strictly speaking, this was true. The actual killing had been done by Yusupov and Purishkevich.

On New Year's Day, the Emperor arrived from headquarters and made Dimitri's arrest official. Two days later he issued orders for Dimitri to be sent to the Russian troops in Persia, where he would be under the supervision of the commanding general, Baratov. He would be accompanied by Nicholas' aide, Count Kutaisov. The later was so upset by the assignment, which he considered to be practically that of a jailor, that Dimitri had to calm him down. Dimitri's tutor, General Leiming, insisted on going along, and was granted permission to do so. Felix Yusupov, a civilian, was merely banished to one of his estates.

By this time Dimitri's mood was very low. He took no pleasure in his popularity, and began to realize that the killing of Rasputin would not change anything for the better. If anything, it would toughen the Empress's stand against any concessions, and it was in itself an opening to lawlessness.

The appeal of several members of the Imperial Family not to send Dimitri to Persia failed, and he was escorted to the station by his sister, just back from the front where she was serving as a nurse, and Grand Dukes Nicholas and Alexander Mikhailovich. The station master offered to give Dimitri a chance to escape by side-tracking the special train. The offer was refused, and thus Grand Duke Dimitri Pavlovich departed for the exile which was to save his life.

He was well received in the Caucasus and by the troops in Persia. Two months later came the abdication of the Emperor, and the provisional government sent word to Dimitri that his exile was lifted and he could return to Russia. Dimitri refused the offer, left the army, and went to Tehran. There, after an initially difficult period with little money and few friends, the Grand Duke was practically adopted by the British Minister to Persia and his wife, Sir Charles and Lady Marling. This was a brave thing for Sir Charles to do at that time, as the British government was refusing help to the Romanovs, and it did adversely affect his career. Nevertheless, Dimitri lived at the British Legation for a year and a half. Not only that, Sir Charles managed to get him an honorary commission as an officer in the British Army. Dimitri had little to do but read the books in the Legation library, which had a broadening effect on him. During this entire time, Dimitri had no information of what was happening to his family.

Leaving Tehran, the Marlings and Dimitri went by a complicated route through the Middle East to Bombay, where a British ship was waiting for them. In Bombay Dimitri caught a bad case of typhoid and almost died. For this reason, when the ship docked at Port Said, Dimitri was taken to Cairo to recuperate. Arriving in Paris, he still had no news of his family. In December 1918, still attended by Lady Marling and a Russian soldier orderly who had stuck with Dimitri through the whole time, Dimitri arrived in London.

In London he had his Aunt Marie, and there was a little money for him from the sale of his St. Petersburg property before the Bolshevik takeover. There, two months later, he learned of the execution of his father. But at least his sister was safe. Grand Duchess Marie Pavlovna had divorced Prince William, and married Prince Putyatin in September 1917. They both made their way south into the German occupied Ukraine and into Roumania. There was a joyful reunion at a station in London when they arrived. Dimitri had known his new brother-in-law in the army during the war, and liked him. Soon they settled in together in a small house in an unfashionable part of London, the loyal Russian orderly acting as housekeeper, while Marie knitted sweaters for sale. Prince Felix Yusupov and his wife and daughter were also in London, but Dimitri avoided them. Felix had funds from the sale of some Rembrandts and jewels, and generally acted as the center of the Russian colony. It offended Dimitri that he kept talking about the Rasputin murder in spite of the promise he had made. Dimitri himself never mentioned it, not even to his sister. In London he took courses in economics, and social sciences.

In 1920, the three of them moved to Paris, where Dimitri found a job in a champagne firm and was eventually made a member of the board of directors. Nevertheless, he was depressed, and began to lose interest in life, and he complained about his health.

Then, at a party in Versailles, he met Miss Audrey Emery of Cincinnati, Ohio, a wealthy, beautiful, and charming American whom Marie Pavlovna had met earlier and liked enormously. Dimitri told his sister he wanted to marry Audrey, but had nothing to offer her. Audrey, though thirteen years younger than Dimitri, disagreed. At her own initiative she converted to Orthodoxy. The wedding took place in Biarritz in 1926. Audrey assumed the morganatic title of Princess Romanovsky-Ilyinsky (after the estate, Ilyinskoye outside of Moscow where Dimitri had been born). They settled for a time in London.

Dimitri was now a changed man. He had an exuberant, beautiful wife, and a home of his own. In 1928 their son was born, Prince Paul Romanovsky-Ilyinsky, named after his grandfather, and nicknamed Paulie.

The couple with their little son lived mostly in France, with frequent trips to England, where Grand Duke Dimitri was a great favorite of King George V (unlike the latter's other Russian relatives in the emigration). He also got along well with all the surviving grand dukes, except Cyril Vladimirovich, whose claim to be Emperor, according to his son, Dimitri did not recognize. In 1918, a monarchist group in Russia had recognized Grand Duke Dimitri[6], and in 1928, the British Foreign Office had notified its Embassies that Cyril was not recognized as emperor, that Grand Duke Dimitri was the heir[7]. Dimitri, however, never laid claim to the throne.

There were also trips to the United States to see Audrey's family. By 1936, however, the marriage was in serious trouble. There were problems with the couple's different life styles, but mainly it was because Audrey fell in love with a handsome Georgian, Prince Dimitri Djordjadze, whom she married after divorcing Dimitri in 1937.

Grand Duke Dimitri was devastated by the divorce, and never really got over it. In addition, he was unwell, showing signs of tuberculosis. In the short time left before World War II, Dimitri lived at the George V Hotel in Paris, spending much time at the Travelers Club, the Ritz in London, and in Switzerland seeking medical help. He saw his son during the latter's vacations from a British school. The last time they met was in 1939, in Genoa. The war had started, but Italy was still neutral. Young Paulie, his nannie, and a World War I vintage British guards officer called Terrence Philips, boarded

6. F.O. W38, 3350, General Golejewski
7. F.O. N5185/665/30, #13298

the Italian liner *Rex* and sailed for the United States. In 1945 Paulie became a U.S. Marine serving for a time in Korea.[8] Eventually he married and had two sons and two daughters.

Left alone now, without his beloved sister, his wife, or his son, Grand Duke Dimitri spent most of the three years remaining to him in Switzerland, trying to find a cure for his illness. The Swiss doctors were unable to do anything, and he died there, in Davos, 5 March 1942, only fifty-one years of age. It was a melancholy ending for a man who had once been the toast of St. Petersburg, an Olympic hero, favorite of the Tsar, war hero, and then had played a short but decisive role in Russian history.

8. Testimony, Prince Paul Romanovsky-Ilyinsky

TSESAREVICH ALEXIS c. 1915

TSESAREVICH ALEXIS c. 1906

CHAPTER XXXII

TSESAREVICH ALEXIS NIKOLAYEVICH
(1804 - 1918)

After eight years of marriage and four daughters, a son and heir to the throne was finally born to Empress Alexandra Feodorovna, consort of Emperor Nicholas II. Grand Duke and Tsesarevich Alexis was born at Peterhof on 12 August 1904. He was the first heir to the throne "born in the purple" since the 18th century.

Alexis was a beautiful, lusty, healthy-looking child, with golden curls. He would have been only the second Tsar to bear that name, the other being the second Tsar of the Romanov Dynasty, who had died in 1676. The godfathers were the German Emperor, William II, and the Prince of Wales, the future George V, and, in addition, all the men fighting in the war against Japan, then in progress.

The delight of Alexis' parents soon turned to horror. Any bruise that the child received turned into an internal hemorrhage with agonizing pain. Alexis had the incurable, genetically transmitted disease of hemophilia, which was impossible to cure then, and now, a blood-clotting deficiency. It is transmitted through the X, or female sex chromosome, and usually only males suffer from it. Males cannot pass it on to their sons, who always get it from their carrier mothers. In this case, it was easy to trace. The Empress was a carrier, because her mother was a carrier, and her mother was the daughter of Queen Victoria, whose faulty X chromosome had passed the disease to her youngest son, Leopold, and through her carrier daughters to other royal families. Empress Alexandra's brother had died from it, and so had one of her sister Irene's sons, Prince Henry of Prussia, at the age of four. Another royal heir, the eldest son of King Alfonso XIII of Spain, born in 1907, was also a hemophiliac. His mother was another maternal granddaughter of Queen Victoria.

The life of Alexis' parents turned into a nightmare of constant vigil and worry. Several times the child was near death. When there were no bruises or other bleeding, there were periods of healthy normalcy, except that the little boy had to be restricted in all of his activities, as almost anything might have been a danger to him. In nearly every other way Alexis was a near perfect child. He was extremely good looking, with splendid dark blue eyes, bright, modest, conscientious, affectionate, and charming. He possessed a very good memory, like his father. His disease did not seem to embitter him. If anything, it made him conscious and sympathetic to the pain of others. He loved to play with other boys, sometimes taking chances with activities forbidden to him, such as riding a bicycle.

The combination of exalted rank and hemophilia assured that Alexis had a degree of care rarely lavished on any child. He was always surrounded by nurses. When he was five he was given a pair of male companions and bodyguards, two sailors from the Imperial navy, Derevenko and Nagorny. By nature, Alexis was mischievous. He would sometimes present himself during dinner and make the rounds of the table chatting with the guests, his tutor, Pierre Gilliard, wrote that he "was very simple in his tastes and he entertained no false satisfaction because he was the Heir; his pockets were filled with string, nails and pebbles."

Sometimes he could be rude. Once he walked into the waiting room where he found the Foreign Minister, Izvolsky, who remained seated. Alexis went up and said in a loud voice, "When the Heir to the Russian Throne enters a room, people must get up."

One of Alexis' dream was to own a bicycle, and he often begged his mother for one. It was, of course, forbidden. One day as his father was reviewing the palace guard, here came Alexis down the middle of the parade riding a bicycle. The Tsar promptly halted the review and ordered every man to pursue and capture the vehicle and its rider.

While usually very kindhearted and considerate, Tsesarevich Alexis was fully aware of his position, and sometimes took advantage of it. Princess Vera Constantinovna tells of an incident in 1916 when she went for a carriage ride with Alexis. "I was wearing a beautiful new dress with yellow flowers on it, and was so proud. The carriage passed through some mud puddles, and Alexis said to me, 'jump.' I did." When asked why, Princess Vera smiled and replied, "He was my Tsesarevich."

Alexis, like his father, loved military pageantry. From birth he bore the title of Hetman of all the Cossacks, and had his own Cossack uniform with fur cap, boots and dagger. In the summer he wore a miniature uniform of a sailor of the Russian navy. ALexis also had an ear for music, and played the balalaika well.

Once his sister, Grand Duchess Olga asked Alexis why he was so quiet. He replied, "I enjoy the sun and the beauty of summer as long as I can. Who knows whether one of these days I shall not be prevented from doing it?"

Gilliard was appointed to teach Alexis French. He wrote that "I found myself confronted with an eight-and-a-half year old boy rather tall for his age . . . a long, finely chiseled face, delicate features, auburn hair with a coppery glint, and large grey-blue eyes like his mother . . . He had a quick wit and a keen, penetrating mind . . . Those not required to teach him discipline as I was, could quickly fall under the spell of his charm. Under the capricious little creature . . . I discovered a child of a naturally affectionate disposition . . ."

Alexis' hemophilia was kept from the Russian people. They, of course, soon knew that something was wrong; the Heir was in delicate health. It was Alexis' health which finally brought Rasputin onto the scene. There is no doubt whatever that this Siberian peasant was able to alleviate and even totally eliminate the boy's episodes of severe pain when none of the doctors could. This also meant controlling or stopping the internal bleeding. It could have been some form of hypnosis or power of suggestion. He appeared to do it through prayer. It is, therefore, small wonder that the frantic Empress believed that Rasputin was a true man of God.

When World War I commenced, Alexis was ten. When he was well, his father involved him in various activities, such as reviewing troops. At his father's side, dressed in a miniature copy of whatever uniform his father was wearing, Alexis was in his element. When Nicholas took over command of the army in 1915, Alexis spent time with him at headquarters, sleeping in the same room or railroad compartment with his father. He was extremely popular among the officers and men; they were particularly impressed that he wore the uniform of a private.

Alexis was interested in everything, and so pleased to be released from the constricted surroundings of Tsarskoye Selo. He had to return there, however, when sneezing brought on nosebleed, especially dangerous to hemophiliacs. Six months later Alexis returned to headquarters for a short time. His last visit there was in December 1916.

When Emperor Nicholas II abdicated on 15 March 1917, he first intended to do so in favor of Alexis, with Grand Duke Michael Alexandrovich as regent, but when the document was brought to him, he tore it up and wrote out another abdicating for himself and Alexis, and passing the throne directly to his brother, Michael. In this document, he declared that, ". . . . not wishing to part with our dear son we hand over our inheritance to our brother, the Grand Duke Michael Alexandrovich. . ." This was quite understandable, but it probably doomed whatever chance the monarchy still had. Alexis, as a symbol, would have been acceptable to a great many people.

Nicholas II returned to the Alexander Palace where the whole family was kept under house arrest until August. Alexis' lessons resumed, this time with his father as one of his tutors. The boy was cheerful through it all. He was still attended by Nagorny, one of the two sailors who had been with him since he was a child. The other,

Derevenko, started being extremely rude to Alexis, then left.

In August the family was moved to the Siberian town of Tobolsk. In some ways life for them was better there. The people were more sympathetic, as well as their guards. Alexis had one of his periods of excellent health, which lasted until the spring of 1918. He was cheerful and active. Meanwhile, the Bolsheviks had taken power, and gradually the atmosphere surrounding the family grew ominous. Alexis, who was hard to restrain, took a spill and had one of his worst episodes in several years. In April 1918, the Bolsheviks decided to move the family again. Alexis' condition was made worse by whooping cough, which caused a blood vessel to rupture. After much soul-searching, the Empress accompanied her husband, along with Grand Duchess Marie, leaving Alexis behind with his other sisters, Olga, Tatiana, and Anastasia, and Gilliard and Nagorny. There was no guarantee of reunion.

By May Alexis was well enough to travel, and they went by river steamer to the town of Ekaterinburg, where the family were placed together at the Ipatiev House, by coincidence, it had the same name as the monastery where the first Romanov Tsar, Michael, was living when he was elected to the throne in 1613.

The Ekaterinburg period only lasted two months. Alexis' faithful sailor, Nagorny, was taken away and shot for making one too many demands on the Red guards on Alexis' behalf. Alexis was still not well, and his father now carried him around. The rest is well known. On the night of 17 July 1918, in a basement room of the Ipatiev House, a Cheka firing squad opened fire on the entire family and four attendants. Alexis, it is reported, still moaning in his dead father's arms after the volley, was finished off with a revolver fired by the commissar in charge, Yurovsky.

Thus died the last Tsesarevich, less than a month short of his fourteenth birthday.

GRAND DUKE MICHAEL ALEXANDROVICH

GRAND DUKE MICHAEL

Eilers collection

EMPEROR MICHAEL II

CHAPTER XXXIII

GRAND DUKE MICHAEL ALEXANDROVICH (1878 - 1918)

EMPEROR MICHAEL II (1917)

The third and youngest son of Emperor Alexander III, Grand Duke Michael was perhaps the favorite child of the Emperor and Empress, and the only one completely at ease with his strict father. Grand Duke Michael was born at St. Petersburg 9 December 1878, third in the succession to the throne behind his two elder brothers, Nicholas and George.

Michael, known in the family as "Misha," or "Dear Floppy," because of his lean, angular body, and habit of throwing himself into chairs in a most relaxed manner, was a highly intelligent, spirited youth. He used to take long walks with his father, who taught him how to build fires and follow animal tracks. They would set out into the deer park with a lantern, spades, and some apples, and would build a fire and roast the apples, returning home by lantern light. On one of these walks, Alexander playfully picked up a hose and squirted Michael. Michael knew his father's habits very well. Each morning, before commencing work, the Emperor would go to a window and stand leaning out looking at the lawn. The following morning after his dousing, Michael lay in wait in the room above his father, and when Alexander III leaned out of the window, he was greeted with a bucket of water from above. None of Alexander's other children would have dared such an indignity, but Michael got away with it.[1]

History was Michael's favorite subject, and he and Olga studied it together, it being a family chronicle as far as they were concerned. Michael's younger sister, Grand Duchess Olga, shared many of the hours with Michael and their father, but both children were a little afraid of their mother, Empress Marie. Their childhood was without ostentation, no expensive presents. Most of their time was spent at Gatchina, outside St. Petersburg.

1. *The Last Grand Duchess*, Ian Vorres

Michael and Olga also shared an English nanny called Mrs. Franklin, who ruled the nurseries in a thoroughly British fashion. She stood for no nonsense. The children were brought up on a very plain diet, porridge for breakfast, mutton cutlets, peas and baked potatoes for lunch; jam and bread and butter and English biscuits for tea; cake was a great treat served only on special occasions. Michael was four years older than Olga, but they liked the same people, shared the same tastes in many things, and never quarreled. When they were grown and attending official functions, Olga would startle people by suddenly calling to Michael across the room, "Floppy!"[2]

When Michael was eleven, the dining room was turned into a school room for them, and they had lessons every day from nine in the morning until three in the afternoon. Part of their education consisted in dancing lessons, which they both hated. The dancing master was Mr. Troitsky, a very dignified old gentleman with beautiful white whiskers, who always wore immaculate white gloves. According to Michael, he "insisted on having a huge vase of fresh flowers standing on the piano for each lesson." Michael and Olga had to bow and curtsey to each other before starting to dance the *pas de patineur*, the waltz or the polka. They knew that despite orders, the Cossack guards outside the ballroom were watching them through the keyholes, and this made them feel very self-conscious. After the lessons, the Cossacks would greet them with broad grins and laughter.

As they grew older, they were allowed to dine downstairs with their parents and older brothers and sister. Being the youngest, they were served last. It was considered bad manners to eat quickly, and they frequently had time to swallow only a few bites before their parents were finished and signalled the servants to clear away the table, so Michael and Olga often went hungry.

One of the favorite times of all for Alexander's children, and Michael in particular, were the annual visits to their grandfather in Denmark, King Christian IX. In Copenhagen they could actually walk around freely, and go into shops, something which was impossible for them in St. Petersburg, where security was very tight. Michael was a particular favorite of King Christian, as he seems to have been with all of the family. Frequently there were as many as seventy family members gathered at Fredensborg, and Michael would be brought in to say goodnight. Later, he and Olga would tiptoe from their bedrooms and peer over the bannisters at the adults.

In the autumn at Copenhagen, the favourite dish served was roast pheasant, and Michael would sniff the aroma with delight. There were other odors as well—the English royalty smelled of fog and smoke; the Danish cousins reminded him of damp, newly

---

2. *The Grand Duke's Woman*, Pauline Gray

washed linen, and he thought he himself smelled of well-polished leather.

Grand Duke Michael grew up to be a very good-looking young man, clean shaven but with a small moustache, not as tall as his various cousins and uncles, but taller than his brother Nicholas. From 1900 to 1902, he was taught economics by the future prime minister, Count Witte, who obviously liked him a great deal, considering him to be extremely 'sweet and honorable,' but, when interrogated about the young grand duke by his grandfather, Christian IX, Witte tactfully answered that he was not as intelligent and well educated as his brother Nicholas, but in his character he took after Alexander III.

Michael was only sixteen when his father died, and his brother Nicholas ascended the throne. Five years later, when Grand Duke George died, Michael became the heir to the throne pending the birth of a son to Emperor Nicholas, and was heir from 1899 to 1904. Even so, he was given no special training, No one seriously considered the possibility that "darling Misha" might actually become Emperor.

After the death of Alexander III, Grand Duke George, Michael's older brother, had been officially named Tsesarevich. For some reason, perhaps because of possible succession problems, Nicholas II did not accord the title of Tsesarevich to Michael, although he was recognized as heir presumptive. The succession question became a serious matter when, during one of Empress Alexandra's pregnancies, Nicholas II fell seriously ill. Had he died, Michael would have become Emperor—but what would the situation have been had Alexandra then given birth to a son? There was nothing in the laws of succession to cover such a contingency. Since it was not covered, Witte argued that Michael should indeed inherit, and if the child were a boy, Michael would be honorable enough to abdicate in the child's favor, and become Regent. Privately, Witte did not think Michael would make a good regent. Nicholas II recovered, and this little-known crisis passed.

Although of a very unassuming nature, and not given to ostentation, Grand Duke Michael nevertheless showed his resentment at being denied the title of Tsesarevich, which he felt rightfully belonged to him—until the birth of Nicholas' son, Tsesarevich Alexis, Grand Duke Michael studiously avoided attending any official function where he would have had to appear as "Tsesarevich," since he did not officially have that title.[3]

This may seem contradictory, since it is generally written that Michael had no ambition, was easy going, and particularly was

---

3. *The Grand Duke's Woman*, Pauline Gray
The Court of Russia, E. A. Hodgetts
Inside Royal Palaces, Countess de Planty

unhappy at his position in the succession, dreading the possibility of becoming emperor one day.

When Tsesarevich Alexis was born, the Emperor issued a manifesto on 14 August 1904, naming Grand Duke Michael co-regent with the Empress in the event of his death before Alexis attained his majority.

Like all grand dukes, Michael entered the military, and eventually became colonel-in-chief of the Blue Cuirassiers. He was given an estate a day's journey outside Moscow called Brasovo. Michael delighted in the business of running this large estate, and did so extremely well, producing a large profit from its operations, not that he had a need for money. As a grand duke and heir, he received an income from the Imperial Appanages of two million rubles a year (at least $10,000,000 in todays money.)

While Michael was still heir, he became interested in one of the daughters of the Duke of Saxe-Coburg (Queen Victoria's second son, Alfred) and his wife, Marie Alexandrovna, the sister of Alexander III. This made the girl and Michael first cousins, and the marriage was not allowed. After this, Michael contented himself with a series of mistresses and temporary girl friends. He had a romance with his sister Olga's maid-of-honor, Alexandra ("Dina") Kosikovskaya. The affair was serious enough that plans were made to elope, but somebody revealed this to the Empress, and they were stopped. His mother gave him a scathing talking-to, and made him feel thoroughly ashamed, and Dina was sent away as fast as possible.[4]

By 1906, however, Michael was no longer heir to the throne, and he was not inclined to be stopped again. This time he was in love with an extremely beautiful woman, the daughter of a Moscow lawyer named Sheremetevsky. Her name was Natalia, and she was called Natasha.

Natasha was married to one of Michael's officers in the Blue Cuirassiers, Vladimir Wulfert, a handsome young captain. She had previously been married to Sergei Mamontov, by whom she had a daughter, Tata.

Natasha and her new husband left Moscow and went to live at Gatchina outside St. Petersburg, where Wulfert was stationed with his regiment. Gatchina was a charming small town, filled with pretty little houses in the middle of parkland; there were many lakes about, and it resembled Windsor in many respects.

A few months after Natasha's arrival at Gatchina there was a grand reception, and she was presented to Grand Duke Michael, her husband's commanding officer. As she curtseyed in front of him, she noticed that he was gazing intently at her. The Grand Duke lost no time in inviting Natasha to be his partner in the mazurka, and later

4. *Mother Dear*, A. A. Polyakov

took great care to stay at her side.

Within a short time, Natasha had become Michael's mistress. At first, according to Natasha, Michael was much more in love with her than she with him. It had been most amusing to seduce the brother of the Tsar. Gradually, Natasha fell deeply in love with Michael. His gentle character, quiet passion, and deep love for her won her over, as did his tall, slim figure, clear blue eyes, and very fair hair. Michael would not allow her to be out of his sight. He even invited her and her husband to be his guests in his private box at the races. Tongues soon began to wag, excitedly pointing out her husband and her in the Imperial box, chatting amiably to the Grand Duke.

There wasn't much poor Wulfert could do, so he took the easy course—do and say nothing. He showed himself to be very much the gentleman: and was seen to smile at the Grand Duke in a polite and friendly fashion. He even went out of his way to be gallant and attentive to his wife in public. When Grand Duke Michael visited their apartment, Wulfert managed to greet him in a friendly manner.

Michael mentioned marriage to Natasha. At first, she didn't take this seriously, but Michael insisted. "Why should we not marry," he demanded. Michael said that he did not care very much about his position in society or his army career. He realized that marriage to Natasha would ruin all of this, but it made no difference. He told her that they would retire from public life, and go to live at Brasovo.

Eventually, Wulfert agreed to a divorce and went to live in the officers mess. Natasha went to her sister's husband, Alexei Sergeyevich Matveyev, a lawyer from Moscow, and asked him to arrange the divorce. Michael frequently joined her on these trips, and they would stay with her family. Her father pretended to be ignorant of who Michael actually was.

This state of affairs could not be kept secret forever, and so Michael wrote to his brother the Emperor asking permission to marry once Natasha was free. Nicholas wrote to their mother, ". . . I will never give my consent . . . it is infinitely easier to give one's consent than to refuse it. God forbid that this sad affair should cause misunderstanding in our family."

As usual, Michael did not stand alone in the family. Grand Duchess Olga fully supported her brother. She had been living in a loveless marriage with Prince Peter of Oldenburg for years. One day while watching a military review at Gatchina, her eyes met a tall, fair man wearing the uniform of the Cuirassier Guards, who was talking to Michael. Michael noticed, and immediately asked the officer, whose name was Nicholas Koulikovsky, to a luncheon party for the next day; he then asked Olga to attend. The party was a great success and Olga fell deeply in love. She went to her husband and demanded a divorce. Prince Peter would not agree, for the sake of his family name and dignity, he said. He did say that he would reconsider in seven years or so. Meanwhile he was prepared to appoint the man as one of his personal aides-de-camp, and allow him to live in their house. Olga and Nicholas were so discrete that no one knew of the strange ménage à trois, which continued until 1914. Prince Peter never did reconsider the divorce, but in 1916 the marriage was annulled, and Olga and Nicholas were quietly married.[5]

Olga and Nicholas often would slip away from home and join Michael and Natasha for picnics, and Olga would drop by to visit with Natasha. Sometimes they would go to Tsarsky Sad, the Tsar's private gardens, where there were many things to amuse themselves with. There was a wishing well, and a tunnel which was said to be a secret passage from the Palace, and was rumored to have been used by Paul I when he tried to escape from being killed, on what he thought was orders from his mother. The park had many small islands on which were pavilions dedicated to various gods of mythology, and a boat house staffed by a crew of sailors from the Imperial yacht.

Occasionally, Michael took Natasha on visits to his own apartments at the Antichov Palace, but concern was growing in the Imperial Family over this state of affairs. Michael and Natasha decided that it was best for her to leave Russia for a time, until the scandal of her divorce died down. After a passionate and tearful departure, Natasha left for Europe. It was in June of 1909, and she stayed first in Vienna, and then went to Chexbres in Switzerland. In those days there was no international telephone system, and Natasha and Michael stayed in constant touch by telegram. She sent 377 of them alone. Some of these have survived, and are in the possession of Grand Duke Michael's stepgranddaughter, Pauline Gray.

Michael soon left Russia himself, and joined Natasha in Copenhagen. She sent him a telegram to Amalienborg Palace on her arrival:

> "Arrived Hotel d'Angleterre room 102 will await you all day impatiently - Natasha."

Only twelve days later Michael had to return to Russia. The parting was extremely painful for both, and Michael wrote to her:

> "Copenhagen 13th August 1909.[6]
>
> My darling, beautiful Natasha, there are not enough words with which I could thank you for all that you are giving me in my life. Our stay here will be

---

5. *The Last Grand Duchess*, Vorres
6. All of the diary and telegram dates are 'old style,' 13 days behind the Gregorian calendar.

always the brightest memory of my whole existence. Don't be sad - with God's help we shall meet again very soon. Please do always believe all my words and my tenderest love to thee, to my darling, dearest star, whom I will never, never leave or abandon. I embrace you and kiss you all over . . . Please believe me that I am all yours, Misha."

It was not long before Natasha, unable to bear the separation, decided to return to Russia. She rented a small furnished house in Moscow near the Petrovsky Park, and they spent the Christmas holidays there together. It was then that Natasha discovered that she was with child. Michael was delighted, and cried with happiness. Even so, he would not defy his brother and marry without permission; besides, no Russian priest would dare perform the ceremony, so there was nothing to do but wait.

Michael rented a house in the country called Udinka, surrounded by lovely woods and a lake with a bathing house. On Natasha's birthday Michael arranged for a magnificent display of fireworks, and decorated a special chair as a throne for her.

Some evenings Michael brought his own chair into the garden and sat for hours playing his flute. His pet poodle, Cuckoo, did not appreciate the music, and would lift up his head and howl until Michael chased him back into the house.

In early August 1910, Michael and Natasha returned to Moscow to prepare for the birth of their child. On 6 August 1910, their son was born, and named George in honor of Michael's dead brother. Michael was very proud of his little son, who was fat and placid, with rosy cheeks and big blue eyes, and a mass of golden curls. During the summer they returned to the country, where they gave parties and played hide-and-seek among the lilac bushes like children.

This carefree life could not go on. There were unpleasant facts to be faced. Natasha was still married to Wulfert, and therefore George was his son, by law. Michael was upset about this. He adored the baby, and wanted to acknowledge him. He had always loved children, and had a wonderful loving relationship with Tata, Natasha's daughter. Wulfert finally agreed to the divorce and to renounce his wife's son. He was paid the sum of 200,000 roubles ($1,000,000 today). Grand Duke Michael promptly recognized George as his son.

The next summer, Michael and Natasha visited Brasovo, a night's journey from Moscow. Michael's private railway car was hooked onto the ordinary train, which made a special stop for them. They took carriages from the railway to the house, a distance of about two miles. Brasovo had a large rambling house with huge rooms and parquet floors. There was a garden with a croquet lawn, swings, fountains and a swimming pool, and stables as well as the home farm.

Michael and Natasha took a vacation and went to Bavaria for a short holiday. While they were there news came that the Tsesarevich Alexis was again critically ill and not expected to live. It is often hinted that this fact determined the course of action taken by Michael. Should the Tsesarevich die, Michael would once again be the heir to the throne, with all probability of one day becoming emperor, as Nicholas and Alexandra were unlikely to have more children.

It seems, however, that Michael would have taken this step no matter what. He and Natasha slipped across the border into Austria and were married in the Serbian Church in Vienna. There was nothing anyone could do about the marriage, it was perfectly legal, but Michael's son remained a commoner, and the marriage morganatic.

When Michael's telegram reached Nicholas II, the Tsar was furious. He complained, "He [Michael] broke his word, his word of honour. How, in the midst of the boy's illness and all our troubles could they have done such a thing?"[7]

Nicholas wrote his mother that the marriage was to be kept a complete secret, in the family only. This was impossible, and he was eventually forced to recognize it, and in 1914 granted Natasha the title of Countess Brasova, but he banished them from Russia.

Grand Duke Michael, Natasha, and their little family spent the next few years in luxurious exile traveling about Europe. They went first to Cannes, where they took a whole floor at the Hotel du Parc. Michael's pranks, a family characteristic, had full reign. He loved to put hair brushes and damp sponges in people's beds, sew up pajama legs and fill them with confetti, set alarm clocks to ring at all hours. They motored to Grasse, to the Gorges du Loup, and elsewhere along the coast.

In August they went to England where Michael leased Knebworth House from Lord Lytton, which became their base of operations. There was a problem with taking their dogs into England, and Michael wrote to King George. Permission was obtained to keep the dogs caged at Knebworth for the period of quarantine.

For Natasha's twenty-fifth birthday, Michael bought her a picture postcard showing distant mountains. On the card he wrote:

> "My dearest Natashechka, With all my heart I congratulate you, and from the depth of my soul wish

---

7. *Tsar's Letters to Empress Marie*, Nicholas II

you the best of health and happiness for a thousand years. I regret that there are very few articles suitable for presents here, but to them is added a Rolls-Royce that will be awaiting its mistress in Paris. Kissing you very tenderly, Your Misha."

Later in the year they were in Paris, and Michael went to the top of the Eiffel tower. From there he mailed Natasha a postcard which read, "Gatchina is almost visible from this height. Kissing you tenderly, Your Misha." Clearly, he was missing Russia.

In 1914 at the beginning of World War I, Nicholas pardoned Michael, and they hurriedly returned to Russia, leaving almost all of their possession behind. Michael re-joined the army and was sent to command the newly raised Caucasian Cavalry Division at the front in Galicia. It was made up of six regiments of volunteers from various Moslem nationalities. This division, which became famous under the name of the "Wild" Division, performed magnificently against the Austrians, and was very proud of having the Tsar's only brother as commander. This combat command of a famous division made Grand Duke Michael popular again in the army.

Michael's diary for this period is filled with entries, for he wrote almost daily. In January 1915 he wrote:

> "At 10 a.m. the Vyazemskys, Johnson [his secretary] and I went to detestable Petrograd. I went to my house on the embankment, where I have a hospital for 100 wounded soldiers and 25 officers and where Shleifer is in charge. Then I went to see Mamma at the Anichkov Palace and stayed until 3 p.m. After that I went with Natasha to do some shopping until 4 p.m. and then I went to Tsarskoe Selo to see Nicky."

Michael's private railway coach was attached to the staff train near the front, and Natasha was able to visit.

Dimitri Abrikosov, an early admirer of Natasha, was invited to dinner at Gatchina. He wrote of the visit, "When I arrived, the first person I met was the Grand Duke, and was captivated by his charm. . . . I have never met another man so uncorrupted and noble in nature . . . In many ways he was a grown-up child who had been taught only what was good and moral. He did not want to admit that there was wickedness and falsehood in this world and trusted everybody.

"The situation in Russia was growing so grave by this time that not even the Romanovs could ignore it. The war was going badly, Nicholas II was at the front and out of touch with the affairs of government, which were given over to the Empress, and Rasputin seemed to be the real emperor."

In December 1916 Rasputin was murdered, and members of the Imperial Family were implicated. Instead of helping the situation, it made matters worse. The real problem had not been Rasputin, but the Empress, who had taken all power at the capital into her own incapable hands. The Tsar was warned repeatedly. Grand Duke Nicholas wrote him letters, as did Grand Dukes Alexander and Paul, all to no avail.

In January 1917, the Empress said to Grand Duchess Cyril, "I have been on the throne for twenty-two years. I know Russia. I know how the people love our family. Who would dare to side against us?" The Empress continued stubbornly on her way.[8]

Michael watched these events from Gatchina. He was not well, and spent most of his time there, but he was aware of the plots against the throne from the Family. The drawing room of Grand Duchess Vladimir was filled with treasonable talk, and plots to seize the Tsar and force him to abdicate, and to imprison the Empress were openly discussed. At the most critical of time, the Imperial Family was divided against itself.

During this time, Abrikosov left a description of Grand Duke Michael. "I remember how . . . I was taken to a small hunting lodge where a magnificent supper was served. Gypsies were singing, and much wine was drunk. The only man who shared my gloom was Grand Duke Michael, but he bowed to the wishes of his wife, who liked crowds and flattery . . . I declined to go for a drive, and remained with Michael, who was not well . . . Whenever I think of this lovable man . . . I see him as I saw him that Sunday . . . He told me that he often thought how difficult it was for his brother, who sincerely wanted to do only what was good for the people, but who was hindered by his wife. 'Several times I have tried to convey to Nicky what people are saying about him and about the dangerous influence of the Empress.' Nicky, he said, seemed indifferent to his fate. Tears choked his voice . . . I was shocked by the utter despair on the pale face before me and had the distinct feeling that we all stood on the threshold of great misfortune."

In his diary, Grand Duke Michael noted,

> "3rd February 1917. (In the train from the front to Gatchina.) We are three hours late arriving, probably due to snow drifts. I write 'probably' as one can never find out the real truth . . . the fact is that everything is complete disorder everywhere."

8. *Nicholas and Alexandra*, Robert Massie

On February 25th ". . . . disorders on the Nevsky Propekt today. Workers were going around waving red flags and throwing grenades and bottles at the police, which compelled the troops to open fire. the main cause of the unrest is the shortage of flour in the shops."

And on 26th February, "The riots in Petrograd have increased in size. On the Suvorov Pospekt and Znamensky Street 200 people were killed."

Grand Duke Michael came to the conclusion that he should try to do something, and see if he could not ease the precarious political situation. But it was already too late.

According to Countess Brasova's account, General Krymov planned to seize the Tsar on his train, and compel him to abdicate in favor of the Tsesarevich with Grand Duke Michael as regent. This plan was aborted by the commencement of the revolution.

Grand Duke Michael went into St. Petersburg to see Rodzianko. After extensive consultations, it was agreed that the answer was a Constitutional Monarchy, headed nominally by Alexis under Michael's regency. Grand Duke Michael agreed to this, but the plan was to be kept totally secret, even from other members of the Imperial Family. Michael wrote in his diary:

"27th February 1917. At 5 p.m. Johnson and I took a special train and went to Petrograd. In the Mariinsky Palace we met M. N. Rodzyanko, Nekrasov, Savich and Dimitriyukov, and later we were joined by Prince Golitzin, General Belyayev and Kryzhanovsky . . . A temporary Executive Committee was formed which began to issue orders; this was made up of several members of the Duma, headed by Rodzyanko . . . I went to the War Ministry and sent a telegram direct to General Alexeyev at Mogilev to pass on to Nicky. In it I enumerated the measures that should be taken immediately to stop the revolution that has already begun . . . the resignation of the whole of the Cabinet Ministers, and that Prince Lvov should form a new Cabinet of his own choice . . . An answer came, 'You must make no changes whatsoever until I arrive.' signed by Nicky . . . After this unsuccessful attempt I decided to return to Gatchina, but this was not possible owing to heavy machine-gun fire . . . At 5 a.m. Johnson and I left the Winter Palace and walked to Princess Putyatin's house and went to sleep on some couches."

On 2nd March 1917, Grand Duke Michael wrote:

> "In the morning I received a reply from Rodzyanko. We were left quite undisturbed today. Heavy movement of traffic continues but the shooting has stopped. Nevertheless I must add that there is complete insubordination in the ranks of the army and total anarchy reigns."

It was later that day that Michael received the most fateful message of his life, a telegram from Nicholas II, which read:

> "To His Majesty the Emperor Michael: Recent events have forced me to decide irrevocably to take this extreme step. Forgive me if it grieves you and also for no warning—there was no time. Shall always remain a faithful and devoted brother. Now returning to HQ where hope to come back shortly to Tsarskoe Selo. Fervently pray God to help you and our country. Nicky."

It was in this way that Grand Duke Michael Alexandrovich learned that he was the Emperor and Autocrat of all the Russias.

At 6 a.m. on the 3rd March, Michael was woken up by a telephone call from Kerensky, advising him that the Council of Ministers were going to visit him in an hour at 7 a.m.. The only comment in Michael's diary for his first day as Emperor was, ". . . actually, they did not arrive until 9:30 a.m."

Some ministers argued that Michael should accept the throne, the monarchy being the only possible unifying force in Russia. Without it, these ministers felt there would soon be anarchy. Others, notably Rodzianko and Kerensky, were adamant against Michael's assuming the throne. Further, they told Michael that they could not guarantee his safety, and that he might be killed.[9]

After extensive consultation with the Provisional Government, Michael, and they, reached the conclusion that he could not reign. A manifesto was drawn up, which Michael signed on March 4, 1917.

Most historians and general writers refer to Michael as "Grand Duke," without ever according him the title of Emperor. Some histories do not even mention that he was emperor; those that do dismiss this fact with a breezy, "Grand Duke Michael abdicated after one day." This does disservice to fact and to a most honorable man.

---

9. *The February Revolution*, George Katkov

Michael's manifesto is of great consequence historically, as it was the last known official act of a Dynasty that had ruled Russia for 304 years. It is also the document which ultimately prevented a 'legal' take-over of the government by the Bolsheviks, and brands their assumption of power as one of force rather than of law.

Examination of the document reveals several interesting facts. First, and most important, contrary to all writers, Emperor Michael II did not abdicate. Nowhere in the document are the words abdicate, renounce, or refuse, used. Michael, recognizing the political and military situation, in effect named the Provisional Government as regent. His exact words were, ". . . . I will not assume the full duties of emperor until a constituent assembly duly elected by the people has decided on the permanent form of government . . ."

By this wording, Michael remained Emperor, but granted to a constituent assembly 'duly elected by the people' the right to abolish the monarchy, or retain it as they wished.

Emperor Michael II may never have reigned, but there can be no doubt that he was the last Emperor of Russia. How long? That, too, is debatable. Had a constituent assembly been elected, and decided to continue the monarchy, Michael would have remained Emperor. The Bolsheviks preempted this by forcibly disbanding both the Provisional Government and the Constituent Assembly, and declaring Russia a republic. The manifesto of Michael did not extend to this.

In August of 1917, the British government inquired as to "what is the exact form of government, is Russia now a republic?" The ambassador, George Buchanan replied, with his answer flagged for Buckingham Palace [to King George V], "Russia is still a monarchy. I myself made the mistake in speaking to Kerensky of calling it a republic. He corrected me most forcefully, stating that Russia was a monarchy with an Emperor, and would remain so unless the Assembly decided otherwise." However, on 1 September the Provisional Government, prompted by Kerensky, declared Russia a republic, although legally it should have waited for the election of a Constituent Assembly.

Thus, from a *de jure* point of view, it can be fairly argued that Michael, "dear Floppy," "darling Misha," remained Emperor until his death, probably in June 1918.

After his manifesto, Michael returned to Gatchina where he remained through the summer, little disturbed by events. Michael's health improved, and during the summer he continued to give Tata riding lessons, and they often went for drives in the Rolls Royce with visitors, and sometimes even went for picnics as in the old days.

On 21 August 1917, the house was suddenly surrounded by soldiers under the command of a Captain Kosmin, the Assistant Commander-in-Chief of the Petrograd district, accompanied by

Captain Svistunov, the Gatchina Commandant. They announced that Michael was under house arrest by order of the Director of War Ministry, Savinkov. Michael wrote in his dairy, "Our guard is 60-70 strong. The sentries are posted on the outer parts of our garden and on the outside of the fence. We have just read the news in the papers of our arrest. . ."

Shortly before this, Michael was allowed by Kerensky to see his brother Nicholas. Michael went to the Alexander Palace, and was required to hold the meeting in the presence of Kerensky. In his diary for 31 July 1917, he wrote:

> "At 12 noon the Palace Commandant arrived and we went together to the Alexander Palace. We entered the Palace from the kitchen side and then went through the cellar and passed to the fourth entrance to Nicky's reception room, where we found Count Benkendorff, Kerensky, V. Dolgoruky and two young officers. From there I went through to Nicky's study where I met Nicky in the presence of Kerensky and a duty officer. I found Nicky looking quite well; I stayed with him for 10 minutes and then I left and returned to Boris (Grand Duke Boris Vladimirovich) and later went back to Gatchina. This meeting with Nicky was arranged by Kerensky, and I found out later that Nicky and his family were leaving that same night for Tobolsk."

What Michael did not write, if Count Benkendorff is to be believed, was that Michael left this meeting in tears.

On 23 August 1917 Michael wrote to Kerensky requesting permission to go abroad. That evening a verbal reply was returned, stating that this was not to be allowed, that for the present the situation made it necessary to keep Michael isolated.

On 28 August 1917 General Kornilov attempted a military coup. He had formed an army and was marching on Petrograd. Michael describes what happened:

> "29th August 1917. I was woken up at 3 a.m. and the Commandant told us that we should prepare for departure and to be ready in one hour's time. We all managed to be ready in time, but did not leave until 5:10 a.m. as the army drivers had trouble starting up our cars . . . we arrived in Petrograd at 9 p.m. On the way we saw the Preobrajensky Reserve marching in the direction of Petrograd, obviously on their way to help defend the city. When we arrived, we were taken

to the office of the Commander-in-Chief, and were met by Captain Filonenko . . . we went to Alesha's flat on the Fontanka . . . we are guarded by 65 soldiers and are under strict arrest. My stomach pains are worse.

"On August 30th, "We are all very tired and nervous. Today's news: General Kornilov's advance has been stopped. The Temporary Government have arrested General Denikin and Markov, but Kornilov has been suspended and it is declared that he will be brought to trial.

"6th September 1917 . . . Captain Kosmin arrived at 5 p.m. It has been decided to move us back to Gatchina . . . It is so nice to be back home at last."

At about this time, Emperor Michael must have commenced serious consideration of escape, for Natasha asked permission to go to visit her bank, pretending that she needed to examine some important papers. An official stayed by her the whole time she was there, but nevertheless she managed to cram a considerable amount of the more important jewels into her fur muff, and returned home safely. Other valuables were packed in cases and hidden.

On 25 October 1917 bands of Bolsheviks laid siege to the Winter Palace, and it fell on the 26th. Kerensky fled, and the Reds had come to power.

Michael was summoned frequently to Petrograd to the Smolny Institute for interrogation by the chief of the local Cheka, Uritsky, but each time he returned. In early March 1918, this changed. Instead of returning, Natasha received a note reading, "Uritsky has . . . declared that we have to move immediately to Perm . . . Uritsky assures me that you and the family will have no difficulty in following whenever you wish."

Natasha immediately commenced making plans. The first was to get George to safety. He was, after all, the son of the Emperor. Using false papers showing the governess to be the wife of a Danish official travelling with her small son, they left for Denmark.

From Perm, Michael was first arrested, then later allowed his freedom to live in rooms rented at the Kings Hotel.[10] Natasha managed to visit Michael in Perm twice. Before she could return a third time, in June 1918, a telegram arrived, "Our friend and Johnny have vanished without trace . . ."

Natasha stormed into the Cheka demanding an interview with Uritsky, demanding to know what had happened to Michael. She

10. *The Last Days of Tsardom*, Paul Bykov

shouted and raged when told that no one knew anything definite. Uritsky lost his temper too, and told her that he suspected that she was the one who knew where Michael was, and had been personally involved in his disappearance. Still shouting, Natasha was taken away. After ten months in prison, Natasha was moved to a nursing home. She had been coughing pathetically and feigning illness. Tata came to visit, and plans were made. That night, Natasha calmly dressed and walked out of the nursing home undetected.

Natasha hid out in the apartment of Princess Vyazemsky until friends were able to obtain a false passport for her, then she left by train for Kiev, wearing the uniform of a Red Cross nurse. She arrived at Orcha, the Bolshevik frontier with the Ukraine, and was soon free to walk the short distance to safety, and finally reached Kiev. They were well fixed for money, as both Natasha and Tata had managed to bring their jewels and furs, including Natasha's famous pearl earrings, each pearl the size of a hazelnut. The Roumanian border was, however, closed, and so they went on to Odessa. Here they finally managed to board the *H.M.S. Skirmisher*, as the sound of gunfire approached Odessa. From here they reached Constantinople, and finally, England. There was still no word of the fate of Emperor Michael.

It was not until 1934 that Natasha knew what had happened to her beloved Misha. Even so, this account may not be true.

A book entitled *The Last Days of Tsardom* by P. M. Bykov, sometime Chairman of the Ekaterinburg Soviet, was published. In this, Bykov recounts what allegedly happened to Michael:

> ". . . . On the evening of June 12-13 [1918] this group came to the hotel with forged documents from the Provisional Extraordinary Commission (the Cheka) . . . Both the arrested men were put into carriages which were ready, and taken out of the town along the track to Motovilikha. After passing the Nobel kerosine dump, six versts from Motovilikha, they turned off into the forest to the right and there shot Michael Romanov."

It should be remembered that Bykov was also involved in the murder of the Tsar, and in the cover-up. This story was in keeping with other false information put out by Lenin and his gang at this time, attempting to absolve themselves of the murderous deeds. The murder of the Tsar and his family were also pretended to have been committed by unauthorized agents. As no other word of Michael was ever had, it is reasonable to assume that the last Tsar of all the Russias, Emperor Michael II, died by murder at Perm in June of 1918.

Natalia, Countess Brasova, died in Paris on 26 January 1952. Her and Michael's son, Count George Brasov, was killed in an automobile accident near St. Tropez, France on 12 July 1931.

BIBLIOGRAPHY

Abrikossov, Dimitri, *Revelations of a Russian Diplomat*, Seattle 1964

Alexander, Grand Duke, *Once A Grand Duke*, New York 1932

Alexander, Grand Duke, *Always A Grand Duke*, New York 1933

Alexandra Feodorovna, Empress, *A Czarina's Story*, London 1948

Alexandrov, Victor, *The End of the Romanovs*, Hutchinson 1966

Almedingen, Martha, *The Emperor Alexander II*, London 1962

Almedingen, M., *House of Romanov*, London 1966

Almedingen, M., *I Remember St. Petersburg*, London 1969

Almedingen, Martha E., *The Romanovs*, New York 1966

Appleton, Nathan, *Alexander II*, Boston 1904

B. W., *Russian Court Memoirs*, Plymouth, 1916

Benckendorff, Count Paul, *Last Days at Tsarskoe Selo*, Heinemann 1927

Beaulieu, Leroy, *The Empire of the Tsars*, 1898

Bilbasov, V. A., *History of Catherine II*, Berlin 1900

Brokhaus and Efron, *Encyclopedia*, St. Petersburg 1912

Burke's Peerage, Royal Families of Europe, London 1977

Buxhoeveden, Baroness Sophie, *The Life and Tragedy of Alexandra Feodorovna, Empress of Russia*, London 1929

Bykov, P. M., *The Last Days of Tsardom*, London, 1934

Catherine II, *The Works of the Empress Catherine II*, Ed. by A. Pypin, St. Petersburg 1907

Catherine II, *Memoirs*, Ed. Dominique Maroger, Paris, 1953

Cole, J. W., *Russian and the Russians*, London 1854

Cowles, Virginia, *The Romanovs*, New York 1971

Crankshaw, Edward, *Shadow of the Winter Palace*, New York 1976

Cyril, Grand Duke, *My Life in Russia's Service Then and Now*, London 1939

Dashkova, Princess Catherine, *Memoirs*, Paris 1966

Dobson, Christopher, *Prince Felix Yusupov*, London 1989

Esterhazy, Comte V., *Memoirs*, Paris 1905

Fields, Leslie, *The Queen's Jewels*, New York 1987

Gabriel, Constantinovich, *V Mramornom Dvortse*, New York 1955

George, Grand Duchess, *A Romanov Diary*, New York 1989

Gerhardi, William, *The Romanovs*, New York 1939

Gibbon, Edward, *Alexander I*, Trenton 1819

Golovina, Catherine, *Souveniers*, London 1910

Grant, C., *Mother of Czars*

Gray, Pauline, *The Grand Duke's Woman*, London 1972

Gribble, Francis Henry, *Emperor and Mystic*, New York 1931

Grimm, A., *Alexandra Feodorovna*

Grunwald, Constantine de, *L'Assassinat de Paul Ier, tsar de Russie*, Paris, 1960

Hanbury-Williams, Sir John, *Nicholas II As I Knew Him*, London 1922

Haslip, Joan, *Catherine the Great*, New York 1977

Helps, Sir Arthur, *The Russian Court*, London
Hodgetts, E. A., *The Court of Russia*, New York, 1908

Jackman, S. W., *Romanov Relations*, London 1969
Jenkins, Herbert, Ed., *Russian Court Memoirs*, Plymouth 1916

Jenkins, Michael, *Arakcheyev, Grand Vizir of the Russian Empire*, New York 1969
Joyneville, O., *Life and Times of Alexander I*, London 1875

Kerensky, Alexander, *Russia and History's Turning Point*, New York 1965
Kerensky, Alexander, *The Murder of the Romanovs*, London 1935
Kleinmichel, Maryia, *Memories of A Shipwrecked World*, London 1923
Kokovtsev, V. N., *Iz Moyego Proshlovo*, Paris 1933
Konovalov, S., *Emperor Alexander II*
Korf, M.A., *Accession of Nicholas I*, London 1857

Ligne, Princess de, *Memories*, Paris 1860
Lloyd, H. E., *Alexander I*, London 1826
Lowe, Charles, *Alexander III*, New York 1895

Massie, Robert, *Nicholas and Alexandra*, New York 1967
Marie, Grand Duchess, *A Princess in Exile*, New York 1932
Marie, Grand Duchess, *Education of A Princess*, New York 1930
Marie Feodorovna, *Letters of the Empress to Emperor Alexander I*, Berlin 1911
Marie, Queen, of Roumania, *Some Memories of the Russian Court*, Liv. Age 303, Cot. 1919
Masson, Charles F., *Memoires secrets sur la Russie*, Paris 1802
Mazour, A. G., *Rise and Fall of the Romanovs*, Princeton, 1960
Morane, *Paul I*, Paris 1907

Nabokov, V.D., *The Provisional Government*, Queensland, 1971
Naryshkina, Y., *Under Three Tsars*, Zurich 1930
Novikoff, Olga, *Russian Memories*, London 1917
Nicholas II, *Diaries*, Paris 1925
Nicholas II, *Letters to Empress Marie*, London 1937
Nicholas, Grand Duke, *Alexander I*, Petersburg 1912
Nicholas, Grand Duke, *Imperatritsa Elisaveta Alekseyevna*, St. Petersburg 1909
Nicholas, Grand Duke, *An Account of Visit to London*, Corp. Council of London, 1815
Nicholas, Grand Duke, *Lettres inedites à Frederick Masson*, Paris 1968
Nicholas, Prince, *My Fifty Years*, London 1928
Nicholas, Prince, *Political Memoirs*, London 19__
Novikoff, Olga, *Russian Memoires*, London 1917

Oldenbourg, Zoe, *Catherine the Great*, Paris 1966
Oldenburg, S.S., *Tsarstvovaniye Imperatora Nikolaya II*, Munich 1949

Paleologue, G., *An Ambassadors Memories*, Paris 1924
Paleologue, George, *The Enigmatic Tsar*, London 1938
Paley, Princess, *Memories of Russia*, London 1929
Pamyantnaya Knizhka, St. Petersburg 1914, and 1917
Pares, Sir B., *Russia*, London 1941
Pares, Sir B., *Fall of the Russian Monarchy*, Cape 1939

du Planty, Countess, et de Sourdis, *Within Royal Palaces*, Boston, 1892
Polovtsev, A. A., *Dnevnik Gos. Sekretarya, 1883-1892*, Moscow 1966
Polyakov, V., *Mother Dear*, New York, 1926
Pridham, Sir. Francis, *Close of A Dynasty*, London 1956
Prodvprmuu Kalendar (Court Calendar), St. Petersburg 1907, New York 1965

Radziwill, C., *Secrets of Dethroned Royalty*, London 1920
Radziwill, C., *Memories of 40 Years*, London 1914
Radziwill, C., *My Recollections*, London 1906
Radziwill, C., *Confessions of the Czarina*, London 1918
Rambaud, A., *Histoire de Russie*, London 1879
Rappaport, A., *Fair Ladies of the Winter Palace*, London
Rodzianko, M. V., *Krusheniye Imperii*, New York 1986
Romanova, Andreya, *Vladimirovicha, Dnevnik*, Moscow 1923

Samson-Himmelstierna, H. von, *Russia Under Alexander III*, New York 1893
Schilder, N. K., *Imperator Aleksandr I*, St. Petersburg 1904
Schilder, N. K., *Imperator Nikolai I*, St. Petersburg 1903
Schilder, N. K., *Imperator Pavel I*, St. Petersburg, 1901
Seton-Watson, Hugh, *Russian Empire 1801-1917*, Oxford 1967

Tarsaidze, Alexander, *Czars and Presidents*, New York 1958
Tatishchev, S. S. *Imperator Aleksandr II*, St. Petersburg 1908
Tooke, Pere M., *Memoires*, Amsterdam 1800
Troyat, Henri, *Catherine the Great*, Paris 1977

Vasili, Count Paul (pseudonym), *Behind the Veil at the Russian Court*,
London 1914
Vorres, Ian, *The Last Grand Duchess*, London 1985
Vyrubova, Anna, *Memories of the Russian Court*, New York 1923

Waliszewski, K., *The Story of A Throne*, Paris 1893
Witte, S. Yu., *Vospominaniya*, Moscow, 1960

Yusupov, Prince Felix, *Lost Splendor*, London 1953

INDEX